The Clinician, the Brain, and *I*

The clinician needs to make sense of many client experiences in the course of daily practice: do these experiences reflect the simple product of complex neurochemical activity, or do they represent another dynamic involving the subjective self? When research findings from the neurosciences are applied to clinical psychology, reductionist thinking is typically followed, but this creates problems for the clinical practitioner.

In this book Tony Schneider draws together the three strands of philosophy, neuroscience, and psychology to explore the mind–body question as it affects the clinician. Taking a position more closely aligned with dualism, he argues for the utility in making distinctions between brain activity and 'I' – the subjective self – both in general psychological functioning and in psychopathology. Schneider considers traditional psychological topics contextualized by neuroscience research and the mind–body issue, as well as applying the ideas to various areas of clinical practice. Topics include:

- the mind and body from the clinician's perspective
- fundamental aspects of the role and mechanics of the brain
- the developing self and the relationship of 'I' with the self and with others
- psychological functioning such as focus and memory, sleep and dreaming, and emotions and pain.

The idea that 'I am not my brain' will resonate with many clinicians, and is systematically argued for in clinical literature and neuropsychology research here for the first time. The book will be of particular interest to psychologists, psychiatrists, counsellors, and clinicians who wish to incorporate advances in neuroscience research in the conceptualization of their clinical work, and are looking for a working model that allows them to do so.

Tony Schneider is a clinical psychologist and educational psychologist working in a private practice in Western Australia.

Explorations in Mental Health series

New Law and Ethics in Mental Health Advance Directives
The Convention on the Rights of Persons with Disabilities and
the Right to Choose
Penelope Weller

The Clinician, The Brain, and *I*
Neuroscientific findings and the subjective self in clinical practice
Tony Schneider

The Clinician, the Brain, and *I*

Neuroscientific findings and the subjective self in clinical practice

Tony Schneider

Routledge
Taylor & Francis Group

LONDON AND NEW YORK

First published 2013
by Routledge
2 Park Square, Milton Park, Abingdon, Oxfordshire OX14 4RN

Simultaneously published in the USA and Canada
by Routledge
711 Third Avenue, New York, NY 10017

First issued in paperback 2016

Routledge is an imprint of the Taylor & Francis Group, an informa business

British Library Cataloguing in Publication Data
A catalogue record for this book is available from the British Library

Library of Congress Cataloging in Publication Data
Schneider, Tony (Clinical psychologist)
   The clinician, the brain, and 'I' : neuro scientific findings and the subjective self in
   clinical practice / Tony Schneider.
   pages cm
   Includes bibliographical references.
   1. Clinical neuro psychology. 2. Subjectivity. 3. Self (Philosophy)
   4. Mind and body. I. Title.
   RC341.S283 2013
   616.8—dc23
   2012051049

ISBN 13: 978-1-138-63571-5 (pbk)
ISBN 13: 978-0-415-83912-9 (hbk)

Typeset in Bembo
by Swales & Willis Ltd, Exeter, Devon

Contents

Preface

In November of 2008, Melbourne's *Baker Institute* ran the inaugural *Heart and Mind* Conference in Prato, Italy, to consider issues relating to the effect of events of the mind on the heart. The value of the conference lay in the bringing together of people from different nations and from different disciplines – medical, psychological, and the research laboratory. After thirty years teaching and practising in clinical and educational psychology, my exposure to interdisciplinary discussion had been minimal. The conference proved inspirational in this regard, and out of this experience was born the idea to write as a clinician on some of the matters raised at that conference – especially on the age-old mind–brain problem in the light of emerging research and clinical practice.

I write this book in the spirit of that conference. I seek to bring together ideas from the philosophical tradition, key ideas from both neuroscience and psychology, and the concerns that arise from the pragmatism of the clinician, with a view to stimulating thinking and discussion that transcends traditional boundaries in a field that always has been and always will be of central importance in the understanding of ourselves. Aspects of the book are necessarily speculative, but if it contributes to new ways of thinking about old issues and if it challenges clinicians to think more deeply about what they are doing, I will consider it having achieved its purpose.

In some ways, this book marks a reverse journey to that of Freud, who began his career as a neurologist, and, finding the neurology of his time to be inadequate in its conceptualizations to account for what he saw clinically, he entered into his pioneering journey into psychotherapy. I, on the other hand, after many years as a psychotherapist, now find an increasing interest in what the neurosciences might have to say in the matters of the human mind. This book details my discoveries and thoughts to this point.

Some may question the breadth of material I cover in such a small volume, and indeed, each section could easily be a volume in itself, more systematically researched and presented. But the point is that everything affects everything else, and the clinician is confronted with complex inter-relationships. I have therefore sought to retain a sense of this complexity by touching upon the various components that make up the whole. The quest to understand the *I*–brain relationship as it affects clinical practice necessarily causes us to consider diverse phenomena.

I dedicate this book to my daughter Kathryn, who has recently entered the great tradition in clinical practice. I also acknowledge with deep gratitude the ever-present support of my wife, Moira, for her spiritual, emotional, and practical support in all that I do. I have no doubt that, without her, this book would not have been written.

Acknowledgements

I wish to acknowledge and thank the following people for their input, for reading and commenting on earlier manuscripts, and for their encouragement: Nurit Amichai; Dr Paul Corrigan; Dr Harry Dumbell; Professor Alan Gijsbers; Rick Mellor; Sean Monahan; Professor Andrew Page; Dr Robert Turnbull as well as Clare Ashworth, Tamsin Ballard, Joanne Forshaw, Jane Harris, Katie Short, Kristin Susser and Richard Willis.

Introduction

This is a book written by a clinician primarily for clinicians. I have included some basic psychological notions familiar to the clinician so that interested others might find value in reading these pages, but the focus is ultimately to explore issues confronted by clinicians in the course of their practice. It is not a philosophical treatise, but given the subject matter, philosophical issues are inevitably raised. Nor is it a systematic review of scientific research, although I refer to research findings throughout, mostly from secondary sources. It does not attempt to be rigorous in an academic sense, although a critique is offered concerning the interpretation of some aspects of brain research in the context of the proposed *I*–brain dynamic.

To make the book readable for the non-academically inclined, I have made liberal use of analogy. But I have also done so because *I* is an intangible entity and its interaction with the brain is difficult to conceptualize. However, I am conscious of the logical error one can make when arguing from analogy. Science purists may not be happy about this, preferring descriptive, 'evidence-based' argument backed by 'research'. But such 'evidence' may not always apply to this particular subject matter.

Many books written for clinicians are 'how to' books. This is not one of those. Rather, it explores the mind–brain relationship (in my formulation, the *I*–brain relationship), with a view to contributing to a working model of the mind that may be helpful to clinicians seeking to make sense of the diverse presentations that come before them. Books about emerging theory and research are generally written by academics, and although rigorous and systematic, these can at times be difficult to access and relate to in clinical practice. This book is written to explore and integrate some of the emerging neuroscience research and theory in a way that is relevant for the clinician.

While for many clinicians the concept of *I* is intuitive and implicit in their psychotherapeutic work, it has neither scientific rigour nor philosophical agreement and remains a continual focus for debate. I propose that I am not my brain. Yet, because it can be neither seen nor measured, the notion of *I* as an entity separate from the brain is regularly questioned in psychological research. From the early behaviourist conceptualizations to the recent neuroscience formulations fuelled by a flood of brain research, clinicians and theorists have developed models of brain functioning and human behaviour that are often reductionist and deterministic, either excluding the notion of *I* altogether or arguing for *I* as an emergent function of a complex neural system, as against *I* being an entity that actively interacts with the abstract mind map the neural system sustains.

Naturally, the question arises: do I really *need* such a notion to help me understand what I see clinically? In considering the utility of the notion *I* as part of an explanatory mechanism helpful to the clinician, I invite the reader to measure it not against the vexing notions of 'evidence' or 'proof', but against the notion of 'goodness of fit' to the data – both research data and clinical experience. I suggest that the idea of 'goodness of fit', rather than 'proof', is the normal criterion we use when assessing the utility of a model in science. The case for *I* as a separate entity rather than as simply the apex of a complex neural processing system is presented throughout the book, and I make no attempt to summarize the arguments here.

The debate is not so much whether *I* exists – in a sense, we all experience its existence. Rather, the debate is whether *I* as an entity is explainable by or reducible to the emergent properties of a complex neural system, as many argue; or whether there is value in returning to a notion that has been around a long time: *I* as an entity distinct from, yet integral with, the neural system. My exploration of these matters emerges from the practical concerns of how a clinician is to formulate psychological problems without oversimplifying them, as the human mind is so extraordinarily complex. I introduce aspects of this complexity as the *clinician's conundrum*, a conundrum best summarized as: is what the client experiences a direct function of his or her brain processes, or of the client's *I* either causing or reacting to those brain processes? Naturally, both are implicated, but I will argue that there is value in differentiating the two, and that understanding their interplay is helpful from a clinical point of view.

In exploring the idea of *I* as an entity separate from the brain, this book covers a diverse range of psychological topics relevant to the clinician. The book's style is to raise questions to consider, rather than to 'prove a point', although my own position will be evident. Topics range from Charlie's dilemma (if his *I* is equivalent to his brain, then how is it that his brain appears to perform functions not 'owned' by his *I*?) to general questions of subjective experience, the role of emotions, and the parameters of moral responsibility. How things are conceptualized also has a bearing on intervention strategies, on the respective roles of 'talking therapies' and medical interventions. It means the clinician might reasonably ask the question: does the problem before me represent an '*I* event' (that is, its origin is *I*) or a 'brain event' (that is, its origin is the brain)? The answer to this question has implications for how the clinician might then deal with the event.

This book is presented in six parts. In Part I, I explore the notion of *I* as a unitary indivisible entity that is not the same as the brain, even though it needs the brain for its expression in the natural world. I look at semantic issues and suggested parameters of *I*. In Part II, I explore basic brain functions potentially relevant to the clinician's understanding of his client's experience and behaviour. We familiarize ourselves with the structure and functions of the brain as an entity separate from *I* and consider the problem of locating *I* within the brain. In Part III, I consider the emerging relationship of *I* with the brain in the developmental context, and then in the awareness and acceptance (or otherwise) of *I* of its own body and brain, and in the relationship of *I* with other *I*s.

In Part IV, I look at how *I* might interact with the brain in the context of various normal psychological processes such as memory, attention, other states of consciousness, and emotions. In Part V, I apply these thoughts to conditions typically encountered by the clinician: depression, psychosis, post-traumatic stress disorder, and so on. Finally, in Part VI, a kind of post-script, I look at some implications of the *I*–brain distinction in the legal context, the conundrum the distinction presents for scientific research, and how the conceptualization of the *I*–brain dynamic might affect intervention and the role of the clinician.

Part I

The search for the subjective self

1

The elusive subjective self

There exists in my body a subjective and expressive self – an entity I will call *I*. Despite the common usage of this term, getting to the heart of what *I* 'is' (or am)[1] is a challenge confronting both neurologist and psychologist. In this book, I explore the relationship of *I* with the brain from a different perspective to one generally taken, where *I* is seen as a function of the brain rather than an entity interacting *with* the brain. I believe the perspective of *I* as a function of the brain does not provide the best account of what is seen clinically, nor is it the only way to interpret the relevant research in the neurosciences and in psychology.

This chapter introduces the clinical conundrum presented in *I* as an entity distinguished from the body and brain. We begin with Charlie's perplexing thought and how a clinician might respond to Charlie's dilemma.

The perplexing thought

Charlie[2] struggled with a perplexing thought whose source appeared to be not-*I*: 'The thought comes to me frequently that I will take a knife, stab my girlfriend, and kill her', Charlie told me in anguish.

> But I really don't feel this way about her – I love her – and I don't want to do her any harm. Still, I'm scared that one day I'll act upon this thought. I have to be careful not to have a knife in my hand when she is with me: that fills me with so much dread.

How can this be? How is it possible for Charlie to experience a thought which does not 'belong' to him? He has no intent to kill his girlfriend, nor reason or desire (so it would seem) to do so. He has not acted upon his thought, showing that he is capable both of evaluating the thought and of resisting what it tells him. But resistance is not easy: it can be exhausting, and he is afraid that one day he may act upon the thought even though he insists that he does not want to.

There are different ideas on how one might deal with Charlie's intrusive thought. It is not unusual to find a clinician moving from one position to another to find something that 'works': clinicians are by and large practical people. Good clinicians also seek to be 'evidence based', which means the intervention they employ has been reported to have worked to a 'significant' extent to ameliorate similar symptoms in others. But such movement from one approach to another bears testament to how little we understand the brain and its relationship to *I*: there is little cohesive theory.

One idea is that Charlie is really kidding himself. For a reason he does not want to admit to or is not conscious of, he really *does* hate his girlfriend, and wants to put her away. It is a decision for which his *I* should take full responsibility. However, the idea is so morally repugnant and his conscience (or fear of subsequent social retribution) is so strong that he manages to separate himself from this powerful thought. Yet the thought really *does* belong to him; its source is *I*. He should take ownership of it, and work through the secret hatred he has towards his girlfriend. Now it is no longer secret, it might be possible for him to set himself free from the impulse this 'intrusive' thought has created, simply by changing his mind. The clinician will help motivate Charlie to make this new decision, after he has come to accept his *real* feelings towards his girlfriend.

Another idea might be that Charlie's girlfriend has become the scapegoat of the *real* object of his hatred, which might be his mother, his girlfriend's mother, or even something he sees in her that reminds him of himself. The origin of the impulse remains *I*; its focus, however, has been misplaced. The adventure of therapy then becomes to discover who the *real* culprit is, so that Charlie can 'deal' with his hostile 'intrusive' thought more effectively by working through his hatred towards this person. Sigmund Freud became famous for such adventures in therapy. He might have used the politics of *id*, *ego*, and *superego* to explain what was going on in Charlie's brain. For Freud, Charlie's rogue thought might represent an *id* impulse; his concern that the thought represents a moral problem might be a message from his *superego*, while his *ego* has to decide what to do. Indeed, *I* certainly *is* in the business of deciding what to do, as we will see.

A third idea is that Charlie is, in fact, right. The thought really *does not* belong to him. It intrudes upon his *I*, finding its origin in some neural distortion. A clinician practising cognitive behavioural therapy (CBT) might want to train Charlie how to 'dispute' this intrusive and irrational thought, replacing it with a more acceptable one. He needs to train his brain to produce 'helpful' thoughts. Alternatively, a 'social experiment' might be formulated to prove to Charlie that this foreign thought would not result in the feared action, by providing him with every opportunity to act upon it, whereupon he discovers (hopefully), knife in hand, that in fact he does not attack his girlfriend. The thought was just an aberrant neural event, not necessarily connected with intent or action. Charlie has to deal with his fear that the thought might lead to unwanted action, and provide evidence for himself that his thought did not in fact 'belong' to him. Yet if Charlie's brain can produce a thought that does not belong to him, who is this *he* (that is, the *I* inside Charlie) that the thought does not belong to, but intrudes upon? Who is this *he* that is separate from at least some of the thoughts in his head and can dispute his thoughts?

For the radical behavioural therapist, the solution is relatively simple: there *is* no problem. Whether or not a thought 'belongs' to Charlie is immaterial: if it cannot be 'objectively' seen or heard or measured, it is not an entity for science to consider. Neither *I* nor the troublesome thought is a concept of real value to the clinician. Not until Charlie has been seen to actually pick up a knife and attack his girlfriend – that is, not until he actually engages in 'dysfunctional' behaviour does a problem exist. Should this happen, a programme would be developed, either to 'extinguish' the problematic behaviour by introducing an 'aversive event contingent upon the behaviour' next time it occurs, or to reinforce an alternative appropriate behaviour by rewarding it with a 'pleasant event contingent upon the desired behaviour'. Seeing some obvious difficulties with this approach, despite its purist scientific reasoning, some behaviourists subsequently conceded that thoughts *might* exist and be a legitimate 'target' for intervention. So they took a similar approach of introducing reinforcing events contingent upon targeted behaviour, but this time the target included thoughts and not just observable behaviour. Nevertheless, the more 'pure' approach would be to target a decrease in *complaints* about the thoughts – the observable behaviour – rather than the thoughts themselves.

For those keeping pace with the latest developments, the 'mindfulness' approach might provide another angle. Who knows if the thought belongs to Charlie or what it might mean – does it really matter? The problem is not the thought itself, but Charlie's *relationship* with the thought: that is, the relationship of *I* with the thought. So the idea is to accept the presence of the thought and observe its distressing nature – do not try to figure it out, do not interact with it, do not be controlled by it.³ Regardless of whether Charlie was the originator or the unwilling recipient of the thought, he should just notice it and let it go. Detach. He should not let the things of mind or heart interfere with his equilibrium. He should remain observer of both internal and external worlds. To use Schwartz's formulation (Schwartz and Begley, 2002): relabel the experience ('It's not me, it's just a thought in my head'); reattribute the thought ('The thought is actually a glitch in my neural system'); refocus on something pleasant instead ('I'll think of the flowers I'd like to give to my girlfriend, instead'); and revalue the thought ('This thought is senseless, not worth the energy to consider its implications'). Such an approach acknowledges the separateness between Charlie's *I* and his thought.

If we do not restrict ourselves to schools of psychological thought, another approach might be considered. Although not promoted within the scientific or clinical practitioner community, it is an approach many people across diverse cultures would consider. That is, Charlie's thought is not his own, but is an expression of a spirit or entity other than Charlie's *I* taking opportunity in Charlie's neural system. If one was to accept such a possibility, how should it be dealt with, and who could deal with such an event? Should a priest come and exorcise this entity? Perhaps the only one who might deal with such a presence (if, indeed, this is Charlie's trouble) is one authorized to do so – from where would such authority come?

In psychiatric circles, there is another way of approaching Charlie's dilemma. Psychiatrists know a bit about the brain events that might produce Charlie's wayward thoughts. They might argue Charlie is unbalanced. Or should I say his neurotransmitter levels are unbalanced. Or *some* of his neurotransmitter levels at least – serotonin, maybe. So we might correct the imbalance chemically with medication. There are many to choose from: in Charlie's case, the psychiatrist might choose a selective serotonin re-uptake inhibitor (SSRI) such as sertraline hydrochloride. Yet what has this to do with Charlie's thoughts? Are we to understand that Charlie's thoughts are, in the final analysis, biochemical events that can be moderated through the application of the right chemical? Has the psychiatrist been able to locate the thought in Charlie's biochemistry?

As it happens, Charlie *was* prescribed sertraline: he reported that it lessened the intensity of his unwanted thought, but did not stop it. His persisting thought was a little easier to manage and he did not get so exhausted with the conflict. His *I* obtained partial relief. But it continued to present itself in regular and apparently random fashion, although more so when his girlfriend was present. Neurotransmitter activity appeared to contribute *something* to the problem, but it did not seem to affect the thought content.

Charlie's dilemma highlights a problem of the relationship between the brain and *I* and different responses a clinician might consider. It seems that Charlie's *I* loves his girlfriend and that for some reason his brain created a thought alien to *I* that wants to destroy his girlfriend, so there is a conflict between Charlie's *I* and his brain. Biochemical intervention seems to help Charlie to cope, but does not remove the essential conflict. How has the conflict come to be and, importantly, what does it tell us about the brain and *I*? Let us begin by taking a closer look at this entity *I*.

The body and *I*

The entity *I* is capable of subjective experience. It is not limited to nor defined by the physical body, although for as long as I have been aware of *I*, it has been in my physical body. Wherever my body goes, *I* go; wherever my body is not, *I* am not, although we will see the reverse may be more to the point: wherever *I* chooses to go, the body follows.

I is not identical with the physical body. If I lose a part of my physical body, I do not lose part of *I*. If I have a diseased organ replaced by another, all of *I* remains in my body – *I* is not fragmented by the loss of that organ, nor has that particular organ any awareness of being *I*, or a part of *I*. The new organ replacing the old does not bring a fragment of a foreign *I* to do battle with the existing *I*, even though the foreign tissue might do battle with the new body: it somehow realizes it is in foreign territory. Likewise, judging from reports of heart transplant recipients, I might experience personality changes should I be given a replacement heart – it seems I inherit not only a heart, but a little of the donor's emotional memory, too – but there is no question that my *I* remains the same, despite my tastes having changed.

Should even a large part of my body be disabled by a broken neck or neural disease, *I* somehow remains unitary and intact. *I* does not become fractured. Should

I lose the function of half my brain through a stroke, I would not become 'half-*I*'. After neuro-anatomist Jill Taylor suffered a massive stroke in her left hemisphere, she wrote: 'I understand that no matter what information is being processed (or not being processed) in my two hemispheres, I still experience the collective of myself as a single entity with a single mind' (Taylor, 2009: 144). However she might conceive of the relationship of her *I* with her brain, she reported that her *I* remained intact, a unitary whole, even though she had lost the use of practically half her brain.

Should my brain be cut in half, as happened to Harriet Lees, the thirty-one year old who suffered debilitating epilepsy and in whom surgeons severed the corpus callosum, connecting the left hemisphere to the right (Sperry, 1964), *I* would not be split in half and become two *I*s: perhaps a left-brain analytic critic fighting a right-brain liberated artist. Harriet's *I* remained one. Granted, her *I* was confused as parts of her body no longer communicated with other parts because of disconnections between parts of her brain, yet her *I* reportedly remained intact – she did not even feel disturbed.[4]

Should one brain be joined to another, however, it may be possible for two *I*s to coexist. This happened to Canadian twins Tatiana and Krista Hogan, who were born joined at the head so that they shared part of their brain (the brainstem and thalamus). They shared sensory input ('one girl drinks and the other feels it') and even thoughts (Dominus, 2011). Nevertheless, each retained her own *I*, as we observe when Tatiana says to Krista, as she reaches for the cup from which her sister has been drinking, 'Now I do it', clearly differentiating her *I* from her sister's. They appear to share aspects of the orientation and perception their conjoined brains allow them, yet retain separate subjective selves and personalities. That is, two clearly delineated *I*s in two separate bodies with a partially shared brain, allowing access to information mediated by each other's brain.

What and where, then, is *I*? Is *I* something I can see or measure? Can I detect its location somewhere in my brain or, more generally, in time and space? And what is the *relationship* of *I* with my brain and body[5] and the external world? And does all this really matter to the clinician? I believe it does: when I am faced with another *I* sitting opposite me, struggling with its relationship with its brain and body, with the world it inhabits, and with the other *I*s in that world, I need to understand how all this works.

I: A unitary entity

I is a unique and undivided entity: I have only one *I*. Though there are tens of billions of neural cells and there is no one neural cell, region, or pathway in ultimate charge, there is one *I* who (normally) *is* in charge.[6] And although many activated neural cells are needed for consciousness, these cells all contribute to the awareness and capacities of only one *I*.

Even those with dissociative identity disorder have but a single *I* that slips from one role to the next, often unaware of doing so: when in one role, it is generally unaware of its other roles. Here *I* is affected by the fragmentation of memory in the neural system through functional disconnections. Yet there are never two *I*s inhabiting the same body – just one *I* playing hide-and-seek, wearing different identities to suit the changing demands of an otherwise overwhelming world.

When I 'talk to myself', *I* is not split in two: there is only one *I* talking, and the same *I* listens to what is said. Even when I have 'two minds' about a thing and cannot decide what my decision will be, it is the one *I* that moves from one position to the next: *I* is not in both positions at once. And it is the one *I* who will make a judgement, for better or worse, between the two options being considered.

So what *is* this unitary entity that inhabits the one body, capable of both subjective experience and initiating actions, but not identical to the body? Australian philosopher David Chalmers suggested that 'conscious experience' may be inherently irreducible to anything more 'basic' – it might be considered an irreducible entity like space, time, or mass (Schwartz and Begley, 2002). This seems intuitively correct, although I would suggest a variation of his proposal: it is *I* that is such an entity, which, like space, time, and mass, is irreducible to anything more basic. It is the fundamental reality I experience – it is one, undivided, and continuous over time. Although *I* is mostly known and understood as conscious experience, these two are not the same, as we shall see. For now, I propose there is an entity *I* present in the living body.

While such a notion might appear self-evident, closer inspection reveals some puzzling phenomena. Thoughts and ideas and sensations can enter a person's head where the question arises: is this thought, idea, desire, or sensation an expression of *I* – that is, did *I* generate it, or did it come from elsewhere? Do these events really belong to *I*; or do these events intrude upon *I*? Such a dilemma might be raised by one suffering obsessive compulsive disorder, or schizophrenia, or severe depression, or post-traumatic stress disorder, or addictions of various kinds. It is a dilemma a person might present to a clinician. Yet their dilemma is one we probably all experience at some time. Along with the question about whether a thought, idea, or sensation is actually mine as against it being produced by a neural initiative or hormonal intrusion comes the problem of responsibility for those thoughts and actions that *I* disputes ownership of – and spouses and upholders of the law begin to look to clinicians for insights into the matter.

An old mystery

A reader familiar with the writings of the ancients will no doubt observe that this is not new. This notion of *I* is another way of talking about the 'soul' or 'spirit' of a person as distinct from the physical body – a revisiting of Descartes' dualism. The philosopher might cite Immanuel Kant or Martin Buber's explorations of 'I', or the latest works exploring the mind–body problem, or the related problem of consciousness, which has stretched the imagination of philosophers over many centuries, and about which many deep and scholarly works have been written.[7] The psychologist might refer to Freud's conceptualization of 'ego', or Jung's 'soul', or Frankl's 'spirit', or to more recent neuro-psychological works on mind or consciousness and the brain.

These all have valuable and relevant insights to offer. Certainly, I do not pretend to have answers where others have struggled to understand the mind–body problem, nor do I dismiss the interpretations and speculations inspired by recent research advances. I do not intend summarizing what has been written, as it would do injustice to these great minds, and there are many well-written books available that introduce the serious thinker to the issues. I simply enter the debate as it affects me as a clinician. But why should I, a clinician, enter this debate? Why not let scientific investigation and philosophical discourse take its course and inform me of what I need to know as new discoveries come to light? Besides, how does this debate relate to the theory and practice of psychology? Yet Charlie's problem shows the clinician's position on this matter affects how he interprets the client's experience and how he approaches intervention.

The current tendency is to define human experience as simply the clever work of neural networks, chemical reactions, and conditioned responses, or some unclear combination of these processes: there is frequently no conceptual room for an entity *I*. Many clinicians have found themselves drawn into such a theoretical position over the decades of psychological research and practice. The position regularly espoused in the recent flow of neurological and neuro-psychological literature similarly promotes deterministic and materialistic explanatory models to explain subjective experience, even if it creates a mild unease that there is 'something more' going on in relation to a subjective self. Researcher and clinician John Bowlby asked: 'Since, then, a clinician must perforce adopt some viewpoint, what is it to be? How is he to picture the relation of private to public, of subjective to objective, of feeling to physics, of body to mind?' (Bowlby, 1971: 107) How, indeed?

Chapter 2

I expressed through the body

My starting point and assumption is the presence of *I* – of self, ego, psyche – whatever you will. I have confidence in this because, of all the things I know, I know this best. Descartes famously said: '*Cogito ergo sum*'. That is: 'I think; therefore I am'; or: 'I am thinking, therefore I exist'. For Descartes, to 'think' embraced mental acts and data: feeling, perception, judgement, will, and so on. Perhaps 'consciousness' or 'subjective awareness' is a more accurate translation than 'think' in the Cartesian sense (Anscombe and Geach, 1970). Of course, Descartes was not defining 'I' in this statement: he was simply arguing for its existence. Now *I* say: *to feel, to smell, to remember, to hear, and to see requires a recipient: I am such a recipient, because I testify (thankfully) to being able to do these – I feel, I smell, I remember, I hear, and I see.* Furthermore, *to initiate thinking, to make judgement, to be able to decide, to plan, and to act requires a source: I am such a source, because I testify (thankfully) to being able to do these things – I think, I make judgements, I decide, I plan, and I act.* This is a step towards my definition of 'I'.

I make no attempt to 'prove' the existence of *I* philosophically or scientifically – to me, its existence is self-evident. *I* constitutes a *source* of events communicated through my brain and body, as well as a *recipient* or *destination* of such communications. And for you, your *I* will be self-evident to you, being similarly a source and recipient of communications.[1] In this chapter, a conceptualization of *I* is considered that reveals a conundrum the clinician faces when interpreting client experiences.

I am not my body

What is the *nature* of *I*, and how does it interact with the physical self? I do not pretend to solve this ancient philosophical mind–body problem – I do, however, present an interpretation for clinical purposes. I begin with the notion that *I* and the physical body are not identical.

If *I* and the physical body are not identical, is it possible for them to have separate existence? That the physical body is capable of separate existence from *I* is evident when we study a dead body. *I* departs when life departs, and the body remains.[2] More controversially though, is *I* capable of an existence apart from the body? Some report experiences which suggest this, as we shall see. Based on their interpretation of such reported experiences, the ancient Egyptian, Buddhist, Judaic, Christian, and Muslim traditions accepted the ongoing existence of *I* in some form or another after physical death.

Only many scientists and philosophers were unhappy with this notion. It was not that they had evidence to the contrary. Rather, they concluded that there was no *I* without a body (if, indeed, they would add, there *is* such a thing as *I*), on the basis of *lack* of 'scientific' or 'objective' evidence supporting such a notion. However, *lack* of evidence is not a valid reason to dismiss *anything* – it proves and disproves nothing. Further, we are constrained by systems of logic and argument that are necessarily limited by the experiences we happen to have, by the language available to us and the concepts that language encompasses, by the assumptions we are prepared to make, by the nature of the evidence we regard as valid, and by what we *want* to believe. But for all the depth of thinking entered into and for all the brilliance of argument, such logic and concepts do not necessarily equate to truth. Sometimes truth is dependent on what is revealed to us (as, indeed, is the 'truth' about a client's experience which the client needs to reveal to the clinician). The issue here is not about logic, but about whether a thing is possible – even if the thing is beyond my grasp. And if it *is* possible, how might I have knowledge about it?

It is my proposition that *I* and the body may be capable of separate existence; yet somehow the two come together, they 'need' each other, as it were, to function in the physical world as we know it, to become a human being. What the *body* is generally attracts little debate, but what is *I*?

Semantic alternatives

What is *I*? Is it simply another expression for self, ego, or consciousness? The difficulty finding a word to represent an idea is that each word has associations that vary from person to person and the word's capacity to communicate an idea is coloured by these associations. Definitional problems are exacerbated when the concepts underlying the words change over time or have different association histories for different people living in different cultures. And how much more difficult when words are translated from one language to another! Alternative words may carry overlapping concepts, but may suggest attributes I am not necessarily proposing, creating potential for confusion.

We come back to the term *self*. It might refer to *experience* of *I*, as in 'self-awareness', or 'self-consciousness'; or it could refer to certain perceived *attributes* of *I*, as in 'self-concept'; or it might simply refer to my body, as in 'looking at "myself" in the mirror'. The term 'self' does not distinguish between *I* and my body, my thoughts, the various social roles I might engage in, and all other things belonging to me. In general usage, 'self' refers to the combined package of *I* and my body. Certainly, when we talk of 'self-esteem', no distinction is made between *I*, the body, and the history of success (or otherwise) that *I* accomplishes in my body.

Similarly, the term *ego*, Latin for 'I', carries the associations of Freud's formulations. While both *I* and Freud's notion of ego are seen as the origin of decision making, Freud ascribes various roles and functions to ego relative to id and super-ego that I am not necessarily espousing. Feinberg distinguished his use of 'ego' from Freud's when he defined it as the 'inner I', that 'most intimate aspect of the self' (Feinberg, 2001: 1). In similar vein, the terms *soul* and *spirit* as alternatives for *I* carry the formulations of theorists such as Jung and Frankl, not to mention prior conceptualizations in the Hebrew and Christian scriptures and in the writings of Greek philosophers. The idea of spirit, or *ruach* in the Hebrew tradition, is related to breath or wind, a term used in relation to the generation of life – the 'life prin-ciple' – as well as referring to the seat of emotions, intellect, and will; while the Greek counterpart of spirit, or *pneuma*, is similarly related to wind, breath, the sign of life, or soul (psyche) – a principle of life, 'bound to the body in life, it escapes it with the last breath and returns to the ethereal sphere' (Bromiley, 1985).

William James, a founding father of psychology, argued for an alternative term with different associations for *I*, proposing that the 'proper field of enquiry for psy-chology' is *consciousness*, for 'that is what the mind is' (Schwartz and Begley, 2002). Yet 'consciousness' carries its own meaning – consider the expressions 'uncon-scious' (would *I* then cease to exist?) and 'subconscious' (a subset of *I*?). When I say 'I am conscious', I am saying consciousness is a state or attribute of *I*. Even though consciousness is clearly necessary for me to know *I* exists, when I have been uncon-scious (perhaps in sleep) and then recover consciousness, *I* is essentially the same *I* as before – for a period *I* lost awareness, but not its existence. Consciousness is the basis for my knowledge about *I* (as indeed it is for my knowledge of the external world), but it is not the *same* as *I*.

Although the traditional distinction has been between the *mind*[3] and brain (and certainly the term *mind* is a popular alternative for *I*), mind has its own nuances and associations, especially given the mindfulness concepts which find their origin in the conceptual framework of Buddhism. Perhaps the reintroduction of mind in clinical literature is reactive to the conceptual void caused by the general avoidance of the terms *mind* and *psyche* in much psychological research and practice in the last sixty years. Speaking of which, why not use the term defining the subject itself – the *psyche*? Yet the traditional focus of psychology as the study of the psyche is on the mechanisms of perception and thinking, of memory and learning, which has more to do with brain processing than *I*.

Perhaps the popular use of these various expressions refers to different attri-butes of the entity *I*. *Spirit* might refer to the life-force embedded in *I* (as in: he is 'spirited'; or: she is in 'low spirits'); or *I* disembodied, present as an intangible entity (as in: his 'spirit' has left his body; or: they sensed her 'spirit' in the house) – although spirit must have a form of *some* sort to be manifest. *Mind* might refer to *I* in interaction with the brain, especially in the decision-making process and the thoughts mediated by the brain (as in: he 'lost his mind'; or: she 'can't make up her mind'; or: what a 'mindless' [thoughtless] thing to do). *Soul* might refer to *I* in relation to aspects of feeling, motivation, or morality (as in: he was 'soulless'; or: she became his 'soul-mate'; or: it was a 'soul-searching' experience). *Consciousness* might refer to the capacity of *I* to apprehend sensory information (as in: he was 'conscious' throughout the operation; or: she 'lost consciousness' when she was hit from behind). But *I* is not *only* spirit, because it also reacts to body sensations; *I* is not *only* mind, because it also feels; *I* is not *only* soul, because it also decides; and *I* is not *only* consciousness, because, as far as we know, it normally stays in my body even in my deepest sleep.

Conceptualizing *I*

But in the end it is *I* that feels – my body perhaps (though not necessarily) a source, and certainly the expression of that feeling. It is *I* that initiates moral judgements – my body acts accordingly. It is *I* that attributes value and beauty – largely from information my brain mediates. It is *I* that normally decides my focus of attention – and accordingly directs my brain, eyes, and body. It is *I* that hopes and imagines – my brain mediates meanings that constitute those hopes and imaginations. And it is *I* that receives and sends messages – mediated by my brain and body. It is *I* that has authority over the body so that I expect it to respond to the direction of *I*. Such authority over the physical self allows moral and legal responsibility for thoughts generated and actions performed. If all goes well, there is a seamless integration of *I* and body,[4] and making such distinction is generally unnecessary. But I believe the distinction becomes necessary in the conceptualization of problems a clinician might confront.

For our purposes, I conceptualize *I* as *source and destination of communications* processed and filtered through the neural systems. *I* is the endpoint of a communication process, both genesis and destination of information flow: it is the active, dynamic receiver and initiator of information.[5] If there is information exchange, there is always an origin and a destination of information: this becomes a key issue in relation to the role of *I* relative to the neural system.

This relationship between *I* and external sources also contributes to the defining of *I* in its uniqueness. Just as the *source* of much information the neural system mediates and processes lies *outside* the neural system (though not all non-*I* information comes from an external source), so its *destination* does not reside within the neural system, despite the neural system's intimate relationship with that destination. No location within the neural system has been identified that might act as an ultimate destiny for the many strands of incoming information – no cell, no neural network, circuit, or region. I am proposing that *I* is the destination, and that *I* is not identical with the neural system. Similarly, *I*, through the agency of my body and the activation of neural networks available to me, is the source of communications to the external world, and especially to other *I*s encountered.

While *I* is located in neither time nor space, we all know its presence. Although the idea of an entity not being in any identified place at any defined moment does not sit well with the neuroscientist and biochemist that prefer to *see* things, it is a more familiar concept in quantum physics, with an accepted basis in theoretical science and mathematics. But for those who need concrete images to grasp ideas, conceptualizing *I* is problematic. Perhaps like the Spirit was said to 'hover' over the waters in the creation story, so I might conceive *I* 'hovering' in the brain. Or like how a magnetic field we cannot see is held in place by a magnet we *can* see, so the confluence of signals locating *I* is held in place by neural structures mediating those signals.

An idea communicated between two people may be encoded variously as a series of sound waves, bodily movements, or marks on paper, yet has meaning and existence separate from the sound waves, bodily movements, or paper markings mediating that idea. The idea itself cannot be directly seen or measured – it is of a different nature. Similarly, *I* exists and has meaning separate from the brain/body that acts as mediator between *I* and the world.[6] And just as something abstract and unseen as an idea has the power to change the physical world, so the unseen *I* has the power to impact the world and others. The power of an idea that has no meaning apart from *I* who apprehends it cannot be overstated. Wars are fought over ideas, people die for ideas, and the neural system is greatly affected by ideas: they play a central role in mental wellbeing. Yet where *is* this thing called an idea and *what* is it? Like *I*, the ideas *I* deals with remain elusive.

What is the *source* of *I*? Some suggest the brain, that *I* is the 'coming together' of complex neural processes. However, I will argue that the 'coming together' of complex neural processes carries the network of meanings *I* accesses, rather than constituting *I* itself. Perhaps the source is other than the brain. Consider a novel presented in a book: the book is not the *source* of the novel; it is only the medium that *holds* it. Although the coming together of those words embodies the meanings and ideas that form the novel, there is nevertheless another source implicated. The author is known by the ideas the novel contains. That the author may not be present does not prove an author does not exist: the novel bears testament to the author. Is this true of *I* also?

My body as an expression of *I*

My brain and body allows *I* to interact with the natural world – to take pleasure in it and to find meaning in it. My eyes and supporting neural software allow *I* to apprehend the visual experience, although it is a quality in *I*, not the neural system, that 'experiences' or makes the judgement that what I see is 'beautiful'. My ears and supporting neural software allow *I* to apprehend the idea you present to me, though it is a quality in *I*, not my ears and their associated neural systems, that 'understands' and makes judgement about what you mean. Similarly, music may activate diverse neural regions creating an internal harmony, but it is *I* that takes pleasure in it. And while it is *I* that enjoys the warmth of the sun, it is my body on which the sun's rays fall, just as it is my body that allows me to plant cabbages in my garden, although it is *I* that plans and purposes to do so. *I* interacts with neural networks to allow information exchange; not just information in the sense of language, but information in the more general sense of knowledge about the natural world, including sensations, abstract understandings and images, and encounters with other realities.

And so I would expect this design purpose[7] – the functional, meaningful, plea-surable interaction of *I* with the world – to be reflected in neural architecture. I believe that building a model to understand neural design on this basis is more useful than building it around superseded (at times) evolutionary adaptive features that may have little to do with the forces contributing to my unique neural devel-opment, my DNA notwithstanding. We need a model of how a well-functioning neural system allows a distinct and unique *I* to thrive in the current natural world.

With every progressive neural or bodily shut-down, its effect is not the diminish-ing of *I* itself so much as a diminishing of the capacity of *I* to interact with the natu-ral world. With increasing neural dysfunction, *I* may encounter difficulties both in its awareness of things and in its attempt to make sense of the world. I am thus reframing the problem of consciousness as one of how *I* interfaces with a dynamic neural system that is subject to corruption. While I do not understand how this interface works, I suggest as a starting point that the interface most likely comprises either a *broad* field or *multiple* fields of neural engagement. I suggest *multiple* fields of engagement because it seems the interface can be compromised, intentionally or otherwise, to varying degrees. Neurological research (Carter, 2010) suggests the various states of consciousness are not simple on/off events. When someone is in an unconscious state such as a coma, the link can be tenuous indeed, although the brain continues to function in many respects normally, dealing with largely internal automatic communication and processing systems. In other states of consciousness and (dis)empowerment of *I*, such as in trance, in sleep, in daydreams and in 'preoc-cupations', in drug-induced stupors, in hypnosis, or in a semi-conscious state, the interface can reflect a *partial* compromise.

If *I* is largely positioned by the confluence of communications mediated by neural networks, its existence in the brain is only possible in the living state: that is, while the communication flow continues. Does it then follow that when the neural network ceases to mediate the communication flow (either from external sources, or generated by the neural system itself), *I* ceases to exist? Is it possible for *I* to continue to exist, provided it is sustained by a communication process that *some-how bypasses the neural system*? I suspect this would be the position taken by those who believe in the existence of a self beyond the death of the body when neural activity ceases. For thousands of years, our ancestors have believed that *I* does not cease to exist when the physical body dies and disintegrates. Rather, they argued that when I die, the body loses its 'grip' on *I*, and *I* lets go of the body. Each goes to its own destination.

Is this really possible? Let us consider Una's experience of the morning when her *I* appeared to momentarily separate from her body.

Chapter 3

I separate from the body

There is only one *I*. The uniqueness of that identity is reflected in a unique combination of feelings and memories, and in the history of the decisions, plans, and actions made. If such attributes are an indispensable part of *I*, are these necessarily held in neural networks? If it were possible for *I* to exist apart from the body, would that *I* retain some or all of these qualities? Or are these qualities invested in my natural time-bound self, restricted to neural capacities that *I* accesses in its earthly sojourn, and largely lost if *I* should have existence apart from the body? Let us consider some unusual experiences.

Looking down from above

An extraordinary experience related by Una Glennon, mother of murdered twenty-six-year-old Ciara, occurred some months after Ciara's death. Extraordinary, but by no means a unique report – neither in literature, nor in the clinician's consulting room. I have heard of such accounts by people over the years in my practice. In fact, there are estimates that some ten percent of the general population experience an event analogous to Una's out-of-body experience sometime in their lives. In her book, there is no underlying agenda: it is simply the telling of her painful story.

It is early morning and Una is lying in bed. She recounts:

> Suddenly I am aware that I am floating upwards. My body remains on the bed but I am rising higher and higher towards the ceiling. As I am just about to touch the ceiling I am gripped by fear and I return instantly to my body . . . Clearly I am not my body. My body is merely the shell that encases the essence of who and what I really am. When I was floating to the ceiling I was whole and entire, with my mind, my thoughts, my awareness and even my fears. What remained on the bed was merely a shell, nothing more than a piece of discarded clothing.
>
> (Glennon, 2010: 57)

What do we make of this? Could Una 'see' without the use of her visual system? Could she understand her circumstances without recourse to neural networks? Or was she still firmly in her body, suffering a hallucinatory experience? Was her experience the effect of hypoxia or anoxia, or of irregularities in her brain's proprioceptive functions,[1] as is commonly suggested for the not-infrequent accounts of out-of-body experiences reported by the dying? Yet there is no suggestion here of body shut-down or 'near death' experience. Further, there are accounts of out-of-body experiences wherein people appear to be able to 'see' things (accurately) that they would not have been able to see from the vantage point of their bodily position and where there was no indication of their having earlier observed those things. The experience is not just limited to feeling 'as though I am outside my body'.

Janet recounted an out-of-body experience she had as she was being raped, after which she had been left for dead. She explained that, as she hovered above her body, she did not feel the pain being inflicted upon her – she felt a peace. Moreover, she recalled making a decision to re-enter her body for the sake of her children: 'No, I have to go back to be with my children.' She had somehow been made aware of the difficulties that lay ahead of her while she was 'out of her body', apparently communicated from an unknown source: 'The future will be difficult for you.' Was this a dissociative experience in that she was still in her body but emotionally separate from her overwhelming circumstances, or was it a momentary disengagement of her *I* from her body? If we are to accept this account as an out-of-body event, it would appear that Janet had thoughts and made a decision outside the context of her neural system. It also appears that, although her neural system was presumably responding to pain messages from the damage being done to her body, the pain messages were not apprehended by her *I*.

There are other published reports that record a range of contexts in which people report out-of-body experiences: when experiencing physical or mental stress or trauma, such as Una or Janet did; under the influence of psychedelic or dissociative drugs; at time of near-death or in a temporary brain-dead state; and in a semi-sleep state, that borderline period between dreaming and waking.[2] The experiences vary, but they have in common the sense of 'leaving' the body, often of being able to see the physical body and surroundings below; of being free of the normal physical sensations the body experiences; of being unable to action the body, but being able to think, decide, and experience emotion; and of re-entering the body after a short period.

Not surprisingly, controversy surrounds the interpretation of these events, with some attributing the experiences to an altered state of consciousness resulting from neural dysfunction, while others present these accounts as evidence of a human spirit having an existence beyond the body, as Una suggested. How data is interpreted is likely to reflect one's assumptions about the nature of a person's spirit, or *I*. But the question remains: might these experiences provide evidence for *I* as an entity distinct from the body, and that it can exist outside the body, even as the ancients believed? Furthermore, if it can exist outside the body as Una, Janet, and others suggest, is it possible for *I* to see, think, decide, and feel separate from the neural support structures we normally assume are prerequisite for such activities?

What if Una's *I* remained outside her body? If the brain requires the presence of *I* as source and destination of communication for its ongoing functioning, without *I* does the brain begin a shut-down process, eventually leading to death? We know that once the automatic internal traffic of communication in the brain (manifested in ongoing electrical activity) ceases, the neural structures that mediate the flow of communication begin to deteriorate and collapse.[3] Not only do the communication processes require the supporting biochemical structures to operate, *the supporting biochemical structures require the communication processes to remain intact.* If *I* is intrinsically bound up in these communication systems, does the brain need *I* as much as *I* needs the brain to function in the natural world?[4] Furthermore, might we find a similar interdependency between 'automatic' bidirectional flow of communication between various parts of the brain, and between the brain and various organs such as the heart, as we find in the flow of communication between *I* and those 'automatic' neural communication systems?

Yet questions remain. How do we differentiate various states of consciousness? How can we reliably distinguish between dreams, hallucinations, illusions, and 'reality'? Can we confirm that during her out-of-body experience Una was in touch with 'reality'? It raises the more general question of the reliability of my interpretation of subjective experience. Moreover, my capacity to reflect on subjective experiences assumes reliable access to my history of past experiences which inform the interpretive process. There is also the troubling problem of how out-of-body experiences might be remembered if they take place while the brain is effectively disabled: *I* must then be able to hold memory. For now, I present Una's and Janet's experiences as reported by credible witnesses: what we make of them is open for debate.

Many reports match Una's and Janet's experiences. Dutch cardiologist Pim van Lommel studied near-death experiences in cardiac arrest patients, of whom some eighteen per cent (of 344 patients) reported 'classic' near-death experiences while they were clinically dead – their brainstem activity had 'flat-lined'. That is, electrical activity could no longer be recorded. He conjectured that continuity of consciousness despite lack of neuronal activity in the brain 'may be achievable if the brain acted as receiver for the information generated by memories and consciousness, which existed independently of the brain, just as radio, television and internet information existed independently of the instruments that received it' (van Lommel *et al.*, 2001).

Van Lommel posited that memory might have an existence beyond the neural storage process, even though activation of the neural system is normally required to store and access memories. If we adopted van Lommel's suggestion, we would need to allow that memory is an integral aspect of *I*. While this notion seems intuitively necessary for *I* to experience a sense of identity embedded in one's history, there are associated difficulties. Certainly, the fragmented, reconstructive, and relatively distorted nature of the memories *I* typically accesses bears testimony to the involvement of neural software processing. Perhaps memories would not be fragmented and distorted if they had existence apart from neural storage and retrieval systems.

Out-of-body experiences have also been reported by people in the borderline state between rapid eye movement (REM) sleep and the waking state, when sleep paralysis persists and dream imagery mingles with sensory input. These experiences provide fascinating but difficult-to-interpret data regarding the *I*–brain relationship. In attempts to induce such experiences, researchers have stimulated theta brainwave frequencies associated with the dream state, with some success. It seems the experience of the relationship of *I* with the body can be manipulated by stimulating brainwave frequencies which possibly mediate between neural hardware and *I*. Nevertheless, differences between dreaming and out-of-body experience have been observed: the out-of-body experience is reported to be more vivid and generally associated with the memory of leaving and re-entering (being 'pulled back' into) the body (Green, 1968).

Some parameters of *I*

Although I suggest that *I* is not defined by brain chemistry, it nevertheless needs the brain to interact with the body and thus to interact with the external physical world. While disabling or removing parts of the brain would not remove or diminish *I*, the capacity of *I* to interact with the world is compromised, as people with brain tumours or with brain tissue removed testify. Some kinds of brain lesions or deterioration may result in *I* no longer operating effectively, perhaps being altogether disabled: *I* can become trapped in a dysfunctional body and brain, distorting communication.

When all is functioning as it should, *I* expresses itself seamlessly and directly through the body. Equally, it can communicate indirectly in mediums outside the body, through music, writing, or art. Nevertheless, all expressions of *I*, direct or indirect, are not the same as *I*. Mostly, *I* finds direct expression through the body through verbal and nonverbal means. The complex interactions within the neural system (for example, between semantic centres, emotional networks, and the associated physiological reactions and motor responses) mean that the expression of *I* has multiple avenues within the body which need to be interpreted by the receiver. It also means there are many opportunities for distortion. The meanings *I* expresses through the body are not always clear to the external observer, as we discover in the case of somatoform disorders. Whatever the medium, the signals *I* sends are not the same as *I*, even though *I* remains the source of those signals and the signals constitute a true reflection of *I*.

If *I* is not limited to the physical body and if it does not follow the destruction of the body when the body dies, perhaps it does not suffer the ravages of time either. Just as a decision or an idea does not 'age', nor, perhaps, does *I*,[5] while the body and brain clearly do. Many have said: 'I don't *feel* any older – it's only my body slowing and breaking apart.' My time-bound body changes, getting older, eventually deteriorating and collapsing, but *I* may be ageless. Ageless, perhaps, yet *I* also changes, but differently to a body bound by natural laws. Over the years, *I* may become wiser, *I* may change position and attitude, *I* may variously embrace or reject people and events, shifting allegiances and embracing or rejecting new information – *I* may change and be transformed, but not in the sense of it 'aging'.

While *I* is in the brain and body, these restrict and largely define *I* – but should *I* be free of brain and body, what then might be the parameters of *I*? At the very least, it remains the ongoing source and destination of communication. Certainly, such it does *within* the body. In this respect, I would describe the role of the brain as *transformational*. It transforms *I* events – decisions, ideas, and so on – into real-time events in the body. Conversely, it transforms bodily events – life experiences, interactions with others, and so on – into *I* events. The brain becomes key to both the freedom and the limitations of the expression of *I* in the physical world.

The body and its sensations and impulses are concerned with physical survival and comfort, and provide a vehicle with which the natural world might be acted upon and reacted to; *I* is concerned with ideas, and decisions, and allegiances. Yet the body's impulses and sensations are managed by *I*, just as *I* uses the body to express its ideas and decisions. *I requires expression*: it is only through expression that its presence is known. This appears to be a fundamental law in the relationship of *I* to the world, the body/brain acting as intermediary.

Although the body/brain acts as an intermediary, there still exists a relationship of *I* with the body/brain in its own right. In this relationship, sometimes *I* is in the ascendancy; sometimes the body/brain. Both are about the business of making sense of incoming signals, but for different reasons and in different ways. Although we would normally expect the body/brain and *I* to act in harmony, the relationship can be vexatious. Mostly, horse (body/brain) and rider (*I*) gallop in the same direction as one, the rider in control of the horse – but not always. For some, indeed, seldom.

And so these present to the clinician their conundrum. The clinician might consider thus about his client: is he witnessing an effective expression of the client's *I*, wherein *I* expresses distress by way of a body/brain that functions well; or is he witnessing a body/brain at odds with the client's *I*, prompting unwanted impulses and sensations poorly managed by *I*? Is he witnessing a body/brain that, for some reason, fails to properly express the client's *I*, making it difficult to know what is happening for the client; or perhaps an *I* that has some inherent difficulty with the body it calls home? Or perhaps the body/brain has made processing errors, distorting memory and meaning for the client's *I*? Then again, the client's *I* may simply have made some poor decisions.

We have considered *I* at some length. We now explore what is coming to be understood about the brain and its functioning, and consider what insights this might grant about the relationship of *I* with the brain, beginning with the computer as a model for neural processing.

Part II

The brain

Form and function

Chapter 4

The brain

Computers and neural processing

The computer and the brain share a number of principles, particularly with respect to information processing. Apart from the fact that viruses can slow both down and lack of electrical power would cause both to stop altogether, parallels can be determined at hardware and software levels. These we outline here, but we will also observe that there are important differences – importantly, because the computer has no *I* to experience sensations or apprehend meanings, there is no parallel for the brain–*I* dynamic.

Computer parallels

The computer's hardware is essentially a binary system comprising boards with an enormous number of small circuits operating a series of electronic on/off switches that govern all processing activity. Each circuit supplies the fundamental unit of information, a *bit* or binary digit, where '0' represents off, and '1' represents on. These circuits in turn are arranged in *logic gates*, where higher circuits control the state of one or more other circuits – whether it is off or on. And so the system is built up into increasingly complex structures. At cellular level, the brain also operates a binary system of on/off switches that function both in synaptic connections and within the neurons themselves, forming the basis of neural software.

The next level in the computer involves *logic operations*, which is capable of creating complex conditional statements around the fundamental circuits. A raft of simple individual processing instructions is stored in *read-only memory* (ROM) as *machine code*, which in turn provides the first level of 'language' the higher-order software needs – the bridge between banks of off/on switches and a useable language. The machine code is normally preset and comes inbuilt with the hardware.

Similarly, processing software in the brain is built on neural on/off switches – the encoding, decoding, and transmission of bits of information – beginning with the basic algorithms or 'machine language' necessary to build increasingly complex strings of neural connections. I suspect this 'machine' software is preset genetically, 'hard-wired' in molecular formations (DNA – the brain's version of ROM), and that needs to be activated to function. This software provides the capacity to make discriminations visually and aurally, to create fundamental connections, to send signals prompting physical movement, and to determine reflex actions to pain and other primary needs. I would expect these systems to be uninterpretable by any investigator trying to 'read' neural 'machine language', just as computer algorithms are uninterpretable at machine language level.[1]

From here, each software 'language' layer in the computer is built on the previous one in hierarchical fashion and kept in memory. Basic algorithms, equations, and sub-programs are built into small standardized programs, which, in turn, make up 'library files'. These files comprise a variety of small functional and logical programs which more complex programs will use. Some programs relate to specific functions so extensive they have their own dedicated 'card', which talks to other cards in the system, each processing its own specialized area of information. It is these complex programs that present me with the graphics and user-friendly language that enable me to use the computer.

The brain also finds a hierarchy of software built around the acquisition of learned material underpinning the development of language, skills in mathematics, reading or music skills, the capacity to predict and develop strategies to negotiate social situations, and so on. It is the higher-level software that carries information in a form *I* can use, from which meanings are abstracted and judgements and decisions are made. I would expect to find 'libraries' of neural software supporting higher-level processing. Mid-level programs may allow the interpretation of information by matching and making associations, filtering information, focusing and selecting, deleting, adding, adjusting, and searching memory systems.

The computer's memory comprises an enormous number of cell sets (or *bytes*) where binary numbers in groups of eight can be placed and subsequently 'read'. Each cell has a numerical address so it may be easily found. These sets of numbers can be made to represent whatever the higher levels of software code them to represent. It is the higher-level software that interprets the bank of data thus established. The way the memory bank is structured varies. It is normally designed to maximize efficiency and speed of access to the relevant stored data. For example, groups of memory cells called *registers* can be set aside from the main memory bank to allow more rapid reading and writing than if the instructions in the main memory had to be continually scanned.

Of particular interest to us are the two principal types of main memory found in the computer: *random-access memory* (RAM) and *read-only memory* (ROM). RAM has the capacity of being read and written onto at any time, while ROM is preset with programs that can only be read, such as its start-up instructions. ROM memory is a given; it cannot be changed and operates immediately when activated. Among other memory systems is 'cache' memory, associated with RAM, which helps speed things up – here data that needs to be moved around more frequently can be automatically and temporarily stored for quick access, rather than the computer having to repeatedly search its whole memory bank – a bit like the brain's 'working memory'.

The material the brain acquires and uses at the higher levels of processing is stored in its 'RAM' memory, which has various forms, of which more will be said later. It is essentially housed in vast banks of synaptic connections. There is continual interaction of incoming information with 'packages' of stored information using mid-level software. The matching of incoming information with existing information leads to recognition, allowing associative processes and retrieval of linked material, preparing the data necessary to create meaning. The brain is continually scanning for matches in its store of patterns to identify faces, landmarks, language expressions, and so on.

The packaging of higher-level information also occurs in other ways, both at the conceptual and at the kinaesthetic level. For example, if I were to play an organ recital or perform a dance routine, my brain would use packages of learned information firmed up in semi-permanent neural packages or templates, not unlike the way computer software is built around small informational packages of algorithms and 'remembered' or 'set' material – 'chunks of information' that become the elements of a higher-level software package. These efficiencies come at a cost: they enhance speed of functioning (where speed is of essence, these packages are utilized automatically), but are not easily adjusted or changed.

There is another form of ROM memory (presumably DNA based) the brain accesses, which is without parallel in the computer. It is chemical rather than electrical in nature. It sends messages throughout the body in chemical information packages called hormones by way of the bloodstream and other fluids, delivering prepared standardized messages to various parts of the body. Here only the timing and intensity changes, not the messages themselves, although there are many different packages, each carrying different information. The two systems talk to each other. For example, some hormones are controlled directly by the neural software in the hypothalamus, which receives information from almost all parts of the nervous system, as it has an interest in the physical wellbeing of the body. However, to the extent that hormones deal mostly with body chemistry, they are only of marginal interest here, except to note that they are an extension of the central communication network of the brain.

Finally, like the computer, the brain is powered electrically and works hard to do its job efficiently. It never stops working. Siegel notes: 'We utilize neural energy when we think, when we talk, when we listen, and when we read' (Siegel, 2009: 52). We also use neural energy when we feel, when we sleep, when we decide a matter, and when we focus on something. But unlike the computer, the brain has no external power source to plug into. Like the brain, the computer moves at extraordinary speed. The enormous amount of work the computer does at such speed draws significant electrical power and generates heat (hence its cooling fan). It is necessary that it can be plugged it into an ongoing non-fluctuating source of power. The brain, in contrast, produces power chemically, not unlike a standard battery, a source vital to its ongoing operation. But problems can arise – if the chemical processes generating the power are compromised, producing too much or insufficient power, the brain's functioning is affected.

Computer design and *I*

Despite the similarities between computer and brain in various aspects of processing, there are essential differences. Importantly, the computer has no entity comparable to *I* in its functioning and development: I would be hard-pressed to attribute my computer with a 'self', and do not expect it to manifest the various associated attributes. For all the 'thinking' and 'remembering' it can do, the computer has no breath, emotion, experience, or sensation; it initiates no moral, aesthetic, or relational judgements, nor does it imagine or understand things; it has no sense of humour, nor does it have a sense of past or future; it has no regrets or hopes, nor does it make future plans. All of which I am generally capable, and perhaps many of which help differentiate the function of my brain as a processing system serving *I* from the entity *I* itself.

But even using the computer as a model of brain information processing, difficulties are encountered. How might I decipher the brain's software? If I was presented with a computer replete with many complex programs and had no access to the program designers, I would not study software designs by placing microchips under a microscope or by subjecting the computer to functional magnetic resonance imaging (fMRI), nor would I disable a part of the hardware (creating a 'lesion') to see what happens. Perhaps I might experiment with input/output relationships to study the computer's capacities, and see what it might do under various controlled conditions, but this would give limited insight.

Cognitive psychologists are about the business of explicating brain software, determining capacities, algorithms, memory systems, and general cognitive design. But the research brief with a brain that processes an enormously complex informational stream has been daunting. The reach and complexity of cognitive processes is extensive, and few researchers have attempted to outline a comprehensive cognitive model accounting for the many interactive brain functions. Our progress in understanding neural software has been slow indeed. It is one thing to design software from scratch for a computer. It is another to go in reverse – to disentangle complex programs we did not design. And such is the challenge of the cognitive psychologist and neuroscientist in relation to neural software, each tackling the problem from a different perspective – the cognitive psychologist studying the effect of various imposed conditions on targeted performances; the neuroscientist studying the effects of failures or artificial stimulation of specific neural pathways on sensation and behaviour.

What is the end result of the neural software programs? Is it to create *I*, or to prepare information for apprehension by *I*? If the latter, how can something as intangible as an abstract idea be recorded in or derived from a tangible neural trace? How are meanings abstracted from neural networks? The problem may be better understood when we consider the words of an unfamiliar language printed upon a page – it is simply a set of markings on paper. Somehow, meaning needs to be imputed to the tangible marks. No meaningfulness can be discerned where no connection to a pre-existing abstract realm has been made. The concrete representation of an idea mediated by neural software is not the same as the idea itself – how does *I* make sense of these?

How are abstractions such as morality, beauty, judgement, and justice managed by the brain? Are they features that can only be unlocked in the presence of *I* because they ultimately belong to *I*? Does it require *I* to apprehend the meaning of material processed by the brain? It does, after all, require someone to find meaning in the end product of a computer's processing. Abstract ideas seem to be created by the simultaneous connection of diverse units of information where, as gestalt psychologists argue, the *whole becomes more than the sum of its parts*. It seems a synergy is created by the coming together of the information itself, not by the means by which the information happens to be carried. Yet how is such synergy apprehended? Apart from *I*, there would seem to be no purpose or meaningfulness.

Finally, a computer is designed by one who determines what it will do, deciding its settings and designing its capacities – it is not self-generating, even though it might be programmed to build on itself. If my *brain* has 'design', how might that come about?[2] I propose neural programming is the outcome of an unknown mix of design intent and natural laws: there are a number of contributors.

One contributor relates to the settings found in DNA,[3] which establishes the 'machine language' mediating between body chemistry and the 'standardized' neural software that allows the development of the many neural processes – essentially the brain's ROM memory. While its immediate origin is an event that takes place at conception, there remains the question of the ultimate design origin. This design origin should also be the source of *I*, given *I* and the brain coexist and 'need' each other. Certainly, *I* is not that source, nor, I suggest, is *I* without source. Yet the nature of the source is beyond my comprehension.[4]

A second contributor is *I*, who interacts with the brain and makes the decisions and establishes the focus that creates neural connections. Just as an author writes ideas onto a page, so the ideas *I* apprehends from without and generates from within are written into the brain's networks. I am not saying that the brain 'sculpts' or changes *itself*, as Doidge (2010) argues. Rather, just as a rock formation is not sculpted 'by itself', but by wind and water, so the brain is not sculpted 'by itself', but by *I* attending to incoming signals and initiating actions. Nevertheless, the resulting unique neural formation is partially defined by the brain's predetermined features (locked in DNA) that are revealed over time, just as the inner characteristics of the rock are revealed by the action of wind and water.

Those external to me constitute a third contribution to neural software design. Others help mould meaningfulness and perception, teach language and interpret emotion, and are the source of communications that the brain apprehends. In addition, mirror neurons in the brain are sensitive to the perceived emotions and actions of others, resonating with their emotions and intentions (Cozolino, 2006).

Despite the limitations of the computer analogy, useful correlates include information processing as found in its software and some aspects of memory storage and retrieval. The computer model helps me understand some aspects of brain functioning – processing, coding and decoding, and storage. But it does not give insight into *I*, how meanings are imputed, nor the interaction of *I* with the brain. Will a review of the physical brain give clues to the way the brain functions and interacts with *I*?

Chapter 5

The brain

Mind maps and meaning

A fundamental task of the client in therapy is to make sense of things – to derive or create meaningfulness from experienced events. It is equally a fundamental task for the neural system. The brain as an information processing system allows *I* to abstract meaningfulness from incoming information from the body, other people, and the external world. Physical signals are transformed into meaningful units *I* can apprehend. The brain also transforms meaningful *I* events into bodily events. The creation of meanings[1] is made possible through the establishing of connections.

Viktor Frankl developed a therapeutic approach around the idea of 'making sense of things' called *Logotherapy*.[2] *Logos* is a Greek word meaning 'word' or 'meaning', and the focus of Frankl's therapy was to help the client find meaning in life. He argued that the search of *I* for meaning animates the brain and provides the focus in life in the more general sense. I would go a step further than his 'the primary motivational force in an individual is to find meaning in life' (Frankl, 2006), and suggest that *the primary motivational force of an individual is to find meaning*. That is, not just to find meaning 'in life', but in all the informational flow *I* encounters. Feinberg, in his thesis that the mind is best explained by a model of 'nested hierarchies', argues a similar point when he states: 'in the hierarchy of our conscious awareness, it is *meaning* that provides the constraint that "pulls" the mind together to form the "inner I" of the self' (Feinberg, 2001: 131).

The question of meaningfulness in clinical practice frequently translates into answering the question *why*? It is a question with wide application. *Why* do I have this pain – there must be a reason. Or for the one with survivor guilt: *why* am I alive when all the others with me died? It is a question post-traumatic stress disorder (PTSD) sufferers ask: how can I 'make sense' of this traumatic event in the light of my life experiences and expectations, and *why* did it happen to me? It is an issue for those suffering psychosis: *what sense* am I to make of experiences of seeing and hearing things not seen and heard by those around me, of apparent meanings not shared by others? And for Charlie the question also arose – *what sense* am I to make of this thought that disturbs me and has no meaning in my circumstances?

The question of meaningfulness also plays a role in the way neurons function. So the process of making meaning deserves the clinician's close attention. In this chapter, I argue that connectedness leads to meaningfulness, both at a physical and at a functional level. But just as connectedness plays a key role, so does *disconnectedness*, which has its own purpose. These processes underlie an efficient brain, but they also underlie neural failings.

Connectedness and meaningfulness

To see something is one thing. To understand what I am seeing is something else. Whether it is the sentence I see on a page, the face I see before me, or the keys that lie on the kitchen bench: each of these is not simply a visual shape. Each also conveys something to me: the sentence conveys an idea someone wants to communicate, the face I recognize as belonging to a friend, the keys I understand are necessary for me to drive my car. Similarly, to hear something is one thing. But to understand what I am hearing engages another process where meaning is created from sound patterns to convey something to me – whether it is conversation with my wife, the music on my CD, or the sound of a police siren behind me as I drive (too quickly) down the freeway.

A fundamental task the neural software shares with *I* is to create 'meaningful units of information' from the steady stream of signals it receives, largely from the body's senses. I am proposing this as self-evident, although there is a supporting body of research.[3] The corresponding fundamental task of neurons is to make connections with other neurons. If a neuron fails to make such connections, it soon atrophies (Cozolino, 2002). Connections are made at two levels: the physical connection between neurons and the functional connection between units of information – a parallel between the physical and the functional. I suspect that not only do neural connections create meanings, but meanings create neural connections. That is, *I* brings about synaptic connections through the imputation of meaning. While neural connections support meanings at a functional level so that neural activation is necessary for a message – images, symbols, ideas – to be carried, this activation is not the *same* as the message being carried, just as the series of words in a book is not the *same* as the apprehension of the intent of the author. Although neural networks carry meanings, meanings are created for *I*, not for neurons.

Meaningfulness can be created through the juxtaposition, ordering, and connection between bits of information. The creation of such connections is foundational to memory and learning.[4] Take, for example, reading – moving from letters to words to abstract ideas. Letters in the wrong order – that is, juxtaposed incorrectly – either give a different meaning or become meaningless. A 'meaningful' word is created by the correct juxtaposition of letters, which gives rise to an idea (of course, meaning can also be imputed to a misspelled word using other cues or connections). 'Correct' means making a match between the perceived word and the memory or template of a learned word carrying an established meaning or idea. The word gains meaning when connected to the idea it comes to represent. For example, the repeated pairing of the letters 'd', 'o', 'g', with the verbal input of the word 'dog', the presence of a dog, or some other abstract representation of a dog connects the idea with the letters, allowing it to carry the meaning.

Next, words, or more accurately the meanings these words represent, need to be correctly ordered or juxtaposed to become a meaningful phrase or sentence. And so the idea 'dog' next to the ideas 'black' and 'agitated' creates an idea that is new and different from the meanings in isolation. In this respect, Lindsay and Norman observe that 'an important part of the meaning or comprehension of a concept must be embedded in its relationships to other concepts in the memory' (Lindsay and Norman, 1972: 387). These units of functional connections that carry units of meaning I refer to as *association strings*.[5]

Although many thousands of neurons physically connect to create *templates* or *neural networks* carrying many association strings, the particular key to the pattern of each association string is, I suspect, kept in each cell that comprises that association string, allowing for self repair should any cell in that system atrophy. Thus the capacity to carry meanings is preserved. The configuring of network keys in the individual cells allows the whole system to be activated when any one cell in its system is activated. Each association string has multiple connections with other association strings within a network, so long as any one cell in a string is also connected with another string,[6] so that complex concepts and deep meanings are possible.

We saw how the process of connection or juxtaposition moves from letters to words carrying simple meanings or ideas, to more abstract concepts and symbols, creating deeper meanings. The need to create meaningfulness of incoming stimuli prompts the brain to search for all possibilities from its existing store of 'meaningful units of information', or association strings, carried in its library of templates. *I*, through the medium of the brain, actively extracts meaning by comparing a signal configuration – perhaps replacing it – with the closest meaningful representation in its neural library, a process called *apperception*. When presented with the meaningless letter combination 'agtated', for example, it will want to replace it with the more meaningful 'agitated'. Illusionists use this principle to their advantage.

Meaning is also established with matches of a different sort. It is necessary that the word another person uses is used the same way I use it – it needs to match their experience with mine, to fit their context in a similar fashion to mine. In making the same associations for them as the word does for me, it becomes meaningful in a shared sense, allowing 'connection' between people. And in another kind of match, when I see my friend, the visual image is matched to the stored representations I have of my friend's physical features and mannerisms, creating recognition. With that recognition, a complexity of information connected with that friend is activated – conversations we have had, shared experiences, and so on.

At all levels, from basic unit of meaning reflected in the synaptic connections of a string of individual neurons, to enormous neural networks made up of templates of many interconnected association strings involving many thousands or millions of synaptic connections – whenever new connections are made – new 'meanings' or variations of meaning emerge.[7] Smaller network systems[8] support larger and more complex networks; simple formulations that become familiar, assumed, and automatic become the foundation of more complex systems. The effective functioning of the whole is reliant on the accuracy of meanings carried in the discriminations and connections of the primary association strings.

At higher levels of the functional hierarchy, complex comparisons are made between emerging life events and the expectations, understandings, and stored meanings established in earlier life experiences. And so meanings carried in mathematics are applied to engineering problems; meanings of language are applied to the development of argument in court; and emotional meanings are attributed to behaviours in the nuances of a relationship. At this level of complexity, *I* makes use of a library of neural templates to create meanings from the ongoing flow of new information and events. But if the foundations are not strong and the pattern of association strings does not hang together well or the meanings they carry are distorted because of dysfunctional connections, the whole thing is liable to collapse, creating internal fragmentation and a loss of impetus and direction in life.

At the highest level, 'meaningfulness of life' is largely established by the connection of *I* with other *I*s, or with larger external realities. Frankl observed:

> the true meaning of life is to be discovered in the world rather than within man or his own psyche, as though it were a closed system... being human always points, and is directed, to something, or someone, other than oneself – be it a meaning to fulfil or another human being to encounter.
>
> (Frankl, 2006: 110)

While ultimately the apprehension of meaningfulness[9] may lie in *I*, the brain through its associative processes makes this apprehension possible.

If physical connection and functional association are required to carry meanings, then disconnection and dissociation must erode meanings and contribute to confusion and disorientation. Neural disconnection and the associated loss of meaning can lead to different psychiatric symptoms – illogicality, incoherence, dissociative states, and so on. Yet disconnection can also have positive effects. Apart from relief gained in the dismantling of disturbing meanings, disconnecting parts of the brain may allow other parts to work better. Blocking access to old information may enhance creativity. It may also serve important protective functions for *I*, as we shall see. Further, there are experiences that, while not causing *disconnection*, fail to create proper *connection* because the brain's store of information provides few connection points. For example, a trauma experience does not normally have the breadth of connections to be meaningfully integrated with other life expectations and experiences, even though the emotional force of the event creates strong but narrow emotion connections that generate their own meanings.

Psychological difficulties generally involve problems in the attribution of meanings, a poor match between my meaningful internal world and the external world. Normally, such difficulties reflect disconnection at higher levels of meaning attribution. A person may still see people as people and still understand language, but, for example, may fail to 'read' and abstract certain meanings regarding what someone is communicating. This interference in higher-level connections can affect how

I interprets circumstances and the decisions *I* subsequently makes, even though lower-level connections continue to operate well: words still mean what they should and trees are still recognized as trees.

I propose that the connection/disconnection dynamic is fundamental to the neural capacity to carry units of meaning (and possibly a key to the mind–brain relationship), as numbers are to mathematics, and will underpin the theory of much of what the clinician needs to understand. Similarly, the connection/disconnection principle underpins the commerce of human relationships. How and why connection and disconnection occurs becomes the basic issue in both neural and relationship enterprises.

Association strings and a mind map

I have suggested that meaningfulness emerges from associations that find physical expression in the connections neurons make. There are many thousands of millions of such associations with an almost limitless number of combinations, although the associations are unlikely to be all of a kind. Network systems comprising webs of association strings are connected by vast informational conduits called neural pathways. In some neural activity, there is a directional flow carrying signals from a defined source, such as in neural pathways carrying information from the body's peripheries, or carrying sensory signals, or neural information travelling from one part of the brain to another. But here we see a rapid sequence of simultaneous firing of patterns of juxtaposed association strings activating meaningful units, each adding its own contribution to the temporal flow of meanings that *I* apprehends. The association strings and encoded patterns remain even when they are not firing.

Eventually, we may be able to identify constellations of association strings that carry particular meanings. We may find that thought and memory processes follow associative pathways temporally connecting such constellations and that the fragmentation of these pathways relate to particular psychological pathologies. Importantly, the vast store of association strings hangs together in an extremely complex framework in which *I* functions, which I refer to as a *mind map*. The mind map comprises a person's unique perceptual framework. As perceptions are infused with meaning, a mind map might be defined as the integrated web of meanings *I* accesses. It provides the context in which new meanings are created. It is this *mind map* that might be considered the 'apex of neural activity' or the 'emergent property' of the integration of complex neural functioning where it all 'hangs together'.[10] It is this mind map that *I* interacts with.[11] The mind map is not the same as the neural networks that carry it, nor is it the same as *I*. Clinically, this distinction between the mind map and *I* is critical.

A mind map is developed over time and reflects efficient neural processing. It creates a familiar, predictable, and meaningful world, the internal virtual world that *I* uses as its reference point, the basis of *I*'s orientation, the context in which all information captured in the internal 'mirror' of the outside world is processed. The mind map is a comprehensive network of meaningful information that creates expectations and that helps *I* identify which new information will be attended to and how it will be interpreted. It is a map that *I* has access to, in part, in sleep and in other states of consciousness. In processing new and complex information streams by matching new material with existing meanings, it can deal with large volumes of incoming information without becoming overwhelmed and exhausted. The matching process is complex, requiring judgement and decisions involving *I*. This framework of reality contains the abstractions and ideas *I* ultimately apprehends.[12]

The mind map is not static, nor is it literal. It changes with new information and meanings, like the image in a mirror. And in some respects, the mind map *is* a mirror. What is seen in a mirror is a representation, not the actual – yet it is accurate enough for me to shave, comb my hair, and avoid accidents on the road. The information my senses mediate provides meanings representing the actual, allowing me to react accordingly. When the actual ceases to exist, its mirror representation is gone too, although neural traces carrying key meanings remain in memory. Although I can have confidence in that representation, it is capable of distortion, as we shall see. Inside the brain is the stored representation of things: of the parts of the body; of the external world, its sights, sounds, and smells, and the people that populate that world and the language and culture they represent; of things that have happened; and of hopes and plans for the future. *I* deals directly with the meanings these representations signify and, through these meanings, it interacts with the body and the world.

The mind map is *functional* in that it serves the purpose[13] of allowing *I* to apprehend meanings. If my brain has a good history of attending to relevant signals, making accurate discriminations, and making network connections that faithfully carry the meanings that exist externally, then my mind map becomes a good functional match to the external world. If distortions make poor functional matches, the brain works harder, temporary disconnections may occur, meanings may get confused, what should be familiar is not, and *I* can become disoriented.

The dynamics of the external world demands considerable flexibility in the mind map. A mind map representing orientation within the body or to external landmarks is one thing – but what about changing social relationships and social mores? People change, both physically and in their behaviour – how does the brain incorporate tolerance for changes that makes exact matching difficult, yet maintain a sense of recognizability and familiarity? How does it establish relevant cues in creating expectancy ('I *expect* to see you in *this* place: I may not recognize you as quickly in another place'), reducing its workload? This is made possible by the abstract nature of stored material: defining features are abstracted from the literal descriptive yet dynamic information the senses receive in the form of units of meaning, so that other representations not seen before may nevertheless be recognized. This forms the basis of *classification* – a tree is recognized as a tree, even though this particular tree has not been seen before, because it comprises features that have meaning to me as being associated with trees.

The mind map that *I* apprehends comprises the 'coming together' of a vast network of units of meaning. Both stored information and information being processed moment-by-moment contributes to this 'coming together', creating an internal world with all its inherent illusions and deceptions that becomes the 'reality' *I* experiences. Some may ask, could not this mind map be the *same* as *I*? Yet I subjectively know the difference between *I* and my memories, sensations, and perceptions: *I* is the *recipient* or *subject* of these. Further, memories, sensations, and perceptions are in constant flux, while *I* has an inherent continuity over time. Some will argue that the experience of *I* being separate from memories, sensations, and perceptions, and of *I* being continuous over time, are illusions created by the process of neural integration.[14] Yet how can an illusion be held responsible for something in the sense that *I* is? I conceive of *I* being *subjected to* illusions created by the mind map, rather than being the *product* of one.[15] Finally, I suggest that the mind map provides the *context* of *I*'s orientation and mediates external information for *I* – it is not the *source* of the actions and communications of *I*.

Dynamic connections: *I* at work

One of the alternative terms to *I* we considered was the term 'spirit'. Given its wind and breath associations, this term emphasizes a *dynamic* aspect. Movement and change are integral aspects of neural functioning which respond to a dynamic *I*. Just as a plane that stalls falls from the sky and a stationary bicycle falls over, so I propose experience would cease if *I* stopped moving across the neural landscape. Just as eye movement is essential for the stimulation of the visual perceptual system[16] and hair cell movement in the cochlea is essential for the apprehension of auditory signals, so there is need for movement between *I* and the brain. The detection of movement of some kind in the relevant receptor cells is essential for apprehension of information in *any* of the sensory inputs. Movement is a function of time: it is the changing position of one thing relative to another. Perhaps a timeless *I* moves relative to a time-bound neural system, and the resulting dynamic gives rise to conscious experience.

It is this dynamic – this changing in focus, in emotion, in thoughts, and so on – that could be considered evidence of the presence of *I*. To understand the *I*–brain relationship may require conceptualizing movement at every level, from basic synaptic connections to the way *I* abstracts meaningfulness. That is, it may not be static juxtaposition that creates meaning, but the fleeting activation of juxtaposed neurons that holds the thought trace and the accompanying meaning in a way analogous to the visual perceptual process. Even memory has a dynamic aspect, despite the common conceptualization of it being a static storage of information, as we shall see.

The essence of *I* as spirit is movement: we cannot see from where the spirit comes or to where it goes – we see it only by its effects in body and brain. Movement from one neural pattern or region to another creating momentary activation may be the essence of the interaction of *I* with the brain. Surely this is how *I* apprehends the information mediated by neurons, just as my eyes move back and forth to read sentences on a page. Yet what measureable thing is it that moves from one neural region to another? Electrical currents? Activated messenger molecules? Magnetic fields?

Indeed, each of these is present – but do these represent the movement of *I*? The 'presence' that momentarily activates one cell network after another is as close to identifying *I* as we are likely to get – although *I* is not necessarily the *only* source of such activation. Functional MRI provides evidence for the dynamic nature of neural activation: however, it only identifies *the resulting neural activity*, not the source of the activity. How do such dynamic processes operate in a neural system developed around enduring and relatively stable connections?

We have observed that establishing meaningfulness requires neural connections, so that a library of association strings that can be referred to reliably over time is established. This library retains integrity so that whole systems of perceiving and thinking have a solid and relatively unchanging foundation to build on. Yet we have also observed the need for flexibility, for temporary connections to allow the brain to respond to a dynamic world and to accommodate the dynamics of *I*, which it serves. In this sense, as every politician and behavioural therapist knows, timing is everything. *When* connections are made is as important as the *location* of which those connections become a part. The synchronized momentary activation of a particular constellation of association strings corresponds to the momentary event of meaningful experience (Singer, 1996). So at the physical level, there must be capacity for permanent or semi-permanent neural networks on the one hand, and for transient activation on the other.

There are thus at least two aspects to neural connections: on the one hand, the establishment of the neural layout – think of the physical electric wiring that connects different electrical components. On the other, an electrical discharge is activated in specific pathways in that layout, with gating mechanisms directing the discharge. One – the neural network – is laid down developmentally or historically: the learning and the memory process. The other is activated as needed. Electrical pulses and neurotransmitters are differentially activated, passing signals across selected synaptic gaps as necessary. Such activation is selectively excitatory or inhibitory, guarding against simultaneous neural events sending opposing messages. A neural path is developed – then used as needed. Constant use develops it further, although over-use may fatigue the system. But the layout itself remains in a state of flux as pathway connections are changed according to the demands of *I* and of the world. The extent of change possibilities in neural layout is becoming increasingly understood in recent research in brain plasticity (Doidge, 2010).

Neurons are involved in both the establishment of pathways and the activation of on/off switches determining network configuration – both are synaptic events. Yet how does the neuron 'know' what decision to make? For indeed, here decision finds expression; perhaps it is here *I* finds physical expression. How does a dynamic *I* manage its neural resources? Although *I* has no conscious awareness of neural processes, does it play a direct role in neural pathway establishment, or is this determined by neural software mediating the fiat of *I*? How much brain activity is determined by automatic neural systems and how much by direct involvement of *I*?

We return to the dynamic nature of *I* and its implications for neural cell connectivity. Movement is normally regulated: it can be too fast or too slow. If *I* stimulates neural activity too quickly or too slowly, it may affect neural processes, creating connectivity problems. For example, if I read too slowly, I can lose a sense of what is being said, and meaningfulness is lost. If I read too quickly, discriminative failures begin to occur, and I begin to make decoding errors. If I scan a crowd too quickly, I may give my brain insufficient time to recognize my friend. Different rates of processing engage different parts of the brain, allowing it to do different things.[17]

It seems different parts of the brain *require* different processing speeds, as reflected in level of arousal to function optimally.[18] Explicit memory, for example, requires slower processing than implicit memory. What would happen if neural speeds were dysregulated as, for example, might happen with the intake of certain drugs or diets, or with neural hyper-arousal or fatiguing that result from chronic emotional states? If making effective connections requires a processing speed within a narrow band, then speeds outside that band may interfere with neural connectivity and associated meanings, and also with general performance. What might be the effect of variation of optimal neural speed or movement on, for example, discriminative ability, memory, ability to make right judgement, capacity to make accurate connections, or general behavioural performance?

Efficiency, proximity, and selectivity

A key principle of brain functioning is the *efficiency* principle. It is a principle that operates outside the awareness of *I*, and seems largely governed by natural laws. It operates at the physical level in the atrophy of unused neurons that otherwise slow overall processing, yet require the energy and maintenance all cells need. The culling of unused neurons begins at an early age, reducing capacity but increasing efficiency. We also find the efficiency principle in the *positioning* of neurons and association strings. Cell networks requiring more frequent or rapid information exchange between them might be expected to be proximal. Nevertheless, long axons allow neurons to effectively connect quite disparate areas of the brain, with the subsequent development of myelin sheath, ensuring rapid and safe passage of information.

If proximity creates efficiency, how is efficiency maximized in regard to the more distal parts of the body? How can multiple signals to and from hand or foot be efficiently integrated with the neural networks in the brain that, for example, might want to integrate movement with music, or writing with thoughts? It does so by creating a counterpoint in the brain for every point in the body. There is a virtual 'body map' (the mind map subsumes the body map) in the brain, an internal representation of the entire body in space, located in the parietal cortices.[19]

When the brain needs to activate the foot (that is, for *I* to find expression in foot action), it 'talks' to the foot's cellular 'ambassador' in the brain. This ambassador processes the information, sending necessary signals to the foot. The foot does no processing of its own, except perhaps to action muscle movements and support cellular healing processes. But the foot sends messages to its brain ambassador, which passes on the information to *I* by way of other neural networks, and in turn sends only the relevant movement-related messages to the foot. The long-range messages carried through the peripheral nervous system are signals of the simplest and quickest kind, with the burden of interconnections, making meanings, encoding, and decoding left to the brain.

When a foot is lost, the foot's ambassador remains: it can continue to mediate bogus messages to and from a now-absent foot. It can end up with some confusing messages in this way: I am not sure if *I* can 'sack' the foot's ambassador.[20] What *does* sometimes happen is that other signal pathways co-opt the foot's ambassador, illegally activating it. For organs like the heart and lungs, the brain has more intimate involvement, with more complex pathways and memory systems directly interacting with those organs. This is reflected in the relative proximity of heart and lung to the brainstem.

The efficiency principle is also reflected in the process of selective attention and selective storage of information. Rather than processing incoming information 'from scratch', a tedious and time-consuming task, the brain uses existing material to its advantage. When new information 'fits' with existing meanings, it is more likely to be retained as less work is required to make the relevant adjustments: fewer neural connections need to be created. This principle has considerable implications for the therapeutic process.

Efficiencies are also found in the brain's discriminatory processes. Just as *connectivity* is the fundamental unit of meaningfulness, so *discrimination* is necessary to create the fundamental units of data between which the brain subsequently makes connections. Effective discriminations need to occur for each sensory dimension: visual, sound, tactile, and kinaesthetic. This discrimination between 'same' and 'different' for each dimension defines the information differentially activating neurons: a neuron is dedicated for each unit of information identified and remembered through the discriminative process. Every act of discrimination requires extra neural resources and more time to attend, process, and establish as permanent memory. But every act of discrimination also contributes to the breadth and depth of an area of knowledge. Brain efficiency optimizes the discriminatory process: there is a trade-off between speed and accuracy.

Finally, as particular skills are developed, the hardware maintaining those skills undergoes ongoing refining to maximize efficiency. Doidge (2010) observes that, as skills develop, fewer neurons are required to represent skill components: they become more precise and selective in when they fire; the relevant neurons process material faster; and the neural signals relating to the skills are clearer and fire simultaneously in neural sets. That is, there is a change in the units individual neurons represent: I suspect these changes may be governed by the meanings such units come to represent. These efficiencies result in less work for the brain, so that errors are noticed more quickly and the skill is practised more smoothly. Doidge notes that 'paying attention' is essential for these neural changes to occur: we later return to this role of attention and the corresponding role of *I*.

Fundamental as making sense of the world is, there are hazards in the brain's drive to efficiency. The goal of 'making sense' of things eclipses the 'lesser' goal of knowing 'the truth', if 'the truth' makes no 'sense' to me at the time and requires inefficient reworking of established connections and associated meanings. If 'the truth' is complex or foreign to what I 'know', it will require hard work for the brain and so is likely to be discarded in favour of meanings that fit familiar ideas. Making sense of new information depends on pre-existing meanings. To the degree these meanings are inaccurate, how I 'make sense' of things will reflect these inaccuracies. Such inaccuracies might emerge when the brain, being wired for creating meaning through association, creates 'false meanings' in relation to associations occurring through coincidence or happenstance.

Deeper peace, satisfaction, and resolution are found when 'sense' is made of new information rather than its actual accuracy. The 'truth' can be disturbing when accurate meanings do not readily fit the mind map. This has implications for memory: I am more likely to remember things that are meaningful in relation to my existing beliefs. Recall of past events tends to be distorted to better fit how I think they *ought* to be, rather than reflect what *was*. Brain efficiencies are maximized when new material links to pre-existing material, minimizing tension-creating dissonance. If *I* really wants to know and remember 'truth', it may need to battle the brain's natural tendency to distort meanings, to the degree it becomes aware of such distortions. I might only ever know truth 'in part'.

Efficiency and accuracy are balanced for optimal functioning. Just as allocation and positioning of neural *space* relative to function is optimized, so is neural *use* – the amount of work any neuron, synapse, or network of cells might be called upon to do in any unit of time. Too *little* use of an area leads to atrophy in the neurons allocated to that function, or the brain might allocate other functions to those neurons; too *much* use may lead to neural failure – either cellular or synaptic failure, leading to lost capacities and dysregulation. This principle of balance operates throughout the body and may be seen, for example, in the need for heart rate variability. There is a dance of work and rest for each neural network, of alternating one area with another for neural focus, allowing each area opportunity for recovery.

Chapter 6

The brain

Neural hardware and software

To appreciate the problems we face in comprehending the interaction of *I* with the brain, it is necessary to have some familiarity with brain hardware, which I provide as a layman. My goal is to provide a framework to help grapple with the mysteries of human experience as presented to me, a clinician.

We have described how brain hardware supports cognitive software concerned with information processing and storage, borrowing analogies from the computer. But there are neural processes of an altogether different order which deal with sensation and emotion, a part of the bread-and-butter of the clinician's work. As expected, we find these involve complex and integrated neural systems. How might these interact with each other and with *I*?

Neurons and their inter-relationships

Brain hardware supports information processing and storage software, but it also releases neurochemicals that allow the sensations *I* apprehends. The neuron and its physical links with other neurons provide the building blocks for both processes, although it is the interaction between large groups of neurons (neural constellations or networks) that we need to study when matching neural correlates with the vicissitudes of human experience. Neural architecture varies across the brain, corresponding with diverse functions: there is a complex of neural pathways or circuits whose activation correlates with various life experiences. This activation involves the release of complex chemicals such as neurotransmitters, neuropeptides, and hormones that collectively embody the link between the body's physical processes and the experience of *I*, one of the frontiers linking mind and body. As such, it deserves our close attention.[1]

The brain is populated with neurons that communicate with each other. The neural population is many times greater than earth's human population, and each cell is capable of connecting with thousands of others. Each neuron looks at one end like a tree with many branches that branch out into ever finer branches (its dendrites), and at the other end supports a substantial leg that varies in length from less than a millimetre to a metre (its axon). The cell gathers information through its many dendritic branches and passes on signals through its axon, thus linking it to the surrounding neurons (Guyton, 1981).

Information is transmitted when the neuron is activated, or 'fires': this can happen many times a second, simultaneously activating many thousands of other neurons. The length of axon can give some neurons considerable reach through the brain and body. This is not done in random fashion, but selectively, in orderly pathways and networks, some preset, many moulded over time, with a large proportion moulded in the first months of life. This hardware carries the communication processes, with many trillions of links between billions of cells. The information flow through the designated pathways is modulated at least in part by neurotransmitters that receive instructions as to whether and when a connection is to be activated.

Close inspection of the brain reveals a large variation in the physical structure of neurons (Birkmayer and Pilleri, 1966) – variations in size, shape, chemical makeup, and function, in rate of firing and duration of effect – and a considerable variation in the neurochemicals that operate between neurons. It is the neuron that produces neurochemicals, and the type of neurochemical varies according to the neurons producing them: each kind of neuron produces its own kind of neurochemicals. These mostly travel between neurons in the space between the arms or dendrites of adjacent neurons called the *synapse*, but not always. Neural pathways may be defined by the particular neurochemical activated at each synapse along that path: some of these pathways might release a particular neurochemical over a large brain area.

Separate from this integrated system are messages carried by neurochemicals between neurons outside their synaptic connections. These can trigger predetermined responses in neurons with compatible receptors. Just as each neuron has many dendrites through which it receives messages along dedicated pathways, it also has many thousands of dedicated receptors. These receptors are constantly opening and closing, allowing the neuron to differentially receive neurochemical messengers, some of which might pass outside the synaptic system.

Neural cells vary throughout the brain, like cells grouped with like cells. Why such variation? Information carried in the neural system comprises many types: visual and semantic knowledge, quantitative values, pain, light, temperature, and so on. These are encoded and mediated by individual nerve impulses. It is likely that the transport, processing, and storage of different types of information require different 'hardware', although there appears to be considerable adaptability. We see that groups of nerve impulses send signals: visual signals, pain signals, and so on. How this happens physically has received some close study, generally of a descriptive sort. How it operates functionally at the higher processing level has, however, been more difficult to study, in part because no neuron operates independently of any other neuron.

The individual neuron appears to be responsible for the creation of the web of dendrite connections with other relevant neurons. It determines the neurotransmitter release in the dedicated pathways that regulates the informational flow, as well as the release of neurochemicals that activates and modulates more distant neural relatives. It houses the DNA that sets predetermined activities. It determines whether, when, and where to transmit inhibitory or activation signals, and the strength and frequency of those signals. It passes on the signals it receives, sending them to relevant neighbouring cells and associated pathways. It provides the electrical action potential and nourishment (by way of glucomate and glial cells) to do the job (Phelps, 2006). Finally, it may hold a key to an association string of which it is part, as hypothesized earlier. The neuron is the brain's powerhouse. Yet any one neuron can only do its job in concert with many thousands of others, and thousands of neurons can be disposed of without affecting overall neural functioning or *I*, because of the capacity to replicate its functioning and because neurons are not the same as the meanings they carry.

From where do neurons get the signals to do their job? They appear to activate decisions, to transmit messages, and to respond on cue (with millisecond timing) when they have a specific role to play. Although surrounding neurons play a role in this activation, the argument becomes circular, with one cell being responsible for the activation of another – but where does the sequence begin, and what role does *I* play in this sequence? Does *I* interface directly with neural networks? Are these neurons the powerhouse that translates information sourced from *I* into physical form, and vice versa? If so, what is the nature of the signals between neurons and *I*?

Gatekeepers and messengers

On the face of it, the idea of neurochemicals traversing a synaptic gap or being released into body fluids to transmit information appears unnecessarily complicated for neurons to communicate – not an idea California's Silicon Valley would have conceived. What can a neurochemical do that an electrical signal cannot? Although an electrical pulse can pass from one neuron to another through electrically continuous tissue called *gap junctions*, neurotransmitters are generally involved in activating a reaction in neighbouring neurons through the synapse. Even less efficient – on the face of it – are neurochemicals released from neurons into the neural landscape like glowing embers in a bushfire, sparking the firing of neurons that happen to have compatible receptors open at the time. If all we are doing is mediating messages, why this complex interaction involving synapses and neurotransmitters, neuropeptides, hormones, and compatible receptors, and why so many different neurochemicals? Neurochemicals must allow the brain to do something computers cannot.

And, indeed, this is what the evidence points to. Neurotransmitters seem to be involved in complex actions, not simply as a means of information transfer (and this in a limited sense). Let me suggest three relevant to our discussion. First, different neurotransmitters can activate or inhibit responses in neighbouring neurons through selected pathways. In defining when and where connections are made, and which and how cells are activated, they help manage the software governing the brain's cognitive processes and the subsequent adaptive responses of the body (Guyton, 1981). Second, they are chemical messengers that mediate drives, sensations, and emotions. This in turn activates other chemicals that cascade into the body, generally through the bloodstream, actioning bodily responses at a physiological level, responses that can linger (see, for example, Cozolino, 2002). Third and closely linked to the second role, I suspect that neurotransmitters in conjunction with the activated neurons create the event which allows *I* to experience feeling and sensation. Neurotransmitters released along pathway circuits may serve as the immediate source of the experience of *I* of various sensations, moods, and emotions.

Returning to the first role, I have presented neurotransmitters as gates enabling or disabling selected information paths. One of the functions of the nervous system is to select out of the vast volume of incoming sensory information that which it attends to. The synapse operates as a junction point which controls signal transmission. Neurotransmitters can amplify, decrease, or altogether block a signal. This allows a particular transmission route to be taken or certain network connections to be made, determining which neighbouring neurons will fire and which associations are made at a functional level. While neurons govern this synaptic process, *I* governs the neural chemistry as much as do incoming signals from the body's sensory system, using it for the communication tasks it determines.

A second role of neurotransmitters is as chemical messengers that mediate the specific drives, sensations, and emotions that *I* experiences, triggering physiological responses in the body. This role appears to be shared by hormones and neuropeptides: it may be that emotion events are linked to cognitive software when the former (neurotransmitters) activate neural pathways (thus emotions become linked with ideas); while emotion events mediated by the latter remain largely separate from the software, resulting in 'free-floating' sensations and physiological responses. Here the need for different types of neurochemicals becomes apparent, given the range of drives and sensations *I* experiences. The unique composition of each neurochemical allows it to carry the particular information relating to a drive, sensation, or emotion.

A third role I am suggesting for neurotransmitters is that they create the sensations *I* apprehends. Is the experience created when neurotransmitters are initially released; in their presence in the synaptic gap or body fluid; when they subsequently engage neural receptors to activate a neural response; or does experience require the complete process? If the latter is the case, we would expect the relevant experience to cease when neurons fail to be activated by the neurochemicals. Critically, how many neurons need to be simultaneously activated to reach the threshold for *I* to experience the event?

I suggested that neurotransmitters act as a means of information transfer in *only a limited sense*. By this I mean that neurotransmitters are not necessarily a processing component of cognitive software; rather, their role may be to activate selected pathways to allow processing to occur. Particular pathways comprise activated neurons that collectively create an event (an emotion event, a readiness event, or perhaps a decisional event). Neural software operates differently to emotion events in that the former require encoding and decoding processes, although the same neurons are probably involved. I suspect that, as in the computer, neural software is mediated by electrical pulses travelling through the network of neurons, the neurons themselves governing the all-important on/off switches encoding the information. Nevertheless, one process interacts with the other, mediating different actions. And so, for example, because a decision is a commitment to an action, it is likely to involve a synaptic event (that is, it is either activated or not), while thoughts are managed by a different process but through the same neural structures.

More generally, neurochemicals may collectively act as an interface with *I*, allowing apprehension of thoughts and feelings. Is it at synaptic level that thought and feeling interface? Individual neurochemical activity may have less to do with the *content* of the message than with enabling its *transmission*. I suspect the message *content* is reflected in the ever-changing specific and momentary *patterns* of synaptic connections the transmitters allow. If this holds true, then problems with thought content as seen in some psychoses may relate to corruption of patterns of connections, rather than problems with neurochemical production per se.

There appear to be some thirty neurotransmitter types (and many more peptides), whose functions we are only just beginning to understand. What role does each have? How do they work in concert with those other complex neurochemicals and the neurons themselves to encode and decode, to store and retrieve, to connect and disconnect, and to activate and inhibit the vast network of neural message carriers, combining, sifting, and separating signals of all kinds to create the meanings *I* (as the destination for all this activity) is able to perceive and respond to? Furthermore, neurochemicals have a central role in the regulation of many physiological systems necessary for bodily function that operate independently of *I*. Not surprisingly, when we look at the research literature reporting on the suspected role and function of various neurochemicals, the findings are suggestive at best, and often confusing.[2]

Generally, researchers seek to detect the activation of a certain neurochemical under various conditions to determine if it is involved in that particular transaction or event. But determining the function of neurochemicals is difficult. To complicate things, when a neurochemical is activated, it is not the only event taking place – other neurochemicals may also be simultaneously released and other intricate regulatory neural processes are also occurring. Further, much research is *correlational*, and correlation does not mean *causation* – there may not even be a direct relationship at all. So we remain cautious in how we interpret these apparent links. Keeping this in mind, let us look at those events with which some neurochemicals have been associated that might interact with *I*.

Different neurochemicals

The neurotransmitter *dopamine* has received considerable research attention. When the hypothalamus releases dopamine, a person experiences, or *expects* to experience, something 'nice' or pleasurable, like food, sex, or drugs: it leads to desire, anticipation, and excitement. Dopamine may be involved in encoding the learned expectation of a reward, so it becomes a mediator of positive motivation, but also a player in addictions. Furthermore, dopamine can stimulate hormone release mediating the body's fight-or-flight response (as does the neurotransmitter *adrenaline*). So it connects one way or another with *both* motivational systems – punishment and reward. Dopamine is released in the basal ganglia too, and is implicated in voluntary movement. And so it becomes a suspect in Parkinson's.

In the frontal cortices, dopamine appears to be involved in the control of informational flow from other brain areas and might play a role in enabling concentration, memory, learning, and problem solving. High levels of dopamine in certain pathways seem to enhance the feeling of meaningfulness in things (presumably through the connections they promote), while low levels in the prefrontal cortex may be related to attention deficit disorder (ADD). Further, it appears to provide a 'teaching signal' to parts of the brain responsible for acquiring new behaviour. Dopamine has been implicated in lactation, in sociability, in social anxiety, in apathy, and in pain processes; in mood, in sleep, and in learning; in fibromyalgia, in restless leg syndrome, in depression; in Tourette's and in schizophrenia. It can even mess with the heart.

Yet I would suggest that dopamine may not be responsible for these events – that is, it does not *cause* pleasure or pain; its relative absence does not *cause* concentration difficulties, memory difficulties, or muscle movement problems; 'imbalance' of dopamine does not *cause* depression, or schizophrenia, or Tourette's, or Parkinson's, or ADD – it only acts as a mediator for the information transmission and dysregulations which contribute to these phenomena. Dopamine activity relates directly to the neural networks it serves: are observed effects due to the dopamine release or inhibition *per se*, or because of the neural networks it activates or inhibits? Its potential action makes a long and bewildering list: what is the common factor? Does dopamine have a particular function that underlies these various manifestations, or does its function vary depending on the neurons and neural pathways activated?

Then there is *serotonin,* which exercise and eating certain foods help stimulate. It originates in the brainstem and is found in the hypothalamus region and many other parts of the body, including (especially) the digestive system – its activation seems to inhibit pain pathways and to affect mood and sleep patterns. It is connected with the management of various bodily functions, such as appetite, sleep, memory and learning, temperature regulation, mood (promoting serenity and optimism), cardiovascular function, muscle contraction, and endocrine regulation. Low serotonin levels are correlated with anxiety, apathy, fear, feeling of worthlessness, insomnia, and fatigue – events linked with depression. Again we ponder: what do these functions have in common, and is serotonin *itself* responsible for these events, or is it the pathways serotonin happens to mediate that are responsible?

Some neurotransmitters also function as hormones. One is *melatonin,* which is involved in the regulation of the circadian rhythm (the wake–sleep cycle) and is associated with drowsiness and lowering of body temperature. Darkness helps to stimulate melatonin. It is found in the reticular activating system (RAS) in the basal ganglia and affects REM sleep and dreaming. Melatonin has been implicated in learning and memory, depression, and autistic spectrum disorder.

Noradrenaline (or *norepinephrine*) and *adrenaline* (or *epinephrine*) also function as neurotransmitters and hormones. Noradrenaline affects brain regions where attention and action responses are controlled (mostly the RAS in the brainstem, and the hypothalamus). Like adrenaline, noradrenaline is involved in the fight-or-flight response and associated with increased heart rate, creating energy. During stress, it is found in large areas of the brain which become aroused, enhancing general alertness. It seems to play a role in attention, and is implicated in attention deficit hyperactivity disorder (ADHD). It also seems to be involved in the processing of 'emotional memory' by determining what is important to remember. Noradrenaline is reported to reinforce biological encoding of traumatic memory, to be associated with increases in anxiety, arousal, and irritability and, in the long term, with increases in level of tension and unmodulated startle response.[3] This, too, is implicated in depression.

Many other neurotransmitters have been identified about which we know little, such as the pervasive *GABA* (gamma amino butyric acid) – an inhibitor found in the basal ganglia, spinal cord, cerebellum, and other areas (it seems to inhibit anxiety and panic responses – depressed people appear to have insufficient GABA); and *adenosine*, which, like melatonin, is implicated in the sleep cycle, among other things.

Apart from neurotransmitters, there are some 200 other neurochemicals that play an important role in emotion, behaviour, and memory, as well as in body processes. Many are peptides that have specific functions distinct from neurotransmitters, although there is functional overlap. Many neurochemicals are not limited to synaptic activity, so they are not restricted to specific neural pathways. A neuron can produce both neurochemicals whose action is limited to synaptic exchange and those that can be released into bodily fluids: that is, a single activation in the one neuron can create multiple outcomes. It can mediate and respond to a thought or cognition, while at the same time activating and releasing multiple chemical messages, stimulating a particular emotion and behaviour. Naturally, such multitasking has immediate implications for attempts to isolate the function of any individual, network, or region of neurons.

Neuropeptides have diverse functions which are only beginning to be understood. Some of these effects on mood, energy levels, pain and pleasure reception, ability to solve problems and memory are relevant to the clinician. For example, the release of *oxytocin* appears linked with feelings of warmth, trust, and closeness to others, and *vasopressin* affects social behaviours and promotes maternal behaviour and pair bonding. *Substance P* is an excitor released by pain fibre terminals in the spinal cord. *Neuropeptide Y* is a peptide implicated in learning, memory processing, eating disorders, circadian rhythm, anxiety, and sexual response. There are also the *enkephalins* and *endorphins* – opioids involved in the inhibition of pain, reduction of stress, and creation of feelings of calm.

What advantage might there be for neurochemicals to bypass neural pathways and networks? One advantage is that, even *before* neural pathways have been established, or if later these neural pathways should be corrupted by disease processes, such neurochemicals can still do their job, travelling from their source neuron to neurons with compatible receptors. This enables ongoing bodily functions, certain behaviours, and emotional responses, regardless of the integrity and effectiveness of the neural networks that mediate cognitive processes. Such patterns of neurochemical release reflect robustness in the system. Nevertheless, neurochemical release is not independent of other aspects of the neural enterprise, given the same neurons are involved in the mediating software and in the production of neurochemicals. The activity of neurochemicals is largely preset by ROM memory – its genetic programming – allowing essential body functions to be carried out in the newborn well before its neural networks are established.

If *I* exercises control over bodily responses through software supported by neural pathways, then it suggests that some neurochemical activity is largely beyond its control, except at the point of initial release. This is useful when *I* loses control over cognitive processes (for example, in an unconscious state), allowing ongoing body functioning, but it becomes a problem when *I* *wants* to control processes governed by neurochemical release. Similarly, if learned behaviour and ideas are contained in association strings, then the activity of neurochemicals bypassing association strings must be largely independent of learned behaviour, except, again, at the point of its release.

We have seen that various experiences appear to involve different transmitters, and that brain regions linked with certain functions contain multiple transmitters. It may be the *combined* activity of different transmitters that makes possible the various neural functions – isolating transmitters in research may prove unproductive. Making 'sense of' complex information may involve simultaneous access to multiple neural regions and pathways enabled by the simultaneous activity of different transmitters. Additionally, the activation of one transmitter and neural region inhibits others, preventing con-compatible signals. The chronic release of adrenaline, for example, inhibits hormones such as oestrogen; the release of serotonin inhibits dopamine, and so on.

There will always be a relationship between the physical and the functional. The particular combination of neural pathway and transmitter activity appears to create unique physiological signatures that correspond to particular experiences apprehended by *I*. The release of transmitters in these signature pathways also accompanies a release of energy, which may be required for the interface of *I*. Perhaps the release of transmitters along particular signature pathways not only creates unique sensations for *I*, but also energizes its capacity for focus, thinking, and decision making.

The dance of *I* with the neural system

In 1986, neuroscientist Sir John Eccles proposed that the probability of neurotransmitter release followed similar principles to quantum mechanics and was influenced by the intervention of the mind, and in the 1990s neuroscientist Roger Sperry suggested that 'mental forces' might direct the electrochemical traffic between neurons at cellular level. According to Schwartz and Begley, Sperry proposed that 'higher-level' mental properties exerted control over the 'lower-level' mental properties of neurons and synapses: 'The causal potency of an idea or an ideal becomes just as real as that of a molecule, a cell, or a nerve impulse' (Sperry, 1965, in Schwartz and Begley, 2002).

This is an extraordinary claim, yet the mind–body problem, or as I have reformulated it, the *I*–brain problem, seems to demand this. Even before Eccles and Sperry, the late neurologist Purdon Martin pondered the complex integration of the *labyrinthine* (relating to the maze of canals in the inner ear responsible for sensing balance), the *proprioceptive* (the sense of the relative position of neighbouring parts of the body), and the visual senses (these three required to provide a functional internal 'body map'). He wrote in 1976: 'There must be some centre or "higher authority" in the brain... some "controller", we may say. This controller or higher authority must be informed of the state of stability or instability of the body' (Sacks, 1985: 78). It seems he, too, was searching for the elusive *I*.

What picture can we use to describe such an extraordinarily complex system as the neural system working simultaneously at multiple levels and interfacing with *I*? The brain has an ongoing stream of incoming sensory information that creates a mirror representation of the external world: the exteroceptive system. At the same time, it has an ongoing stream of information from the body, comprising the *interoceptive* (information from body organs) and the *proprioceptive* (information about balance and movement) systems. These three subsystems interact, providing essential orientation. They in turn interact with stored information that helps create meanings from the incoming data. These meanings are established by a dynamic of ever-changing patterns of neural connections and disconnections (paralleling associations and dissociations at a functional level), accessing yet other subsystems – discrete software packages serving as information-processing equipment. It is a system with many internal regulatory features – when one circuit is activated, others automatically shut down.

It is this integrated system that sustains the mind map, the field of reference for *I*. But it is also the avenue through which *I* finds expression, providing focus that activates relevant neural pathways and allowing decisions that translate into actions or position statements integrated into the evolving mind map. *I* does so without awareness of how it does so, and, I suspect, without the *capacity* for such awareness. The strength of the presence and capacity of *I* to manage the system varies, as the system can create its own impetus, activating its own pathways independent from *I*. There is thus a dance between *I* and the neural system, each responding to the other; each needing the other in the natural state, the primary driving force fluctuating moment to moment. It is a dance that may be glimpsed in the fluctuating neural activation patterns whose associated oxygen flow is measurable with an fMRI, or whose resulting brainwaves may be measured with an electroencephalogram (EEG). Yet neither captures the flow or content of meanings, the currency *I* uses in its interaction with its neural host.

The way *I* interacts with synaptic activity in specific pathways or in broader fields of engagement might be through electrical fields or wave signals, as Sperry suggested. Yet *I* has no awareness of electric fields or wave signals, much less of neurons, neural networks, or synaptic activity. For *I* to manage such complex systems without awareness of the process, it must utilize software that translates meanings, bridging the gap between the promptings, attention, and decisions driven by *I* and the neural structures that translate them into neural and bodily activity.

Yet there can be awareness in *I* of brain activity that appears to *exclude* the involvement of *I*, as we saw with Charlie's perplexing thought. Here neural pathways were activated that Charlie's *I* apprehended, but of which his *I* did not admit to be the source. Instead, the thought seemed to be activated by neural initiative. *I* became the destination, not the source. Such dissonance between *I* and the brain is not restricted to thoughts, but might also encompass moods, feelings, and urges. That I can choose to distance myself from what my brain wants to do and resist the 'pressure'[4] to conform to an unwanted urge, for example, points to the capacity of *I* to over-ride powerful neural events, underscoring the distinction between the entity *I* and neural processes.

If the nature of *I*, which cannot be located in time and space, is difficult to comprehend and study, the functional aspects of the brain are no easier to scrutinize and comprehend. Understandably, the researcher tends to focus away from software which cannot be seen or measured to hardware which has a better chance of being seen and measured. But even here the dynamic and interactive nature of neural processes makes the enterprise surprisingly difficult, and there is not a lot to report at the microlevel to help the clinician's conceptualizations. Might we have more success standing back and looking at whole regions of the brain, performing some kind of functional analysis of these various regions?

Chapter 7

Neural cartography and *I*

What might I gain in understanding by mapping the neural landscape? What do I gain in understanding by mapping *anything*? Maps provide a visual perspective of location. Places are labelled so that we can more easily describe where to find something, but it explains little else. Yet a close study of an accurate map allows hypotheses to be developed, depending on the information provided. A map of brain functions also allows the development of various hypotheses. However, there is a difference between a static map and dynamic processes. Even if we could successfully name physical regions of the brain and describe the apparent functions of these regions, it may give few clues to the functioning of the subjective and changing mind map.

After considering how maps can be helpful, I will give an overview of the brain map in the light of current research; both its hardware structure and its hypothesized software. We will consider how the brain layout reflects a fundamentally efficient design, but we will discover that finding neural addresses is a problem, both in regard to specific neural functions and in regard to the elusive *I*.

The purpose of maps

In addition to place names, some land maps provide information about various features and their functions, allowing us to develop explanatory hypotheses. Take the location of a town relative to a mine-site, or the location of a power station relative to various geographical features: we may hypothesize what draws people to that town, or why the power station was built where it was. Frequently, the location of various built features relate to maximizing efficiency relative to the existing landscapes, although historical events and unseen socio-political forces also play a role. Some maps might include localized features, such as soil type, allowing for predictions of a specific nature: predictions may be made as to the type of minerals that might be found there, what plants might grow there, and what animals might be attracted to the region.

Then there are maps featuring arrows representing a dynamic relative to the places detailed on the map – they might represent the migration route of a bird or of a nomadic people, or the movement of an army. This allows other hypotheses: a bird's route might be over certain waterways and end in certain wetlands, so we can hypothesize about feeding and breeding patterns. So maps can help our understanding of things, especially if we move beyond the simple naming of places by mapping features and their functions, or dynamic movements across the landscape.

The brain is dynamic, adjusting to incoming information and reflecting the experiential history of a person. So we need to think of mapping the location of flora and fauna, rather than streets and buildings. The position of a particular plant may be static but short-lived, and new plants may quickly grow. The soil type might provide approximate boundaries wherein you might find the plants, but actual plant locations vary and are subject to change. This is even more so for animals who may call a geographical area home, but whose precise position is fluid. Similarly, software functions and their relationship to specific neurons, neural regions, and pathways are subject to change. But most importantly, the dynamic presence of *I* interacting with the brain adds a dimension of unpredictability.

And so we need to allow that the more precisely a function is located, the more subject it may be to change, both over time in an individual and between individuals. Each brain map is as unique as the person it represents. While certain brain regions might commonly correspond to particular functions, it may be better to think in terms of general neural regions to allow for individual differences in brain history and development in relation to those functions, rather than making precise delineations. To reflect the imprecise nature of things, I refer, for example, to 'the amygdala region' when attributing functions to the amygdala. I also avoid expressions such as 'the amygdala does such and such', as this assumes the origin of the said function is the amygdala itself, making it a separate and specific entity rather than an integrated part of the whole. More accurately, the amygdala region contains hardware and software corresponding to certain functions.

It is not inevitable that certain functions are found in particular regions of the brain. Other regions may be capable of such function: this reflects brain plasticity. Returning to our land-map analogy, many major cities are built along major waterways or the coast. The location was generally determined by accessibility to transport routes – it was efficient and practical. Could we re-site these cities? Theoretically, yes; practically, it would be difficult, given the cities have developed an infrastructure they now depend upon. Yet the infrastructure was not a given: it developed over time, according to what the city demanded. But there are also some major cities whose sites were determined by historical socio-political reasons to which no land-map will give a clue. A map may tell me *what is*, but not necessarily *why*, or *what is possible*.

And so it is with the brain. Most aspects of language are normally processed in the dominant hemisphere of the brain (for most people, the left hemisphere): the capacity to speak relates to an area called *Broca's area*; the capacity to understand language is associated with *Wernicke's area*. These locations are roughly the same from one brain to the next – but not always. Other locations can and do take over the language function. For some people, language is largely processed in their *right* hemisphere. That certain brain areas are the ones normally dedicated to particular functions may be because these are the most efficient and best suited in the developing brain. The relative location to other relevant functions may play a role, as might the structure and composition of the neuron types found here. But it was not inevitable. These might be the preferred sites where we expect these functions to occur. However, the *exact* locations in function and the *exact* patterns of neural networks reflect the brain's developmental history and the patterns of focus and decisions of *I* over time. Once established, changing location becomes difficult as it would require changes in the supporting infrastructure – a comprehensive reworking of network connections.

Technological advances are allowing the creation of functional brain maps.[1] The degree of interpersonal variation reflected in such mapping is unknown, but that there is variation is generally recognized. And while clear and detailed descriptions of brain terrain and the functions that generally correspond to specific regions is a necessary starting point, it does not explain brain dynamics. I offer some basics in neural mapping of hardware and function, and provide a limited summary of what researchers are agreed might contribute to explanatory hypotheses – especially those helpful for the clinician. In this undertaking, I am indebted to Cozolino (2002, 2006) and Carter (2010). It is not my intention to replicate or summarize what they have written, but to review the particular findings relevant to our thesis – the exploration of the *I*–brain dynamic.

A layman's neural anatomy

If for you, like me, the physical brain is relatively unfamiliar territory, it is worth a quick review to become familiar with basic 'place names'. I give the simplest of cartographic orientations. The brain is made up of two halves, the right and the left, joined by a bundle of nerve fibres called the *corpus callosum*. This means that nearly all the regions we identify are pairs – one to the right, and one to the left. Beginning at the centre, in the *subcortical* region, we work our way outward. Imagine two small almond-shaped areas at the lower centre of the brain: these are called the *amygdalae*.[2] These lie adjacent to and above the *brainstem*, which reaches down from behind the amygdalae towards the heart and lungs by way of the spinal cord and the *vagus* (an integrated message system relating various key organs to the brain's emotion centres). A pair of seahorse-shaped *hippocampi* lies close by, behind the amygdalae, and also adjacent to the brainstem in which we find the *reticular formation*. The *medial forebrain bundle* emerges from the hippocampi. A little above the amygdalae, at the very centre of the brain, mid-point between the brainstem and the cerebral cortex, is the *hypothalamus*. Immediately above the hypothalamus lies the *thalamus*. These are the key areas in the centre region.

The surface area of the brain, the *cerebral cortex* (*cortex* and *lobe* meaning the same thing), comprises a number of regions and subregions. These include the *frontal* cortex, which predictably is towards the front of the brain, approximately where I might perch my sunglasses when I am not using them. Below this is the *prefrontal* cortex, immediately above my eyes (this comprises a number of subregions, such as the *dorsolateral* region). Behind the frontal cortex is the *parietal* cortex, which lies on the roof of the brain, about where balding normally starts; and the *occipital* cortex, which is at the back. The *temporal* cortices lie to either side, just above the cheekbones and ears. Then there are the sub-surface areas, which lie just below these cortices.

Towards the rear of the temporal cortices, a little below the surface, lays the *insula* cortex, while the *orbital-medial* area lies within the prefrontal cortex. Within the parietal cortex at the top of my head is a strip called the *somato-sensory* region, which is next to the *motor* cortex (in the posterior frontal cortex). Another largish region that lies below the cerebral cortex, separating it from the thalamus, is the *anterior cingulate* (the one closer to the front) and the *posterior cingulate* (towards the rear). The cingulate cortex forms a belt that wraps around the corpus callosum. Just behind the prefrontal cortex is the *septal* area. Close by, moving back towards the centre of the brain, is a largish area called the *basal ganglia* (there are two: to the right and left). Between the cingulate gyrus and the thalamus is another region central to the brain, embedded in the basal ganglia: the *caudate nuclei* and associated *putamen*. These are the main surface and sub-surface areas.

In the 1950s, Penfield found that electrically stimulating various points in the brain activated specific mental events – in his case, the reliving of specific memories. Since then, technological advances have led to the systematic use of fMRI that has allowed detailed functional brain mapping, and I outline some of the recent findings. I do so, however, with some notes of caution. First, each brain region has multiple links to the one next door, so we cannot isolate functions – we may need to conceptualize the apparent functions of various brain regions as *key contributors* to complex and multifaceted functions (Arden and Linford, 2009a). Second, we need to remember the issue of individual differences and variations over time in regional functioning. Third, relatively large areas of the brain are busy when I engage in various cognitive, sensory, and motor tasks: we have to allow that this activation reflects neural *readiness potential* (allowing the relevant parts of the brain to respond as quickly as necessary), not just actual processing and engagement. Fourth, brain region activation may at the same time reflect *different kinds of activities*, as each neuron and neural region is capable of multiple tasks.

Finally, the discovery that as we engage in various activities, specific regions of the brain are activated, lends itself to the conclusion that these neural areas are *responsible* for the event. But is it not equally possible that *I*, or the neural software *I* might utilize, is responsible for the cognitive activity, which is *mediated* through the activation of this specific group of cells? If, for example, I have two telephones before me, and one rings, can I logically say that the telephone that rings is *responsible* for the ringing? Further, is the active telephone responsible for the content of the message? Is it possible for the other telephone to be used for the same task? All I can safely say is that the ringing telephone, *at that point*, is the medium through which the message comes. To say the telephone is *responsible* for the event or is the only one able to do the job makes invalid assumptions. Herein lays the risk of a new sub-cranial phrenology.

The inner regions

What has been associated with the inner regions?

First, the region of the amygdala, centrally located and part of the *limbic system* with major pathways linking it to the *autonomic nervous system* (ANS), the thalamus, the hypothalamus, the hippocampus, and the orbital area of prefrontal cortex, appears to be involved in our experiences of fear and attachment, of early memory, and of general emotional experience (Cozolino, 2002). Connections are here made between arousal (associated with fear) and experienced events, people, thoughts, and sensations. In this sense, 'emotional memory' relates to the amygdala region – a connection between fear and the remembered event or person; between fear and a particular thought or bodily sensation. The amygdala is activated when danger is perceived, being well-connected with the visual system. Its activation enhances the capacity to attend to specific aspects of the environment, so that small details judged to be relevant to danger are noticed and remembered. Unfortunately (sometimes), it also seems to be involved in generalizing these connections. The amygdala's activation in the face of perceived danger stimulates the fight-or-flight response through the ANS pathway, resulting in the classic symptoms of racing heart, perspiration, shallow breathing, and so on.

Not surprisingly then, the amygdala region is activated with perception of abandonment (especially in the young child) – the fear of disconnection with significant others. Subsequently, even before the feared abandonment takes place, when estimates are being made of another's approachability and trustworthiness, this region is again activated, its software scanning and matching for those details it has connected with danger. Nor is it surprising given its role in emotional learning, in perception of abandonment, and in appraisal of safety and danger that its neural networks are strongly established from the beginning of a child's development, sustaining the attachment and affect regulation software subsequently relied on in interpersonal encounters.

In its work to differentiate safe from unsafe, the amygdala region is worked hard when facial expressions are being 'read'. It fires both when we express fear in our face and body, and also when we read fear expressed in the face and body of another. These are neural correlates to the well-documented phenomena of emotional transfer from one person to another. There is moreover a location in the amygdala which, when stimulated, results in a person experiencing feelings of anxiety, of déjà vu (a form of momentary temporal disconnection experienced as an illusion of recognition), and of memory-like hallucinations.

A number of neurochemicals are associated with the amygdala. Among them are receptors that absorb endorphins, which play a role in reducing pain perception. Endorphins seem to inhibit some pathways in this region, creating a sense of calmness and safety (as does the opioid cocaine). Close contact of a parent with child – the process of bonding – releases these 'feel good' endorphins. Conversely, separation and the anxiety of uncertainty are associated with decreased endorphin levels. Noradrenaline and glucocorticoids are also released through the amygdala's activation, enhancing (among other things) memory storage, especially in 'negative emotional' (danger) situations. In addition, the frontal cortex is activated by the release of dopamine by the amygdala. The amygdala region is thus implicated in many of the challenges facing the clinician.

The basal ganglia play a role in motor control and activate decisions made in relation to voluntary motor behaviours, or movement. In this way, they appear to be involved in the decoding of decisions from information they receive from elsewhere, including the prefrontal cortex, translating into signals prompting behaviours. Dopamine is released in this system. Within the basal ganglia are the caudate nuclei, which contain neurons that connect simultaneously to the thinking regions of the prefrontal cortex and the emotion region of the amygdala. The basal ganglia are linked to practically everything in the brain, and appear to play an important role in the brain's learning and memory systems as they affect behaviour, and are linked to feedback systems.

Then there are the hippocampi. These play a role in the regulation of the amygdala region, mediating the traffic between various parts of the prefrontal cortex and the amygdala as part of the limbic system. Here the rational incoming messages the client hears from the clinician are pitted against the opposing irrational fear and anxiety messages that find their power in the amygdala. Perhaps through its access to diverse information, the hippocampal software allows proper consideration of events, inhibiting or slowing responses, attention, and stimulus input. It allows discriminations of detail, is 'logical' and 'cooperative' in matters of social function, and 'tests', for example, whether the apparent abandonment activating the amygdala region is, in fact, occurring (Cozolino, 2002). In making these discriminations, it allows judgements about what is and is not safe.

The centrally located hippocampal software seems to find its way around the many facets of the mind map. It is involved in the organization of spatial, semantic, and temporal information, and compares memories, making inferences from previous learning to new situations. It helps transfer short-term memory into long-term memory, making possible the encoding and storage of explicit (conscious) memory and conscious learning (Cozolino, 2002), as well as of directional memories, contributing to a virtual map of the environment. Damage in the hippocampal region results in difficulties in the creation of long-term memories. This might happen in chronically stressed children in whom prolonged high levels of glucocorticoids results in neuron degeneration to the point cells can collapse and die, compromising hippocampal functioning.[3] Conversely, maternal care and soothing appears to be protective, enhancing hippocampal functioning. Atrophy in the hippocampal region is found in those suffering prolonged depression, in those suffering schizophrenia, and in the elderly.

The software in the thalamus region relates directly to the cerebral cortex and the midbrain region, relaying sensation, spatial sense, and motor signals that allow physical interaction with the environment. Cozolino describes the process thus: 'An organized sense of the body in space forms in subcortical and cortical networks involving the thalamus, cerebellum, and parietal cortex' (Cozolino, 2002: 107). Representations of things encountered in the environment appear to be created here, allowing rapid fear signals to be sent if a match to a frightening image is made. We observe the interactive nature of brain regions and how the memory system is distributed throughout the brain. Furthermore, the strong connection the thalamus has with the cerebral cortex (the thalamo-cortico-thalamic circuits) implicates it with consciousness, alertness, and sleep. It is involved in the regulation of arousal, level of awareness, and activity, so that failure in this region could result in a coma.

The hypothalamus controls the pituitary gland, which in turn controls the endo-crine (hormonal) system, through which glucocorticoids (cortisol), adrenaline, and noradrenaline are released into the bloodstream, creating general arousal and the energy to fight or run. When it is not activating the fight-or-flight response, hypo-thalamus software regulates basic drives: hunger, thirst, and sexual desire. It also regulates the circadian rhythm, defining when I feel energized, when I want to sleep, and my body temperature. Neural activators in the hypothalamus, along with those in the neighbouring amygdala region, control the ANS (which car-ries messages to the heart, lungs, liver, intestines, and muscles), arousing through its *sympathetic* system, or inhibiting through its *para-sympathetic* system the pro-cesses necessary for physical action. The hypothalamus carries software necessary to translate the decisions *I* generates into physiological responses, and presents *I* with bodily desires about which decisions need to be made. Further, there are two small regions called *mammillary bodies* in the hypothalamus which play a role in recognition memory and possibly in the memory of smell. When this area becomes corrupted, as commonly happens in Korsakoff syndrome, amnesic syndromes can result, a complete blacking-out for extensive periods.

The brainstem serves as a highway between the brain and body by way of the spinal column, mediating signals to motor action. It also regulates pain signals, the signals relating to kinaesthetic and tactile senses, and the signals regulating the heart, lungs, and respiratory system. The complex two-way neural pathway system carry-ing information between the brain and organs in the far reaches of the body is called the *vagus*: this is essentially an extension of part of the regulatory system managed by the *reticular activating system* (RAS). The vagal system carries and integrates the emotional messages *I* expresses through the body. Meanwhile, the RAS, which may play a role in various psychological dysfunctions, is stationed at the top of the brainstem and relates closely to the limbic system, as well as playing an important role in nervous system arousal, which is integral to attention. The wake/sleep cycle is managed here, overall brain arousal or level of activity is regulated here, and staying conscious is largely determined here.

Nevertheless, consciousness is managed in diverse areas of the brain. Carter observes:

> Although consciousness emerges from the cortex it requires an entire brain to
> feed it. The brainstem, midbrain and thalamus are essential because they are

part of a system that directs and controls attention by shunting neurotransmitters to various parts of the body.

(Carter, 2010: 300)

She also notes: 'It seems there has to be a certain amount of excitatory activity in the brain before consciousness arises and a large number of neurons need to be firing in synchrony' (Carter, 2010: 303). A great deal of energy is required to activate the brain so *I* can find conscious expression. And importantly, although at any point only selected regions of the brain are activated, generally through the focus of *I* enlivening the corresponding software, it seems the RAS needs to keep the whole brain in readiness to allow it to respond to whatever *I* requires of it.

The surface regions

The frontal cortex region has no primary sensory inputs: rather, its software appears to deal with processed information from other neural systems – it seems to participate in constructing ideas about beliefs and intentions, and allows a perspective of others (empathy). This software seems to enjoy a controlling function in emotion and behaviour. It is largely inhibitory in nature, putting the brakes on automatic neural responses – perhaps an avenue through which *I* retains control over the brain generally, by way of intent and associated decision making. To enable this, this region has strong and extensive connections throughout the brain, not least the limbic system, right down into the brainstem. This provides it with visceral, behavioural, and emotional information, allowing connections to be made between attention, emotion and cognition, and subsequent action.

The right side of the frontal cortex tends to pick up emotions of disgust, sadness, and fear, while the left side emotions of happiness. The software in this region governs the ability to predict, based on past memories, the likely outcomes of behaviours (Cozolino, 2002). In addition, there are important links to the brain's language centres, making complete the pathway between language (spoken and internal) and aspects of explicit memory, abstract reasoning, intent, decision making, affect, and behaviour. And so injury in, or corruption of, this region messes up control of *I*, leading to impulsive, irritable, violent, or disinhibited behaviours, and a poor capacity to predict the effect of one's own actions. Problems in this region's software also compromise emotional resolution processes, which are so dependent upon language.

In a subregion of the frontal cortex called the orbital area of the prefrontal cortex, we find software linked with the coordination of behavioural regulation through reward and punishment, conditioned fear, and bonding and attachment. The direct connections to the limbic circuits allow *I* to inhibit and modulate the firing of the fear-creating amygdala region by activating the neurotransmitter GABA in the prefrontal cortex, so inhibiting subcortical firing. GABA helps put out the emotional fire created in the amygdala.

The prefrontal cortex also plays a role in the integration of data from both internal and external worlds, connecting it with motivation, emotion, and reward systems. Software in the dorsolateral sub-area helps distinguish whether signals are of internal or external origin – this software is shut down in dream states and in those suffering schizophrenia. From here the ANS can be influenced, mainly through the inhibition of pathways allowing the regulation of emotional responses. Finally, this subregion appears to be associated with the development of abstract concepts such as time, a sense of self, moral judgements (and so the emotions guilt and shame have connection here), the coordination of 'internal maps' (that comprise the mind map), and the capacity for insight and empathy, allowing connection to the social world of others. This region may be central to integration and regulation, creating equilibrium in the neural systems, suggesting a central role enabling *I*. Yet here, too, lays a tiny region called the *septum*, which activates the pleasurable feelings associated with drug use, and which in turn can altogether deregulate and disintegrate the associated systems, disabling *I*.

Also in the frontal cortex is the anterior cingulate subregion, an area concerned with 'melding of emotional reactions with thoughts and judgements' (Carter, 2010: 281). Neural software here relates to maternal behaviour, nursing, play, and bonding; and to attention, reward-based learning, and autonomic arousal (Cozolino, 2006). It 'fires up' when there is cocaine addiction, bonding the person to cocaine instead of mother. It is further associated with visceral, motor, tactile, autonomic, and emotional information. 'Deficits' in this region relate to mutism, loss of maternal responses, and infant death due to neglect. This region plays a role in pain perception – both physical and emotional. It lies between the thinking centres of the frontal cortex and the feeling signals coming through the limbic system. Siegel observes that, because the anterior cingulate region links body, emotion, attention, and social awareness, it plays an important role in the resonance circuits[4] that allow me to feel connected to others and to myself (Siegel, 2009). Neural activity here allows *I* to know sensation and consciousness. Finally, this same centre that integrates my emotions and bonds me to cocaine looks after my heart: it mediates angina (pain) signals, alerting me to lack of oxygen, warning me to stop straining my cardiac faculties (Carter, 2010).

Functions connected with movement, orientation, calculation, and certain types of recognition are found in the parietal cortex. Here we find the somato-sensory region that relates to the nearby motor cortex region in the frontal cortex, which houses software controlling movement. The somato-sensory region provides an internal representation of the body to which the mind map relates. It is where the 'ambassadors' of the many body parts reside. These ambassadors deal with the ongoing brain demands and continually receive and send information on behalf of *I* (some of this information being filtered through the frontal cortex) directly to distant and not-so-distant body parts. The incoming information generally deals with sensation, but information is also sent and received by way of the motor cortex, orchestrating the body's movements. This is done both on instruction from *I*, but also from automatic neural processes – that is, implicit memories reflecting habits learned over time, and protective reflex actions. It is in this region that the *processing* relevant to body parts takes place, as very little processing takes place in distal body sites.

It comes as no surprise to find the temporal cortex, situated as it is above the ears, is dedicated to the processing of sound, speech comprehension (though this is usually on the left side only), and some aspects of memory. A little below the surface of the temporal cortex lies the small insula region. Integrated with the insula is software linked to Broca's area, which controls expressive speech (conveniently located next to the area of the motor cortex controlling the lip and tongue), and its next-door neighbour, Wernicke's area, which helps decode spoken language for *I* to apprehend. The insula region may have a role in 'social' emotions such as lust, pride, humiliation, guilt, and atonement. As such, it has to do with empathy and moral intuition, but it also makes the connections necessary to respond emotionally to music. Curiously, software here appears to read bodily states like hunger and cravings for things like cigarettes and cocaine.

Finally, although I do not have eyes in the back of my head, I certainly have my visual system there. The occipital cortex deals with complex visual processing and the changing internal visual representation of the external world, providing powerful orienting cues of the outside world for the mind map. It is a representation that provides the context for attentional activities, from which *I* can abstract targeted material for memory.

As we considered the functions related to various brain regions, you may have noticed that many functions were not limited to one region but overlapped into others, or needed to connect with others to function. So, for example, the orbital area of the prefrontal cortex is strongly related to the anterior cingulate (and also the amygdala). 'Deficits' in this *combined* territory are typically associated with deficits in maternal behaviour, in emotional functioning and empathy, in inappropriate social behaviour, impulsiveness, sexual disinhibition, and increased motor activity (Cozolino, 2006). Another example is the organized sense of the 'body in space' that appears to be stretched over the thalamus, cerebellum, and parietal cortex.

Then there is that point where the perceptual input of sound and language processed in the temporal cortex, visual images processed in the occipital cortex, and spatial relationships and integration of information from different senses processed in the parietal cortex meet. It is a juncture where perceptual input is 'brought together and associated'. Here connections are made between different perceptions, between different symbols (where words become sentences), and where parts of things become wholes – where meanings are processed. At this juncture, not only does the brain connect word with word, but also concept with word, visualizations with sounds, and so on – complex connections requiring efficient juxtaposition are made possible (Doidge, 2010). There are many other examples of such complex inter-relationships which may be tracked through neural circuits that act like informational highways connecting different regions, forming the overarching mind map.

We have observed how certain brain regions appear to be associated with particular cognitive, behavioural, or experiential functions. These regions vary in their neural architecture. That is, the type of neurons typically found in each region varies, although the regions we have identified comprise large swathes of neural territory, incorporating many different neuron types. Just as soil type varies from place to place in our land map, so does the makeup of the brain – both the structure of neurons and the neurochemicals that are released vary. Even within specific regions there can be great variation, as Koelliker observed long ago regarding the brainstem reticular formation: 'If these cells are accurately traced throughout the medulla oblongata and the pons, it is seen that they never form dense masses with a characteristic and constant form' (Birkmayer and Pilleri, 1966: 14) This, I suspect, allows each brain region to support many different kinds of function. It may also draw the boundaries of what is possible in brain neuroplasticity. Each neural function prefers or perhaps requires a certain kind of hardware, and thus utilizes the appropriate hardware found in a particular region.

We also notice that the software mediating emotional processes is in the central region of the brain – connecting emotion with thoughts, perceptions, and bodily responses such as heart activity. This suggests that emotions, not thinking processes, are more central to survival and day-to-day functioning, both in rapidity of response and in frequency of access. An organ intimately related to emotion – the heart – is closer to the centre of things than we generally appreciate. Although central, the area dedicated to emotional processes is relatively small, suggesting that it is not complex – which does not mean *I* might not have difficulty *interpreting* emotional responses. The cerebral cortex, on the other hand, comprises a large but peripheral area of the brain, suggesting it is structured for considerable storage of memory and learning. The material might be of great complexity, but rapid access to this for day-to-day life is less vital and necessary.

We observe these principles of location, space allocation, and proximity for each of the brain regions: the proximity of sound-decoding software to language comprehension; the proximity of the visual system to the balance centre; the proximity of software controlling the motor movements of the tongue and lips to the expressive language area, and so on. But are there any clues as to the engagement points of *I* within the brain structure?

Searching for the address of *I*

What have we really 'located' in terms of the brain's software? What are we looking for? Each neural region covers a lot of territory – we are talking billions of cells, which is a lot of software potential. There is an infinite number of cell combinations that can momentarily fire to reflect complex meaning combinations. A detective knows that, in volumes of information, only a small amount will be relevant to the case. Many facts may have interest in themselves, but do not further the understanding of who the criminal was or what he did. Similarly, neuroscientists can amass a lot of information, but what are the 'right' questions to further our understanding of the *I*–brain dynamic, especially as it relates to the various psychological problems facing the clinician, the things that burden the client?

What neural cartography *does* reveal is that neural processing and memory systems are at least *to some extent* localized. But the interactive nature of processing requires higher-order functioning to simultaneously relate to multiple regions in the brain. That a lesion, observed electrical activity, or artificial stimulation of any targeted point or region gives rise to an observable effect indicates that that part of the brain plays a role *at some level* in the complex software relating to that function. Yet malfunctioning of any one subprogram could cause widespread disruption at a higher level of processing, so that locating the subprogram could be difficult indeed. Although the more basic subprograms and algorithms are no doubt more localized in the brain than higher-order processes, the roles these subprograms play are likely to be difficult to measure or decipher based on endpoint behaviours and cognitions, given their collaborative role with other subprograms. I would anticipate no little confusion and many apparently conflicting results as the architecture of the brain continues to be scrutinized.

Studying the neural map, there is one thing I do *not* see: neural pathways converging to a central point or region integrating the diverse neural functions, creating a unified experience of events,[5] nor importantly, a location for *I*. Do not the unity of *I* and its seamless apprehension of meaningful experience require some kind of central integrating point in a brain made up of distinct regions performing different functions, with different circuits dedicated to different emotions and sensations? My experience is not of different parts of the brain doing different things in the way I experience my body doing. Although the fear circuits are separate from the pleasure circuits, it is the same *I* that apprehends both. Even though vision is processed separately from sound, the same *I* experiences both simultaneously.

If I accept there is no location for *I*, what about the location of an integration point? Many suggestions have been made: the limbic system that connects diverse parts of the brain; the medial prefrontal cortex, the centre of thinking and decision making; the anterior cingulate, involved in the regulation of focus; or the insula that some believe integrates mind and body. Others point to brain regions that appear to support conscious experience as against those that do not. But there is no consensus. Higher-level abstract material may not even be of a kind to be located this way. Nevertheless, the brain needs to integrate information, and over-riding software needs to manage this information in a manner accessible to *I*.

The experience of *I* is not normally fragmented – it is one seamless whole, a unitary *I* experiencing a single integrated stream of consciousness; but also a unitary *I* that uses the brain and body for *its own expression*, so that there is a 'top down' movement where the intent of a unitary *I* is disseminated into a brain that allocates the required functions to the appropriate regional centres for software processing and neurochemical activation. What is the bridge between these various component neural regions and *I*? How do those measurable neural events form the abstract meanings for the unitary presence of *I*, and how are meanings apprehended by *I*? How does *I* in turn cause neurons to fire? Might brainwaves play a role? How can such a dynamic be mapped? If *I* is indeed a dynamic entity, mapping its location might be like mapping the wind.

Nevertheless, we have been able to map *some* dynamic processes. *Some* pathways have been identified. A central pathway system that has been linked to the mind because of its apparent integrative function is the limbic system, which traverses many regions, including the orbital area of the prefrontal cortex. Some believe this system to be involved in shaping meanings through its appraisal processes. Yet the dynamic relationship between the software of the frontal cortex and the language centres, the emotion centres, and the points of interaction between these pathways would also be of interest, sites where major synthesis must be established. But of the activity of these sites, exactly where they are and how they work, we know practically nothing. And the bridge between operations and *I* still eludes us. For now, *I* remains of no fixed address.

There is another dimension of interest that might relate to *I*–brain interaction – that of *electroencephalographic waves*, or *brainwaves*. This dimension concerns neural activity and excitation but is not confined to any location, nor does it represent the activity of any specific neuron, though it may reflect network activity. Brainwaves are normally measured on the brain surface (though there is wave activity throughout the brain), and they have been found to vary in different states of consciousness, in different emotional states, and in different regions of the brain. They are created by the rhythmic oscillations of neurons, and show characteristic changes according to the type of brain activity (Carter, 2010).

Five different types of brainwave have been identified, each reflecting a different state of consciousness and emotion: alpha, beta, theta, delta, and gamma. Perhaps these waves carry information formulated by the neural software that is apprehended by *I*. However, the waves that are currently measureable are only those of sufficient robustness and accessibility – those generated from synchronous neural electrical activity occurring near the brain surface. The electrical activity of billions of neurons firing in rapidly changing constellations must produce signals of far greater complexity than that represented by the measured brainwaves. The point is that the signals generated are not limited to neurons or pathways, and are capable of carrying information beyond location-specific entities, perhaps of a form that may be apprehended by *I*, or perhaps even *defining* *I* as the source and destination of such signals.

In this, there is a paradox. On the one hand, I am suggesting that brainwaves may point to the presence of *I*. At the most robust level, as brainwave patterns change, so does the level of engagement of *I* as experienced in the level of consciousness. On the other hand, the possible existence of *I* as an entity separate from the body has been argued on the basis of conscious experience in the *absence* of brainwaves, as reported in the literature on near-death experiences. Furthermore, are brainwave patterns necessarily *secondary* to neural activity: can the reverse take place, where neurons respond to brainwave activity? Either way, because brainwaves are non-localized phenomena that appear to vary with the level of engagement of *I* with the neural system, they need to be considered as a measure of *I*–brain interaction.

We have explored the extraordinary relationship of *I* with its neural host in general terms. In Part III, we turn to more psychological matters, looking at the implications of this relationship for the developmental process, and for the relationship of *I* with itself and with others, before we turn to matters directly impacting the clinician's role.

The brain and *I* interact

Development and relationships

Part III

The brain and I interface

Development and relational

Chapter 8

Early development
I weaves a mind map

From the beginning, there is an interaction between *I* and the developing brain. *I* adjusts to the growing capacity of the brain, taking active involvement in the establishment of the emerging mind map, and making decisions within that framework. *I* plays a vital role in the things attended to, around which unique neural networks are created. But equally, the brain plays a vital role in the limitations and parameters within which *I* operates – *I* is reliant on the brain's resources for its expression through the body. It is an intricate dance, one in which many things can go wrong – whether in neural failure of some kind, in the failure of *I* to assert authority over the brain, or in inadequacies in the emerging mind map.

I takes up residence

When did *I* begin – when was the spirit imparted to the developing organism? Was *I* present from the very beginning, at the union of egg and sperm in my mother's womb? Was *I* interacting with my brain as it began to form? Or did *I* 'enter' when my lungs first drew breath – when the *ruach* entered – the hour of my birth, well after my nervous system had begun to remember and react? Until that hour, my nervous system had been altogether dependent on mother for its life and functioning; its source of communication was by way of a 'broadband' cable, mother's umbilical cord. Its earliest implicit memories were reflections of mother's experiences and sustained by the decisions of mother's *I*, passed on through her life-giving cable and captured in newly forming neural networks. Perhaps my physical body needed to be separate from mother and its nervous system free of the influence of hers to begin the process of becoming a functional and separate 'home' for *I*. Thus *I* begins its interactive journey with a receptive but largely unformed neural foundation upon which it builds unique networks, creating meaning from incoming signals.

Or was *I* 'formed' as awareness began,[1] somewhere between my physical birth and fights with siblings and others for 'my rights'? Perhaps somewhere between eighteen months and two years, when I began to understand that what I saw in the mirror was *me*, the body I saw was the body in which *I* resided, so that I came to recognize myself as unique and separate from others (not that I thought about it in this way – I just came to *know*). Was it when I first learned to say '*no*', and '*more*', or as I discovered that what *I* wanted was different from those around me? Was it the time *I* first became aware of being alone, of consciously trying to make sense of others and the world, of coming to develop a 'theory of mind', of becoming self-conscious in the presence of others? Yet although *I* is needed for self-awareness, *I* is not identical with it: the emergence of self-awareness may have more to do with neural development than with the establishment of *I*.

Whenever it was that *I* found a home in my body, there came a time when *I* began to learn to manage that body, and, as much as the brain allowed, *I* began to discover the world in which that body lived. Then the baby became a child, a teenager, an adult – did *I* develop and change over those years? Or was it my body and the capacities of my brain that developed and changed, while *I* remained essentially the same? Such is the mystery that remains to this day, as old as recorded history: what am *I*?

A child is born: mother Rachel names her Sarah. Sarah needs Rachel. Not only does Sarah's body need to be held by Rachel as she can go nowhere on her own accord, Sarah's *I* also needs to be aided by Rachel, as many of the neural capacities her *I* requires to interact with her world are still to develop.

One of the first capacities Sarah's *I* needs to establish is *focus*. Rachel actively encourages this, drawing Sarah's *I* to attend to particular things so that Sarah practises tracking visual and auditory stimuli. What she tracks becomes distinguished from the background. She was born with little ability to discriminate what she sees, feels, smells, or hears, and her neurons have yet to be programmed to distinguish one thing from another. But she actively seeks to do so. A rhythm commences between Rachel and Sarah as Rachel plays visual, sound, and touch games, seeking to connect with Sarah's *I*.[2] Sarah in turn searches out what Rachel does, and so learns to discriminate: mother's breast from her own thumb; light from darkness; the sound, smell, and sight distinguishing her mother from her father and others; one face from another. As discriminations are established, associations are made and corresponding neural connections begin to be etched around the meanings her *I* apprehends. The importance of the alternating processes of discrimination and association in early neural development cannot be overstated. Poor attention predisposes to poor discrimination, in turn interfering with the associative processes necessary for learning.

Much of Sarah's neural development follows a predetermined order, with 'critical periods' in which there is a temporal neural receptivity for certain learning needs to occur, laying the foundation for the next stage. This order reflects neural software hierarchies: basic software 'programs' and algorithms need to be in place before more complex 'programs' and connections carrying more abstract meanings can be developed.

Sarah's *I*, still with minimal self-awareness, has begun its dance with its neural inheritance and with the incoming sensory signals it needs to decode. Before her neurons begin establishing the networks of association strings necessary for language development and social understanding, meanings are already being reflected in gestures and make-believe play. Sarah experiments with sounds imitating language, gradually matching them with meanings. From the beginning, attention to detail is required to accurately create the neural firing patterns reflecting the sound patterns that comprise Sarah's emerging language: 'Infants normally become attuned to the sounds of their native language, including their peculiar accent – particular clumps of neurons in the auditory cortex come to represent the phonemes they hear every day' (Schwartz and Begley, 2002: 227). Poor attention to auditory stimuli in the early years can lead to poor phoneme development, which, in turn, can later contribute to poor reading, spelling, and comprehension.[3] Other developments occur. She begins to ponder permanency, looking for hidden objects where they were previously found. Her mind map weaves together remembered events, forming the basis of expectations.

The establishment of basic cognitive capacities is not the only development taking place. Just as the discrimination/association process is central to Sarah's emerging cognitive capacities, so the establishment of early secure attachment – connections of another kind – becomes a key to Sarah's emerging emotional and social patterning. This happens around the time her capacity for explicit memory becomes established as hippocampal pathways are forged, a time of growing self-awareness and language capacity. Before this, from before her birth, Sarah had to rely on implicit memories which allowed behaviours and some emotions to be remembered. Before her frontal cortex capacities are developed, her central brain region's capacity to mediate emotions is operating well. By six months, she expresses fear, anger, surprise, amusement, and shyness (pride and embarrassment a little later), emotions contributing to a growing store of implicit memories.

Attachment: *I* and others

From the beginning, Rachel seeks to make contact with Sarah's *I*, cooperating with Sarah to lay the neural groundwork for Sarah to be able to communicate and make 'connections'. And, increasingly, connections *are* made. Her desire is not only to 'care' for Sarah, but also to 'know' her. It is this connection between Rachel and Sarah, this communication between one *I* and another – however fleeting, however tenuous at first – that becomes key to the all-important bonding process. It is central to the establishment of secure attachment as the toddler Sarah prepares for her foray into the social world of kindergarten, if she has not already encountered day-care. Sarah meanwhile seeks to retain contact with Rachel's *I* through increasingly innovative 'attention-getting' behaviours.

As increasingly complex social connections are learned, a foundation for attachment is established.[4] When all goes well, secure attachments are established that create the life pattern for relationships and intimacy[5] through the network of meanings and expectations held in her mind map. Sadly, some pre-schoolers fail to establish secure attachment with mother or father. Instead, a pattern of *insecure attachment* is created where the child is oriented to negative expectations and associated coping responses.

Researchers describe three forms of insecure attachment: *avoidant* attachment, where parents are frequently indifferent to the child's emotional state, leading to indifference and withdrawal; *ambivalent* attachment, where parental response is highly inconsistent, leading to wariness and anxiety; and *disorganized* attachment, where parental response can be frightening to the child, leading to agitation and severe stress.[6] When the early attachment history carries such disturbance, a style of interpersonal relationship based on fear and distrust results, an inherently stressful style that stimulates the hypothalamic-pituitary-adrenal pathway[7] and compromises the neural pathways activated by love and connectivity. The child's *I* becomes ambivalent in human relationships, expecting indifference or rejection, which makes for hard work for the neurons (activating chronic stress responses), as well as for parents, and later for lovers and the clinician.

Secure attachment is not only about consistent availability or providing for her bodily needs, but also about parental recognition of Sarah's *I*; insecure attachment is not only about inconsistent physical availability, but also about the ignoring, dismissing, or attacking of Sarah's *I*. Over time, the chronic stress response created by patterns of insecure attachment can weaken aspects of her neural system, making her vulnerable to fatigue, dysfunction, and shutting down. In such event, *subsequent relationships can become a source of stress, rather than of nurturance*. On the other hand, positive nurturing experiences result in the stimulation and growth of receptors capable of absorbing the stress hormone glucocorticoid, allowing Sarah to grow up more resistant to stress and, by extension, to depression.

The power of language

The revolution of formal language acquisition begins wherein Sarah establishes the cognitive tools for her *I* to communicate with increasing specificity and complexity with other *I*s, allowing increasingly sophisticated relationships. Between twelve and eighteen months, she begins to discover the power of language to express meaning: her growing vocabulary sets the basis for further cognitive, personality, and social development. Into her third year, she begins to articulate emotional states, and her growing grammatical versatility allows her to ask questions, express negative feelings, and talk in past tense. Self-awareness develops as she learns to converse and discovers a distinction between her own and another's perspectives.

Sarah has become a toddler who is confronted with Rachel's 'no'. A major shift in her mind map begins, a small Copernican Revolution: no, the universe does *not* revolve around the world, and the world does *not* revolve around Sarah. Yet she will always be centred on her *I*. It is just that Sarah's *I* discovers other *I*s, and with these other *I*s, interpersonal boundaries and the intentions and wills of other *I*s need to be understood and accommodated; her *I* apprehends increasingly abstract intentions and communications.

As Sarah enters her third year, she also consolidates the capacity to *decide* – to make choices, to go left or right, to say 'yes' or 'no'. This is necessary for Sarah's *I* to interact with her world, and is enhanced by her nascent language. The dance between Rachel's *I* and that of Sarah continues: the parameters Rachel sets create the boundaries for Sarah's own decisions. The more practice in focusing, the more sophisticated her language, and the greater the opportunities for decision making, the more robust Sarah's *I* becomes, and the richer and sharper the neural capacities at the disposal of *I*. If all goes as it should, learned external rules are gradually transformed into abstract internal moral principles of 'ought' and 'should' that Sarah's *I* can use as reference for judgement and action.

In the third year, a revolution occurs in the relationship of Sarah's *I* with her brain, particularly her frontal cortex. With the development of language comes a consciousness of personal autonomy, allowing for the emotions of shame, pride, and embarrassment. In her fourth and fifth years, Sarah develops further emotional vocabulary that promotes emotional self-awareness and new capacities for emotional resolution – it is the time where her limbic system goes through substantial development. She now also recognizes emotion in others, making empathy possible. Erikson identified this period as one of 'shame and autonomy', followed by 'initiative and guilt' – a period where Sarah's *I* begins the struggle to manage the impulses and emerging habits generated by her neural home. She becomes aware that she does what she does not want to do, and fails to do what she wants to: 'I'm so sorry, mummy', she says with tears in her eyes, having had a consequence pronounced in response to forbidden behaviour she has engaged in, '*I don't know why I did it – I didn't mean to.*' As authority of *I* over her brain's activity increases, moral responsibility becomes possible.

By middle childhood, Sarah masters logical reasoning for concepts that can be seen, measured, and manipulated.[8] She develops literacy and numeracy skills and her *I* becomes increasingly adept at regulating attention and apprehending meanings. There is increasingly conscious involvement of *I* in the decisional process, reflected in advances in deliberate strategic memory, problem-solving, creativity, evaluative thinking, and executive functioning. Sarah's developing limbic system carries the increasing level of abstraction of which her neural software becomes capable.

Sarah's *I* takes an active role in the development of communication with Rachel. From the beginning, each reaches out and responds to the other – Sarah's neural system supporting an emerging mind map her *I* accesses; Rachel's supporting a well-developed mind map. Although Sarah is dependent on Rachel for survival, dependency is never passivity. Even before her language has begun to develop, Sarah actively seeks to engage Rachel. Each develops an attachment to the other, reflected in endorphin release in both (Cozolino, 2006). This process is foundational to the orientation of *I*, which reaches out through the medium of brain and body towards the other *I*, commencing a life-long dance of communion and differentiation – of connection and separation; of being energized and then exhausted by another; of discovering another; of growing and developing because of the other; and then discovering self, developing an internal communion, and resting from the input of others. Language is central in the unfolding interchange between *I* and the other. Where these processes do not unfold as they should, the reverberations can last a lifetime.

Sarah's developing language profoundly influences her growing sense of self and of her external world because it sets the parameters of her reasoning. These parameters vary in different languages and cultures, as each makes its own associations matched with particular words; each sets its own order of priorities and values that determine which words are learned first; each makes its own classifications that implicitly direct the focus for the characteristics of events deemed important. The language and culture expressed in Sarah's home set a unique framework for meaningfulness and her emerging mind map. The units of language which Sarah shares with her parents provide the tools for her conceptual understanding and abstract reasoning. Her mind map will at first have many matches with theirs, so that Sarah's *I* apprehends a world strongly coloured by her parents' outlook – at least until her teenage years.

The emerging mind map

An extraordinary amount of activity has taken place within Sarah's developing brain as her malleable neural structures respond to incoming information, matching her external world with a functional internal map. Her body map is among the first aspects of her mind map to be established, after which her physical and social worlds become represented. And although the order of development and the allocation of neural regions for particular tasks are largely set by genetic codes, there remains a vast landscape of undeveloped territory ready to be shaped by Sarah's experiences. Neural networks are created in the virgin forest of neurons. Unused neurons atrophy. As Sarah's hippocampus develops into functional maturity, network is superimposed upon neural network, creating an increasingly complex and detailed mind map, one that not only echoes Sarah's experiences, but also sets her expectations and the parameters of her understanding and interpretation for subsequent experience.

As it is with language and cognitive development, so it is with emotion: there is a transfer between Rachel and Sarah. Rachel stimulates the development of neural networks and pathways in Sarah through this interactive process. When, for example, Rachel draws close to, or away from, Sarah, there is a match in the changes of their endorphin and dopamine levels (Cozolino, 2006). Neural networks build on the fundamentals of emotion, movement, and nurturance – between hypothalamus, brainstem, and the essential organs. Just as the mastery of complex mathematics begins with the simple sequencing of numbers, of learning to add, subtract, multiply, and divide, so the mastery of complex emotional responses begins with the simple connecting of emotion with expression, expression with social responses, and social responses with language. Sarah's basic drive to survival begins with emotional communication. Rachel understands and responds to the emotion signals, and Sarah in turn watches Rachel's response patterns, learning what needs to happen to get her needs met. This process remains a significant theme between one *I* and another throughout life: the bridges of communication between people are as important as those within the brain.

The physical development of Sarah's brain is reliant on her experiences as much as her experience is shaped by her brain's emerging physical capacities. But already brain efficiencies seek to short-cut processes, which can lead to inaccuracies and distortions that need to be corrected and managed by joint efforts of Sarah's *I* and the interventions of significant others. The brain succumbs to short cuts, preferring approximate to exact discriminations, preferring the familiar to the novel, sometimes lumping similar sounds, visual features, and movements together to hold a common meaning when they are better kept separate. The more quickly Sarah's brain processes incoming material because of informational overload, anxiety, disinterest, or impatience, the more likely such errors are made. An impoverished discrimination data-base will compromise her brain's subsequent capacities in developing functional networks.

Young and Klosko (1993) undertook to describe and categorize aspects of the unique mind map each person relies on – not so much mind *maps* as mind *traps*, where brain efficiencies and distorted perceptions result in later problems. As Sarah progresses through childhood, she develops internal representations of the world she lives in and expectations of the key players in that world, and she discovers her own place in that world. These become her basic belief systems – Young and Klosko call them 'schemas' – which become the context in which new information is interpreted and understood. Her schemas become the basis for future neural efficiencies, helping to screen and interpret information. They comprise meanings that are not re-processed, even though sometimes they should be. They become the assumptions her brain builds on, generally surviving the turmoil of adolescence, but sometimes retaining distorted perceptions and inaccurate beliefs.

We see in the early years an accumulation of associations which support a network of meanings for the young mind. We see early learning that becomes implicit and automatic, subsumed by later, more complex learning, allowing for increasingly abstract meanings as the frontal cortex software and limbic system develop. In effect, *I* writes its identity onto the neural template in the early years: an identity not based on that template, but reflected in it. But in the teenage years, changes occur that no longer fit with established meanings – it is a time of questioning, a time of rupturing old connections and of creating new ones.

Chapter 9

Entering adulthood

Mind map transformations

You may reasonably have thought that after twelve years, Sarah's brain would have formed a complete foundation for all subsequent needs. But no, another reorganization of neural networks takes place, of severance of old pathways and creation of new ones – perhaps the neural equivalent of losing baby teeth and developing adult ones. The earlier pattern recurs: decommissioned neurons and pathways atrophy, maximizing brain efficiency. This adolescent reorganization largely involves the frontal cortex, resulting in a revised mind map with new meanings and associations: but the changes in neurotransmitter and hormonal processes can create instability. Nevertheless, if all goes well, the changes will enable *I* to make effective judgements and decisions about relationships, and career, and lifestyle, and self.

We follow the passage of *I* through the turmoil of adolescence into the adult world and discover that the adult continues to carry memory traces of early experiences that have tentacles reaching far into the future, colouring that adult's perceptions, expectations, and reactions.

Teenage turmoil

At mid-primary, Sarah's ability to be audience to her own thoughts becomes established: she becomes aware of self – of being both source and destination of communications. As her prefrontal cortex develops new capacities and a wide array of new neural connections are enabled throughout her brain, her *I* begins to 'wake up', so that by age twelve, her *I* is generally a self-aware, discerning, interactive entity, beginning to separate more fully from other *I*s, such as parents and siblings. What has been learned is questioned and another kind of self-awareness develops as her *I* increasingly differentiates itself from the brain processes and accumulated memories that have allowed it to function in the early years. It is a process of 'awakening' of *I*.

Yet it is also possible for Sarah's *I* to remain 'asleep', to remain largely undifferentiated from others and the world she has known. When her *I* is 'asleep', it flows with her brain's thoughts and implicit memories; it does not question remembered material and the demands made of her – she remains an 'extension' of her parents.

But when awakened, Sarah's *I* has better ability to 'dispute her thoughts', and probably also to dispute much of what her parents have said and believed, ideas which were a part of her.

Remaining an extension of her parents prevents Sarah's *I* from taking full authority over her body and brain. Around the age of twelve, a new relationship between her *I* and her brain begins to emerge, a new interactive capacity reflecting a new kind of self-awareness and self-responsibility and 'other' awareness. As hormonal releases trigger internal changes, so begins a preparation for the responsibilities of a committed relationship, of taking leadership in a new family and in society. She begins to ask herself the question: 'who am I?'

The focus is now on creating new reference points between her *I* and the other: reference points largely replacing her parents. She begins to perceive that what she knows and understands – her mind map – is not the complete reality. A set of new positions are negotiated – new responsibilities and a greater authority, changes recognized in law, a change of life roles. The meanings she had previously found in relationship with the 'other' begin to change: new connections and meanings are established because of these new positions; a revised mind map is developed. It is a revision – yet fundamentals remain. No longer is her family the primary reference point – her *I* becomes oriented to a wider context, to the world at large.

This larger context can overwhelm Sarah's *I*, and she may withdraw into a world of introspection over which she has control, the familiar world her mind map encompasses, enabling her to make sense of things from a limited perspective. But her *I* then develops distorted perceptions of the larger context and of her emerging role and purpose in the world. This period of individuation establishes clear boundaries between her *I* and other *I*s in anticipation of healthy encounters between adult *I*s. It is a process of discovering and connecting with another without the loss of her *I* as a separate entity – that is, without compromise of 'ego-boundaries'. Meanwhile, there is often a growing awareness and search for the source of being – the origin of *I*. She begins to ask questions of a different sort: who am I in the larger world? What is the point, the purpose of my being?

Sarah's *I* is faced with many new decisions as her brain reorganizes key structures, allowing new cognitive capacities.[1] This allows her to:

> imagine unobservable and futuristic scenarios . . . to reason logically about personal and social problems, including health, ethics, relationships, politics and future plans. As a result, [she becomes] preoccupied with moral values and the search for a personal identity that integrates [her] present skills, ambitions and philosophy of life with future options across the looming span of adult life.
>
> (Peterson, 2004: 385)

But dangers abound. Sarah may experience an 'imaginary-audience reaction', producing an alternation between painful shyness and fear of relationships (leading in its extreme to withdrawal and paranoiac fantasies), and exhibitionism and invulnerability (leading in its extreme to fantasies and delusions of grandeur). The delusional extremes can surface where the judgement capacities of *I* are compromised, contributing to emerging mental health issues.

Emotionally, Sarah enters a stage of psycho-social conflict in personality development that Erikson refers to as the creation of a sense of personal identity.[2] This process of personality organization accompanies neural reorganization, and a review of decisions by Sarah's *I*, which is establishing her position about many things. These include a philosophy of life incorporating moral values and an orientation to religion; a personality pattern that integrates enduring temperamental qualities and basic dispositions into a comfortably fitting adult character; a stance about herself as a sexual being; a stance in relation to politics and social issues; a blueprint for her future intimate relationships; and her ethnic and vocational identity.

There is much at stake. For some, a supportive environment allows easier transition – and surely there is a need to maintain solid external structures and values to minimize the stress of internal changes. For others, there is little to acknowledge and support the emerging parameters. A smooth transition may require 'managed passage': that is, structured changes, such as rites of passage. Too much uncertainty would create anxiety and further brain stress, and the search for clues for a guide to manage decision making may be found in the wrong places.

What is the optimal balance between stability and change; between structure and freedom; between conformity and self-discovery? Some cope better than others: why? Do they have better brain organization due to optimal early life experiences, conducive to the reorganization taking place? Is too much practice in the 'child role' and making few decisions in the early years going to create problems now? What is the best childhood foundation for later life? The neural changes in adolescence are of a different nature from the original work done: for the child, the brain is being *organized*; for the teenager, it is being *reorganized*. Because of the neural work involved in the changes, a vulnerability to depression emerges.

This period comes with its own hazards as neurochemicals activated by the changes flood Sarah's brain and body, and old neural pathways and networks are fractured and reworked. These hazards create a vulnerability to psychological disorders such as anxiety, depression, bipolar disorder, and schizophrenia. There is vulnerability to searching for meaning and connection and reassurance in the wrong places; and vulnerability to discovering new possibilities in life adventures, such as partying, testing the speed capacities of motor vehicles, and drug experimentation, which can lead to tragic results. As Sarah's *I* adjusts to a shift in her significant 'others', the ones who now constitute her primary reference point, her *I* can become disoriented by the new parameters moulding her mind map and lose its bearings. This in time can reflect in fractured meanings and attributions. When she cannot 'make sense' of her world, she experiences neural stress. Sarah's *I* needs to make adjustments to brain changes that she does not altogether control nor understand: there is a need for re-integration, and confusion easily results.

Sarah's brain seeks to organize its functions efficiently – but what was efficient before is no longer necessarily so. The neural reorganization of teenage years is not altogether a predetermined event: rather, the reorganization of Sarah's brain interacts with the reorganization of her life experiences. Sarah's body grows in size and capacity – this predetermined – and then her brain makes adjustments, and her *I* makes new decisions. The life she lives shapes her brain as much as does the genetic input and the decisions of her *I*. But too rapid a change may overwhelm the capacity of her brain, and judgement is compromised. Her *I* gets deceived, and meanings are confused. Her brain can get tired and begin to malfunction or become vulnerable to disease. Conflicts occur, activating amygdala software, releasing cortisol, putting pressure on her reorganizing brain. Further stress results from a lack of the accumulated knowledge and experience she needs to make satisfactory decisions in her emerging world.

One would think that, with such difficulties accompanying the passage into adulthood, the monumental struggle of the individuating *I* in the rapidly changing brain and body might cause a flood of struggling teenagers to wear thin the steps into the clinician's office. But no – there is only a trickle who take the trouble, and that generally initiated by desperate parents. Yet this is not surprising: the very point is to establish a sense of independent self – it is hardly the time to seek counsel, least of all from that from which individuation is taking place. And so parents watch from afar, hoping that their offspring will not make a shipwreck of their lives – indeed, many emerge in good shape. By now, if all has gone well, the teenager's *I* has negotiated the rapids and is rewarded with a fully formed brain and an effective mind map mediating the information necessary to make the decisions and judgements life will require.

The politics of control

It is one thing for Sarah's *I* to take up residence in her body; it is another for it to take authority over its new home. In the early years, the neural foundations were formed for such authority to be established, allowing her *I* to express effective judgements and decisions in ways understandable to others. This authority established a sense of self that was both confident and assertive: a strong sense of *I*.

But in those early years before Sarah's *I* had taken proper authority of its natural home, it depended on other significant *I*s to maintain the integrity of its relationship with its body. Sarah's *I* depended on others not to exploit its early vulnerabilities or to violate the right of that *I* to manage its own body. Yet, all too often, violations are experienced. Such violations may have a sexual dimension, but not necessarily. Any invasive action enforcing an external will on that which belongs to another *I* is a problem. By 'invasive action', I do not mean the normal setting of boundaries and teaching processes. I mean indifference to what the child's *I* communicates and a lack of respect for the body belonging to the child's *I*.

Such violation when *I* has limited self-awareness will leave implicit neural traces that influence its behaviour in later years. For a toddler, violation may result in confused interpersonal boundaries; for a pre-schooler, confusion in the emerging emotions of guilt and shame; for those in the mid-primary years, issues of authority – a lack of respect for the other may emerge. For a teenager where *I* has begun to exercise proper authority over its physical home, a failure to protect from violation may result in a sense of 'real' guilt and shame by *I* and loss of self-esteem.

Taking authority over the body implies a level of control over that body.[3] But *I* discovers that the body creates its own desires, impulses, thoughts, and emotions that do not necessarily find origin in *I*. It is in those crucial teenage years when *I* seeks to come into full authority of its body that it may find itself in a battle for control, trying to make an apparently recalcitrant body do what *I* determines. It may find itself hostage to the body's demands – whether in relation to powerful sexual urges, physical appetites, or unpredictable mood states. And what a battle it can become, where *I* can feel the shame of failure and defeat, or the empowerment of victory and control.

Yet true control is the capacity to effectively manage the body for the expression of *I*; rather than directly controlling and subduing the impulses, drives, and desires of the body. Such attempts can result in *I* being controlled by the very body it seeks to control. At some level, whatever I engage in battle with influences me because I am reacting to it. That from which I am independent does not control me. Yet I cannot be independent from a body I am to manage. I must therefore enter into a dance of equilibrium, a compromise between two forces: my brain and *I*.

The authority I have over my body must be exercised in the understanding of the dependence I have on my body – therein lies my body's power. I have to learn to use it with wisdom and respect in order for it to do my bidding. I have to learn to love and understand the body in order to properly manage it. While my body is an avenue of expressing *I*, it also makes its own demands on *I* as much as it can manipulate the external world. Who is in control? *I* has authority over the body, but *I* is reliant on the body so that its urges are capable of overwhelming me: this even *before* *I* begins to deal with the possible violations and manipulations by others – whether in my early vulnerable years, or as I enter adulthood.

The politics of control begins around age two and reaches a climax of opposing forces in adolescence, when the question emerges: who is in control? The answer needs to be: *I*. But it can be a confusing time as the adolescent seeks to discriminate between perceived and actual control. The battle finds expression in different ways, and can reach desperate dimensions in those suffering eating disorders or obsessive compulsive disorder (OCD). Does fear control me, or my parents, or the opinions of my friends or work colleagues? Does my past control me, or my bodily impulses? Who *is* in control? And indeed, there are other unseen players in the battle for control of the body and brain over which *I* properly has authority. The question of who is in control is a vexing one – even when I *think* *I* is in control, what is influencing *I*?

An ongoing dynamic

And so we come to the adult years, each brain emerging different from every other, with neural pathways formed in response to years of information input, creating unique configurations and unique patterns of meaning, yet with underlying brain structures relatively similar to one another. Genetics defines some of the neural structures and connective capacities, the developmental timing, and the basic software configurations that account for individual differences and for family similarities in cognitive capacities, physical mannerisms, and personality styles. By the mid-twenties, the prefrontal cortex has finally matured, the region that manages beliefs, intentions, and empathy, and whose software provides a controlling function in emotion and behaviour.

Brain plasticity notwithstanding, the combination of genetic memory and memory formed early in life's learning creates the basis for subsequent expectations and interpretations of life experiences. In the early years, the seeds of the future are sown, the 'plant' positioned; and from this position and these parameters, life unfolds. Not in an inevitable, deterministic fashion; yet the more established the neural pathways, the greater the challenge for *I* if it were to veer away from that path. What has been focused on and how things are remembered has tremendous bearing on what happens in subsequent years. Early memories influence later ones; early habits of focus are generally maintained in adult years.

Sarah's mind map is now well developed: the work of creating a functional internal representation of the external world is now largely complete – so long as life experiences oblige and stay within the range of familiar life patterns. That is: so long as traumatic events or altogether different interpretations of life by significant others are not encountered. Sarah's mind map reflects the culture of her family and society and the rhythm of her physical world. It is only within this framework that the meaningfulness of events can be measured and that subsequent experiences need to connect. It is this framework with which the clinician needs to become familiar for his interventions to be meaningful to his clients.

Although Sarah's brain reaches maturity in her mid-twenties, the making of adjustments to her mind map never really stops: neural networks organizing behaviours, emotions, thoughts, and sensations will be built and rebuilt throughout her life, even reworking whole new brain regions where necessary in the event of a stroke or brain lesion. Repeated external messages are literally able to reform the structure of part of the brain (Doidge, 2010): in a sense, 'the word becomes flesh', as new information transforms neural hardware and chemistry. The decisions of Sarah's *I* also find expression in her neural regulatory systems – in sleep patterns, weight management, level of general alertness (reflecting the perceived safety of her environment), the neural adaptation to ingested chemicals (nicotine, alcohol, and other drugs), and eating habits. Such adjustments are variations of the neural default settings established genetically or early in Sarah's developmental history – once established, they may be difficult to readjust.

But there is a cost to the accumulation of knowledge: decision making can become cumbersome as the increasing volume of information to access requires more processing time. Like the computer whose hard disk is largely full, the rate of processing can begin to slow. In its dedication to efficiency, Sarah's brain may compartmentalize incoming information, restricting the number of possible connections and reducing the readiness of access to stored material so that its benefit is lost.

While the tasks of adolescence are now complete, the issues of life meaningfulness and direction periodically re-appear – especially in transition times, such as children leaving home, the loss of a loved one or of employment, and in retirement. The task of making sense of life continues to the end of Sarah's sojourn upon earth. Similarly, the task of her *I* to embrace and manage its body and the world, and to overcome challenges, making optimal use of its neural resources, continue, with new challenges in every chapter of life.

There is no rest in 'retirement': the demands of life and of her body generally *increase* in the latter years. As the years take their toll, Sarah's body becomes increasingly fragile, and the neural structures on which her *I* depends begin to atrophy, creating anxiety. The old issues of control and the potential for exploitation and violation can re-emerge, creating further apprehension. The question of mortality looms: making sense of life in the face of death. Where will she go when she departs from her body? What *is* she apart from her body? Will Sarah's *I* still be able to know, experience, and be a source and destination of communications after death?

Over the years, my body changes, yet I am the same person. How is this possible? Am I recognizable only by outward physical features?[4] I as a five year old and I as a fifty year old will have changed every imaginable external feature; indeed, every cell in my body will have been renewed – yet *I* remains the same entity. Am I to be recognized by internal features? Even though my mind map retains some memory of the years, providing continuity and a core to identity, this also changes: the memories stabilizing my identity are coloured with time. How is it possible for one *I* to recognize another when these features are in constant state of flux? Does recognition somehow happen 'in the spirit', where the outward form might change, but *I* stays the same, and is forever recognizable as such? What is the enduring essence of *I*?

Chapter 10

I considers self

The questions of shame, guilt, pride, and confidence, of joy or despair, of embrace or rejection of life itself are generally questions of the relationship of *I* with itself, a relationship where *I* evaluates itself, taking the position of judge. Here roles are split, being simultaneously actor and judge! Such judgement is made both of *I* itself – that is, judgements about the decisions *I* has made – and of the body and brain that *I* inhabits – that is, the acceptability of physical aspects of the body to *I*, the acceptability of levels of performance and achievement, and even the acceptability of life itself. Self-appraisal is a critical aspect of the dance of *I* with the physical self. A negative judgement in relation to a decision *I* has made may result in guilt. A negative judgement in relation to physical aspects of the body, to capacities of the brain, or to levels of performance or achievement may result in shame, poor self-confidence, self-alienation, or in the perceived rejection by others. A negative judgement of *I* in relation to its relative efficacy in the world may lead to passivity, anxiety, low self-esteem, despair, and the rejection of life itself.

The capacity to make judgements and decisions about *I* presumes a capacity for self-awareness mediated by my brain, in that it is a conscious process. This chapter begins with the question of self-awareness and self-identity, and then looks at the process of self-evaluation and its relationship to self-esteem. In self-evaluation, the judgement establishes the relationship of *I* with its body: one of embrace or alien-ation. In embrace, *I* makes effective use of its physical home to relate well to others and to thrive in the natural world. In alienation, *I* enters a struggle of self-conflict and self-sabotage that affects its relationship with the other and the world generally. Yet it is not just a question of the perceptions *I* has and the judgements *I* makes of itself, and of the ensuing relationship *I* has with itself and the body. There are also related questions of the capacity to change aspects of *I* on the basis of such evaluation, of the actual *strength* of *I* to do so – a question of self-efficacy with significant ramifications.

I, self-awareness, and self-identity

We have seen that *I* and self-awareness – a dimension of consciousness – are not the same. While in my body, *I* cannot reflect upon itself, on its decisions and experiences, without involving its supporting neural software. It is even perhaps necessary that *I* does not become aware of a decision it makes until moments after the decision is made because of the intervening neural activation required for conscious apprehension of the decision. Like thunder comes after lightning, yet finds its origin in the same event, so awareness of a decision made may come moments after the decision is executed, although their origin is a single event. How is this possible? How can *I* function without immediate awareness of the fact? And how can *I* make the distinction that it is *I* that initiated a decision about which *I*, belatedly, becomes aware, rather than it being the independent product of neural activity? This is tricky territory indeed.

When I say that I am 'self'-aware, of what *is it* that I am aware? Both *I* events[1] and neural events can occur outside awareness. Regrettably, my brain does not give an account of its own neural activities to *I*. It has no mechanism by which to analyse itself, and I have no capacity to be aware of neural events in their own right – only of the meanings and sensations they mediate. So of what am I aware when I consider the self? I am aware of events that originate in *I* that are expressed neurally and physically – I take ownership of them. But it seems that, as I become aware of *I* events, I momentarily suspend *I* activity: activation of self-awareness leads to inhibition of self-expression. I enter the role of the *recipient* of events initiated by me, momentarily relinquishing the role of *author*: at that point, *I* becomes the *destination*, not the *source*. And so, to properly express myself as author of communications, I momentarily suspend self-awareness. Conversely, to become properly self-aware, I momentarily suspend self-expression. To do both simultaneously interferes with performance, like the feedback in a sound system. It is no doubt because of the potential for such interference that neural activity occurs below awareness, especially that involving intricate and split-timing neural feedback systems, such as in proprioception.

Self-awareness detracts from the efficient functioning of *I*. We see this when I focus on balancing on my bike, rather than on where I am riding: the focus on balance easily leads to overcorrection, as *I* interferes with a process that has its own automatic regulatory systems. Generally, focus should be on *external*, not *internal* messages, as neural software systems are built around the flow of incoming information – not around their own functions. The simultaneous awareness of self and focus on performance overwhelms the neural system with too much information, leading to anxiety. It is therefore necessary for *I* to activate physical responses *outside self-awareness* to allow rapid responses. Introducing the self-awareness loop hinders smooth and effective performance, as every musician, sportsman, soldier, and public speaker knows. But while awareness of a decision or performance needs to come *after* the actual decision or performance, *I* is no less the origin. Nevertheless, performance may be rehearsed so it reflects automatic neural activity (implicit memory), with neural 'decision trees' enacted that minimize the involvement of *I* in the process.

There seem to be two kinds of self-awareness. There is the awareness of body function, a consciousness (to a degree) of processes going on within, the exercise of which generally does not cause discomfort. Then there is the awareness of *I* as an entity in encounter with another. This second circumstance more easily causes discomfort as if it is something unnatural: a sense of self-consciousness, of exposure and possible shame. The natural position for *I* is to be in interaction with the other, not to be turned in on itself. In becoming aware of *I* from the perspective of another, I become audience to myself. The experience of self-consciousness is not just one of being self-aware, but of *being aware of another's awareness* of me; an evaluating awareness wherein I feel exposed to them. My *I* has insufficient cover; it feels unclothed. Perhaps too much has been revealed, leaving me vulnerable to judgement and possible ridicule or condemnation. Such awareness may generate an immediate impulse to cover-up, so that any natural expression of *I* through the body is interrupted, or altogether ceases.

Yet there is a positive role for reflection and self-awareness, especially in self-understanding. This has its own complexities in that my essential nature cannot be separated from the context of my neural home, even though that neural home has the capacity to do violence to my sense of self, creating confusion and distress when dysfunction occurs. But normally, there is an integration of *I* with my neural home and associated mind map. The schemas, memories, coping methods, learned repertoires, and positions of *I* that comprise my mind map become my identity. They inform the natural expression of *I* and the way *I* perceives things – my familiar world. Awareness and understanding of that familiar world of the self also allows for self-judgement and sometimes desire for change.

This becomes a classic clinical (and marital) problem: if *I* finds identity in what is familiar, then when I seek change through psychological therapy (or through insistence of my spouse or partner), I enter the unfamiliar – that which I consider not-*I*. This becomes a point of resistance as my instinct is to retreat into the familiar territory of *I*, especially when under stress. There is normally such correspondence between *I* and this neural reflection of *I* that, if there is any sense that what is encoded neurally is unhelpful and in need of change, it can lead to an identity crisis. Understandably, here there is natural resistance: *I* becomes locked into its own history and emerging identity, regardless of how dysfunctional it might be. To change, *I* has to do things that appear 'ego-alien', things that are unfamiliar and awkward, because the new make a poor match (at least for awhile) to the existing mind map. This is hard work and stressful, and requires a conducive and supportive environment. It requires clarity about what *I* wants to 'become', and finding sufficient energy, focus, courage, and commitment to bring about the change and to enact the new decision.

But it is not so much that *I* changes, as it is the mind map *I* relates to. And it requires 'strength' in *I* to change the existing neural network. A weak *I* tends to retain well-established neural patterns. But what does it mean for *I* to be 'strong' or 'weak'?

Self-esteem and strength of *I*

With the capacity for judgement comes the capacity for self-judgement and self-condemnation. Yet by what standard – moral or otherwise – is this done? Where did I learn to condemn? From where do my expectations, standards, and self-criticisms come? This judgement can relate to that over which *I* exercises direct control, such as the decisions *I* makes or the manner in which *I* expresses itself through its body. Equally, such judgement can relate to that over which *I* has no control, the 'givens' *I* has to work with: of body shape and features or gender, of given name or social class, of general intellectual capacity or specific abilities. Whether or not *I* has control over that which is judged, self-condemnation primes the mind map towards the expectation of rejection by others and self-alienation.

If *I* finds expression through my body, then self-evaluation can happen on two fronts. The capacity of *I* to express itself in my body with all the restrictions my body places on *I* (how well I do a thing, how successful I am) can be judged; and *I* itself (typically, the decisions and intentions of *I*) can be judged. Negative self-judgement or positive self-regard, therefore, may be based as much on bodily or neural failures as on *I* itself.[2] Either way, self-evaluation forms the basis of self-esteem, which relates to many aspects of living. The creation of positive self-esteem has become a primary goal for many. Seligman (1995) argues that self-esteem generally relates to level of mastery: my capacity to act upon the world and make a difference – to have a measure of control or, at least, a perception of control even under adverse circumstances. The measure of my *value* is based on my *efficacy* – the ability of *I* to express itself effectively.

Positive self-esteem requires that *I* can effectively manage the activities of the brain, achieving self-efficacy. Loss of self-esteem generally results when *I* is helpless in the face of external or internal neural demands; when the brain (my natural impulses) or circumstances control me. Theory and research dealing with self-efficacy speak of the perceived empowerment of the self in relation to others and the world:

> Self-efficacy is a generative capacity in which the individual organizes and orchestrates his skills to cope with the demands and circumstances he faces. It is the capacity to use one's personal resources well under diverse and trying circumstances. Formally, self-efficacy is defined as one's judgement of how well (or poorly) one will cope with a situation, given the skills one possesses and the circumstances one faces.
>
> (Bandura, 1997, in Reeve, 2005: 228)

Yet self-esteem is increased not just through 'success experiences', but also through the successful imposition of my will over the body's inclinations. When I do the things *I* does not want to do – things on impulse, things unplanned – *I* is diminished and loses power, resulting in a poor judgement of self. Intrinsic to the wellbeing of *I* is its capacity to remain true to its own values. To do so may require a capacity to resist bodily inclinations it has not authored or authorized. Where do such impulses come from – past learning? Rogue neuropeptides? But more importantly, how do I find the capacity to resist the very things that arise within me?

In this there is the assumption that *I* is accountable and has the potential for failure. Moreover, it assumes that *I* is capable of doing what it is held accountable for. *I* appears to have this attribute: the capacity to be 'strong' or to be 'weak'. *I* may have the strength to manage neural demands, or it may fail to do so. How is it possible for *I* to be 'strong'? Is this a quality of the entity *I* itself; does it simply reflect a position *I* takes; or does it depend on aspects of the engagement of *I* with the neural system? *I* needs this quality to make and to action decisions; it is this quality that determines its capacity to over-ride neural inclinations rooted in past history, in internal drives, or in emotional imperatives. This quality varies from one person to another. A 'weak' *I* lends itself to *external locus of control*, the perception that events happen *to* me; a 'strong' *I* to *internal locus of control*, the perception that events happen *because* of me – I *make* them happen. A person with a 'weak' *I* is easily overwhelmed and influenced by others, often preferring not to engage in the commerce of life over which it has such little control. Its inclination to avoidance then becomes a root of anxiety: 'It's all too hard; I want out.'

This quality of *I* – its strength or weakness – plays a role in the capacity of *I* to manage its mind map, and by extension, its neural home. A 'weak' *I* is reflected in a passive, disempowered spirit which takes no initiative, and is reactive rather than proactive, where the 'fire of life' is reduced to a weak and intermittent flicker. It may result in 'failure to thrive', or in the 'loss of will to live'. Its lack of strength is reflected in the neural capacities that mediate this quality – there may be a gradual shut-down of neural activity and a weakening of integrative processes and neural connectivity. Herein is created a condition for depression, but also vulnerability to other psycho-pathological processes such as anxiety, fed by the perception of incompetence and inability to meet expectations. A strong *I*, on the other hand, is proactive, harnesses good energy, has better capacity to resist neural inclinations to distraction allowing effective focus, and has better capacity to regulate emotions and resist urges that underpin addiction. Either way, the qualities and values upheld by *I*, finding expression in emotions and behaviours over time, come to be reflected in the mind map, which in turn provides the context of the judgement of *I* of itself.

Well-known empiricist Martin Seligman cautions us when associating self-esteem with a plethora of variables: this is correlational research – it gives us no indication as to what *causes* what (Seligman, 1995). It makes sense that self-esteem as a measure of self-evaluation is established largely in the context of events occurring to the self, wherein the capacity of self to deal effectively with events is evaluated. Yet, given the dynamic nature of all things human, we might expect a two-way process: high self-esteem is as much a *result of* as it is a *causal factor* in high mastery levels. This two-way process notwithstanding, Seligman argues that optimism acts as an inoculation against depression, suggesting that the *position of I* over time (in this case, of optimistic expectations relating to self-efficacy) positively affects neural processes at a physiological level.[3]

Many struggle with themselves, with their body image or their various cognitive and physical capacities. Their negative self-judgement leads to self-rejection and self-alienation, which can lead to chronic internal tension and eventual depression. But the task of *I* is to *cooperate* with its body, not to *judge* it – the body is given as the medium of self-expression, not of self-adoration or self-deprecation. When I am inclined to competitiveness, I might make comparisons with others or with some inner ideal, so that I judge my body's weaknesses and failures. But I need to work cooperatively with my physical home, not in competition. In part, the attribution of value to the self is a function of what is *invested* into *I* as the entity valued. To invest time into activities that give pleasure to or that contribute to my development, for example, contributes to the valuing of *I*. But ultimately, my focus needs to be external, not internal: my body is for the *expression* of *I* and, although such expression may be frustrated because of neural or bodily limitations, it does not follow that *I* should be devalued because of this.

Now, one area in which level of self-esteem *does* appear to be causal is in my relating with others. My identity is largely contained in a stable mind map developed over the years. When another communicates perceptions about me, those that fit with my mind map I receive readily. Those that do *not* fit my self-perceptions I discard. When, therefore, the other communicates my value to them and their love for me and it does not fit my mind map – if I do not see myself of value or worthy of their love – I will not embrace those messages. And so my friend finds the relationship is affected by my poor self-identity and self-esteem. This is difficult to address, given the stability of my mind map and its resistance to change.

Chapter 11

I encounters *thou*

A woman glances at a man. He sees not only the look of interest in the woman's eye; he sees the promise of intimacy. How is such information communicated? She has said or written nothing. There is no past history. Many women have looked his way and not communicated this promise. No, not just a promise: already intimacy has begun. She has touched something. His *I* has received a powerful message about which it is compelled to make a decision. Not only has eye encountered eye, *I* has encountered *I*. What meanings have they communicated without words? How does he now respond? The encounter has left him changed; he cannot do nothing, nor will he forget the moment of encounter.

There is a mystery of simultaneous intimacy and separateness in the relationship of one with another. *I* discovers another *I* separate from me, yet one with whom I want to be 'connected'. In my separateness, I cannot fully know the other, yet my desire is to know and be known by the other. Frustration, distress, and loneliness result when the process of meaningful connection is thwarted. In this chapter, we explore the mystery of intimacy, of the encounter of one *I* with another in bodies and using mind maps that both mediate and frustrate that closeness. We will see how critical the relationship is between *I* and the brain in the context of interpersonal relationship.

Connection: A life purpose

Just as neurons quickly atrophy when they are disconnected from surrounding neurons, so *I* becomes impoverished when disconnected from other *I*s. When trapped in extreme circumstances, such as in solitary confinement or an isolated place, considerable distress can result. *I* typically responds by replacing the information flow normally existing between *I* and the other with memory and fantasy. If *I* does not take charge in this way, hallucinations may result. The connection with the other is fundamental. Frankl (2006) argues that meaningfulness and purpose in life is embedded in connection with another, and some would argue that the purpose of a community is in turn embedded in its connection with the source of all things.

Entering into a relationship with another is entering into an ongoing exchange of shared experiences and associations, of a thought stream that connects my meanings to the meanings of another. A dynamic *I* follows a 'thread of thought' in its mind map: in conversation this thread becomes a shared thread, moving from my mind map to that of the other and back again. A 'meeting of minds' occurs when that shared thread becomes tightly woven, with two *I*s enabling the process. Meaningfulness emerges from the shared associations that connect the mind maps, and from recognition by the other as *I* begins to be known. It is in such encounter that my existence is recognized, my value affirmed, and my perceptions of the external world validated.

The idea that my meaningfulness derives in large degree from my relationship with others is unsurprising. If *I* am partly defined as the source and destination of communication, there needs to be another destination and source to complete the interchange without which the meaningfulness that derives from information exchange would be eroded. It becomes a fundamental purpose for *I*. The clinician sees in depression a withdrawal from others that results in loss of meaningfulness, purpose, and reason to live. Similarly, the loss of a significant other results in multiple disconnections – both loss of encounter of *I* with the other, and in the network of connections that represents the other in the mind map, potentially leading to some disorientation and meaninglessness.

In the encounter between two *I*s, the dance of each *I* with its neural host plays its own role. Each *I* seeks to know the other by way of the mediating systems available: one the source; the other the destination; then reversing roles. Each encounter is necessarily mediated by the respective mind maps and neurochemical activity. And so the adventure of discovery begins. Who is she? What did he really mean? How do I feel about her? There is a complexity in the communication process in nuances in language, tone, facial expression, and so on that is necessary to capture the abstract ideas and meanings exchanged. It is difficult to break these down into component parts without compromising the message – it is the *whole* that expresses the intended meaning. It is not the physical body communicating, but *I*. The complexities *I* seeks to communicate require all the physical resources at *I*'s disposal to accurately convey the meaning. And thus we come to 'know' each other. If we are successful and I feel 'known' by the other, then there is a measure of satisfaction and completeness in the 'we' that emerges. When this happens, there is a sense of lightened burden: the beginning of healing.

Yet what is this sense of 'we', of communion, that heals? Do the shared meanings validate and integrate mine own? Memories about me are now within the other, a perceptual framework wherein *I* plays a part. And similarly there is such within me regarding the other. The other is not only 'out there' in a physical sense, but also 'within me' in the sense of 'integrated into my mind map' in shared memories. This is what it means to be 'known'. It is also about sharing a common position and making shared decisions. The more my perceptions, memories, and position overlap that of another, the more familiarity and comfortableness there is with the other. There is also the awareness that the other cares enough to do the work of knowing me, to be focused and attentive enough to remember these things and reflect on them. *I* now partakes of meanings shared in our respective mind maps.

The encounter: Another *I*, or another body?

Existentialist philosopher Martin Buber is famous for his book *I and Thou*. He explores at depth the *I–thou* relationship, differentiating the experience of *encounter* with the other *I* from the experience of knowing the other as an *it*, an object to be analysed and 'understood', something that might be described by various observed characteristics. It is a crucial distinction. To encounter another *I* is to relate to another who, like me, feels, smells, hears, sees, thinks, makes judgements, decides, plans, and acts. Only, the other is likely to experience these things differently from me, and therein lays the adventure of encounter. The experience of connection and intimacy is found in the encounter between the two *I*s: not an encounter between two brains.

I does not encounter the profound mystery of the existence of another sentient being just in knowing facts about the other, viewing the other as an external object, an 'it'. This not only retains separateness from the other, but ignores the presence of *I* in the other physical body, one capable of knowing the *I* within my body. Yet in another sense, there is *always* separateness, and it is this very separateness that creates the experience of the 'other'. Just as discrimination precedes connection and constant movement defines the relationship of *I* with its neural host, so the encounter between two *I*s is governed by a dynamic alternating between separateness and connection between two sources. I need to experience myself as separate in order to enter meaningful intimacy.

While the act of evaluating the other creates a separation that is quickly understood, there is another kind of separation that is poorly defined – both hinder rather than aid meaningful intimacy. The latter occurs in attempts to connection or closeness without the proper self-disclosure that discriminates one from another, preventing one *I* knowing the other. Instead of authentic dialogue, there is a pseudo-encounter where the other *I* becomes an extension of one's own needs and desires – a subjugation by one of the other, an apparent closeness at the cost of a sense of self. Due to uncomfortableness with difference and the potential for conflict because of difference, thoughts, feelings, decisions, plans, and judgements are aligned with the other, so that I no longer admit to the activities that define me. My apparent closeness to the other is at the cost of alienation to my own identity. Here the one subjugated is neither one with whom I enter into dialogue nor one I treat as an object to know *about*; but one that I attempt to make an extension of me by closing down the other (or my own sense of self) as a separate entity.

We find a parallel in principles of neural functioning. Like neurons, relationships are about connection and disconnection; and connection only has meaning after 'differentiation' (discrimination) has been established. Only in the context of two clearly separate *I*s does the connective event of relationship create a new meaning – only then does it add anything. The extent to which I am different from the other is the extent the relationship creates new meanings for me.

We have seen how *I* establishes the sense of separateness developmentally, first during the boundary-testing toddler years, and then the conflict-ridden teenage years of individuation, to make possible entry into a meaningful relationship in the sense of an encounter between two individuated *I*s. Both the decision to love and the revelation of *I* in intimacy with another begins with a clear sense of *I*, because it is the things of my heart and the integrity of my being that I express to another. If love and intimacy is based on what I think I *ought* to be (that is, to fulfil the expectations of the other, so avoiding relational conflict), I lose the sense of who I am, and internal conflict, self-alienation, and a sense of being trapped (eventually leading to depression) generally result.

Still, there is a mystery in the encounter. How do I encounter you? Is it the sharing of 'peripheral information', the everyday events each experiences, in addition to connecting with the 'heart' of the other, his or her emotions, values, and life position? The practicalities of relationship must require knowledge of habits, expectations, and so on, of the other – an understanding of the mind map that orients the other *I*. Can encounter be said to occur when there has simply been information exchange, accomplished by such efficient means as Facebook, Twitter, MSN, or swapping of text messages? When the other *I* is not present, is encounter possible?

There appears to be a dimension in encounter that is different from simple information exchange. It involves *my* awareness of *your* awareness of my 'presence'. My *awareness* requires my neural system to be operative, but my *presence* relates to the entity *I* itself. What *is* 'connection' between two people? Is it when *I* encounter *thou* with minimal interference of neural distortions (including misleading associations and incomplete perceptions)? Does true connection require the accurate expression of *I* in brain and body – a fully integrated self? It is possible for neural activity to take place with minimal involvement of *I*: likewise, it is possible for interaction to take place between two people with minimal involvement of *I*. I can relate to another person as a body – an 'it', to use Buber's expression – rather than as *thou* who happens to reside in that body. This may happen in one without capacity for empathy, but it more commonly happens in those capable of empathy, but in whom self-protective impulses or dysfunctional mind maps create problems.

And so it is that two *I*s seek to relate to each other using their physical selves as avenues of self-expression, yet these very physical selves can interfere with the encounter. What are the inclinations of the brain that cause it to interfere with a true encounter, inclinations that each *I* needs to manage so that the relationship accomplishes what it should? There are a number: let me suggest three.

The first inclination is for the brain to seek to protect and preserve the body it dwells in, and for this reason it seeks to predict and control its environment, including the other, for its own comfort. The second inclination is for the brain to try to 'make sense' of the other by finding a 'best match' with existing concepts in its mind map, reducing the other to something the brain can put into easy conceptual compartments, minimizing stress by minimizing difference (that is, preferring not to notice difference), and 'labelling' the other in familiar categories. Knowledge of the other becomes distorted by what the efficient brain has been programmed to 'understand': that is, seeking meanings it already 'understands'. The third inclination is for the brain to follow its own regulatory functions governed by neuropeptide release (such as oxytocin and vasopressin), including the search for pleasure and the avoidance of pain. It wants to interact with the other (perhaps even exploit the other) to satisfy these drives. Given these inclinations, *I* needs to manage its brain and body so that the other *I* is not exploited or manipulated by the self-preserving, information-distorting, and self-gratifying brain which can subvert the *I–thou* encounter.

There is a challenge here for the clinician. What should be the nature of the clinician's relationship with the client? Can I at the same time treat my client as *it* for the purposes of analysis and objective judgement, making observation of various characteristics and behavioural tendencies, yet enter into meaningful dialogue with my client as *thou* for the purpose of therapeutic process? How can I simultaneously enter into the much-lauded role as scientist-practitioner, yet engage with my client's *I*? Herein is another formulation of the clinician's conundrum: but instead of the problem being the reduction of the entity *I* to a function of neural processing systems, here the clinician needs to avoid reducing the client's *I* to an 'it', an object for scientific analysis.

Love, sex, and intimacy

William looked at me with an air of helplessness and resignation: 'I just fell out of love – I don't know why. I fell in love with someone else, and so left my wife Susan.' It was as though he had no say in the matter – he was a victim of circumstance. He hoped Susan would understand, but she said she still loved him and was at a loss to understand what happened. A shame, that – but what could William do?

Is it really true that love can befall someone and just as easily evaporate, altogether beyond a person's control? Is love like sleep – something that *I* 'falls' into, losing control as natural brain processes (gravity, as it were) take over? Can it be that love is sometimes ego-alien, happening to me *in spite of* what I know to be true or *in spite of* what I might really want, like Charlie's perplexing thought? Let us consider the relationship of *I* and brain in this most delicate of matters.

I begin with a key distinction: 'love' is about the valuing of one another; 'intimacy' is about the encounter of *I* with another. In love, *I* makes a decision of good-will to value and treasure the other, to promote a person's wellbeing, or to seek to please the other. Because of love, *I* might invest in a relationship, or even commit to share all of life with the other, necessarily at a cost of some personal freedoms. Intimacy, on the other hand, is about the encounter between two *I*s where *I* draws close to another. *I* makes connections through the sharing of ideas, values, and feelings, and through the enjoyment of the presence of another; *I* may also enter into physical and sexual closeness. Intimacy involves self-disclosure – the revealing of *I*, and by extension the mind map orienting *I*. The sharing of judgements and values, of experienced feelings and memories provide an important context to the encounter.

At every level, *I* uses the physical self both to love and to draw close to the other. But one can love and not know intimacy; one can also be intimate and not know love. Furthermore, one can 'love' in a way that values the feelings of love but not the other; and one can know physical and sexual intimacy without encountering the other. Marriage, a socially recognized covenant designed to safeguard the investment each makes in the other, requires both love and intimacy to function effectively. Where honoured, it protects against the loss of the valued other and against the associated emotional pain of fractured mind maps, ensuring stability for both. But *I* and the brain remain in constant flux as *I* seeks to retain ascendency: should *I* not retain ascendency and fail to effectively manage internal and environmental pressures, the agreement entered into may be jeopardized. This does not make the agreement bad; rather, it reflects a poor capacity to 'keep faith', which assumes the capacity of each *I* to properly manage brain and body. If I cannot trust myself to properly manage my own neural processes, how can another?

The encounter between *I* and the other in the context of sexual relationship is a complex situation because it reflects the delicate balance between powerful sexual forces that find their origin in neural processes, and the separate desire for *I* to find meaningfulness through encounter with another *I*.[1] Dopamine is released as *I* anticipates the sexual encounter, generating desire and excitement and a tendency to obsessive focus and growing addiction to the object of desire. As *I* embraces the feelings of warmth, trust, and closeness in the physical and sexual encounter, oxytocins and vasopressins are released, generating feelings of attachment and bonding that linger (Cozolino, 2006). Here we see the mixed motives of the neurally driven desire for sexual satisfaction, the desire for personal and social acceptance, and the search of *I* for love and intimacy.

There are many other motives too, such as the adventure of discovery, a memory of met needs, or a 'need' to experience power by making a 'conquest'. Given such possible mixed motives, it is necessary for *I* to be at the helm of its own neural processes and to properly manage its impulses for a satisfying and meaningful encounter to occur. One, I suggest, that requires a valuing and honouring of the other. And not only does *I* and its neural processes need to be aligned during the sexual encounter, but these same processes need to simultaneously resonate in the other. Not surprisingly, the intricate balance of these motivational forces is easily upset, and confusion and frustration can quickly result.

Just as we might share our home with the one we love, so we share events in our bodies – the residences of our respective *I*s. That is, the body reacts to the presence of the other *I* by way of the peptides and endorphins that leave powerful imprinting or conditioning events in the 'home' of *I*. In a sense, one body comes to be shared in a remarkable way by two *I*s as it becomes an expression of both. Pleasure-creating peptides are released within one in the presence of the other – at the very *thought* of the other – creating desire and physical responsiveness. The two 'have become one flesh'. How is it possible for *I* to find expression in another body? Yet it is the encounter between two *I*s inhabiting separate bodies that imbues the physical experience with meaningfulness. Biochemical signals tell not only about *I*, but also about the other *I* it has bonded to, whose presence is now longed for and to whom there is a sense of belonging. *I* needs to relate to the other *I* as '*thou*' (to use Buber's term), to *connect*, to retain meaningfulness for the body's pleasure and pain. Without connection, the body's reactions to the other create alienation – as though *I* is no longer in control. Indeed, *I* is not in control of desire's addiction: emotional bonding without meaningful connection is surely a confusing thing.

There is a profound mystery in the sexual encounter: one of beauty, but that easily becomes one of pain. The physical body is frequently used to entrap another for unwilling or pseudo intimacy, or even 'purchased' for the temporary satisfaction of a drive. A physical body may be used to stimulate desire in another, later to find a stranger within: the physical body may be known, but not the *I* within. The subsequent compromise of integrity in *I* is subtle but powerful. It can create alienation between *I* and its own body – a body that has drawn *I* into unsafe self-disclosure, often resulting in self-disgust, feeling 'dirty', or loss of self-value; but also a disgust or indifference towards the other. When the territory of *I* has been entered without the proper engagement of *I*, a feeling of being used or dishonoured, or a degradation of self, may result.

Whether it is through prostitution, pornography, heroin, or one-night stands, neural drives create the conditions for desire and bonding. But bonding with what? In these situations, it is essentially a bonding with emptiness: where there is no connection, no meaning is created. When the delicate balance between neurally driven sexual inclinations and the desire for *I* to know and be known by another is compromised, it can create alienation in the human encounter which only becomes complete when not only does body meet body, or brain meet brain, but *I* encounters *I*.

And William? I would argue he had more control in managing the love and intimacy required in his relationship with Susan than he admitted to. Although William now appears committed to a new decision, earlier intervention might have resulted in a different outcome. In such circumstances, a clinician might usefully focus on the facilitation of better communication, but also on restoring the *I*–brain balance in the relationship, addressing factors compromising both love and intimacy and promoting the skills assumed in each. He might address self-preserving behaviours that undermine an otherwise functional relationship, or work with how William might 'make sense' of and value Susan, how to 'know' her and establish meaningfulness in the relationship itself. But the clinician may also need to work with the resolution of self-preserving but relationship-alienating emotions which discourage self-disclosure and intimacy, such as anger, fear, shame, and guilt.

Part IV

The brain and *I* interact

Memory, consciousness, and emotions

Chapter 12

I preserves experiences

Focus and memory

How memory works is of considerable interest to the clinician: either his client wants to remember things difficult to remember or wishes to forget things difficult to forget. Geraldine remarked:

> I find myself apprehensive whenever the bedroom door is shut and my husband approaches me, even though I love him dearly and have no memory of him or anyone else harming me physically or sexually. Why am I like this? Surely something must have happened for me to react like this: if only I could remember.

Or Liam's complaint: 'If only I could forget the terrified look on the cyclist's face the moment before the car hit and killed him. That moment haunts me daily. How can I block it?'

How indeed? Can a clinician help Geraldine remember what she wants to remember or help Liam forget what he wants to forget? What is this memory we sometimes want, and sometimes do not? How does it work? It is not the same as *I*, as *I* can both gain and lose memories, thus distinguishing between *I* and memories. Should I lose memory, I would lose knowledge of *I*, though not *I* itself. Memory is of interest not only from a clinical perspective, but also in our grappling with the *I*–brain relationship.

The computer analogy only helps us understand certain aspects of memory. It is a complicated process involving direction of attention, selecting material to remember; encoding the material and connecting it with existing material to help establish meaning; establishing a neural trace through repeated exposure or interest in the material; trimming off related material *not* to be remembered; and long-term storage of different kinds of material in varied neural templates. Finally, it involves the capacity to know what is held in storage, a reason to seek it out again, and the capacity to locate the material allowing retrieval – in whole or part – with connected other material.

A distinction might also be made between remembered material and the emotions the material may activate. In both the selection of material to remember and the process of accessing it again, *I* may or may not be involved: the memory process may be largely automatic and even unwanted, or *I* may direct the endeavour, making multiple choices along the way.

Memory, meaning, and *I*

Unlike the mechanical recording of information using film or audio, the brain is directed to search for meaning from a stream of incoming information. Its focus is drawn to elements that seem to belong together – elements the brain matches, or between which *I* makes connections. Because the active drive towards meaning shapes attention in that I look for information that makes sense, and because attention plays a central role in memory, meaning shapes memory. Indeed, 'making sense' of my life story is more important than the accurate recall of remembered events. It allows *I* to inhabit the brain with minimal conflict. It creates an integrated perspective, limits dissociation in its various forms, and maximizes interactive potential with the external world. Subsequent access to memory is also governed by the drive to meaning. Meaningfulness is mediated by the neural events *I* relies on, involving the matching of stored templates with assigned meanings.[1] The *loss* of meaningful understanding generally reflects a failure in the *memory process* (either in difficulty locating necessary matches or because the necessary templates have not yet been created), rather than a corruption of *I*, although *I* can become disabled in the process, and poor focus of *I* can certainly compromise memory.

But the drive to meaning is not the only parameter guiding the complex memory process. Memory systems are integrated into the overall mind map which needs to be both stable and flexible: stable to allow an enduring sense of identity and place in the world; flexible to allow for the dynamic nature of life experience. The memories comprising the mind map need to endure over time yet remain open to reinterpretation and change. And so we expect memory systems to be *dynamic* and *flexible*, capable of continual adjustment to make sense of a changing world; to be *selective*, preventing the brain from being overwhelmed and creating inefficiencies; to be *accurate*, providing a good representation of external realities; to be *practical*, distinguishing between that which I need to know and that which I do not, and between that which will change and that which will not; and to be *current*, seamlessly combining old and new information, overcoming reference to time, yet maintaining an up-to-date reference base to keep me oriented. Even my sense of time is bound up in memory – without the ongoing change and updates of memory, time stops – *I* has no way of knowing time. As such, the sense of time is a function of the neural system rather than of *I*, although paradoxically, the actual *passage* of time is poorly represented in memory.

The brain makes temporary matches between the flow of incoming information and information stored in neural templates. These templates relate to different sensory modalities – visual, auditory, tactile, kinaesthetic, and olfactory. These temporary matches allow *recognition*, a form of *implicit* memory required but not driven by *I* and foundational to the memory system, including the aspects of memory driven by *I* (that is, the conscious process of recall – *explicit* memory). Recognition requires the identification of an association string; the capacity to make approximate matches (unlike computer matches, near enough may be good enough – the meanings represented may be the more important issue); the making of connections to related association strings (allowing for recognition in the wider context); and the matching event to take place in a fraction of a second, then 'letting go' to allow a new match.

Because life experience is dynamic, it is stored in abstract form, although some memories may represent static events, which allows more concrete details to be stored. So, for example, it is difficult for me to bring to mind a specific image of my wife's face, which I see daily over long periods, even though I instantly recognize her; yet I have no problem conjuring a specific image of my grandfather's face (whom I have never met) by remembering a static photograph. Unlike my grandfather's face, the memory of my wife's face is a composite of a multitude of expressions and continually changing angles, represented by complex meanings, in a way a picture is not.

But even the meanings represented in memory can change. Old memories are liable to be reinterpreted with new information. This retrospective connecting of new material with old, of new frameworks of understanding and conceptualizing with old data, creates different meanings and compromises the integrity of the original perceptions and memories. When I discover a man was on illicit drugs, I reinterpret his inconsistent responses to me over the past few months as reflecting his addiction rather than a bid to avoid me because he did not like me: my picture of him changes – how I remember our past interactions changes on this new interpretation. Similarly, new information is interpreted using old memories in the making of meaning. Thus, I choose a particular interpretation of my children's behaviour based on the memory of my own experiences as a child; I may choose a particular interpretation of my wife's behaviour on the basis of my experiences of my mother's behaviour, and so on. So memory may be fragmented and patchy in its initial coding, quickly distorted by various biases, and modified each time it is brought back to conscious awareness through the context and triggers for recall.

But if memory can be so fickle and meanings can change, how can it form the enduring basis of a sense of self? In *The Man who Mistook his Wife for a Hat*, neurologist Oliver Sacks quotes Buñel: 'Our memory is our coherence, our reason, our feeling, even our action. Without it, we are nothing' (Sacks, 1985: 25). Does this mean that without memory, *I* no longer exists as an entity? If *I* can only be known by enduring memories, if the past experiences captured by neural networks constitute the sense of self and provide the context in which *I* has relationship with another, then what is *I* without this neural foundation? How can *I* as an entity have any meaning without a stable memory system? Yet how unstable and unreliable memory can be!

Nevertheless, a partial loss of memory does not correspond to a partial loss of *I*: *I* remains one. Long before a newborn has built a network of memories and meanings allowing self-awareness and creative interaction, its *I* has taken up residence and the interactive process of communication with others has started. And although memories contribute to the identity of *I*, this is because they are shaped by *I*. That is, memories are in part a *product* of *I*, and a product is not the same as the one who produces. How am I to understand *I* without the memories that comprise the mind map defining and orienting *I*? Yet if *I* is defined in part as the origin and destination of communication with others, it is defined by a relational dynamic, rather than by memories *per se*. I become 'known' by others not by *my* memories, but by *theirs*. Long after I vacate my body, I will (hopefully) be remembered by them, I will be defined by my impact on them, by our shared history and our shared meanings. My memory is *our* memory, and any failure in my neural system will not change that reality.

And so it seems to me that if I am pursuing meaningfulness and identity, the proper investment is in building relationships with others, because herein a memory and meaningfulness is created that never needs to be lost in the way that investment in memories and meaningfulness stored in my own brain can.

Different memory systems

To 'remember' means to access aspects of the past in the present. This touches every aspect of my identity, as there is nothing I can know, understand, or do without reference to the past, whether it is walking down the street, recognizing a friend, doing a crossword, or dreaming in my sleep. Ascription of meaningfulness requires memory. Yet what *is* memory? It seems it is invested in the neural system, not *I*. At a physical level, it requires the connection of neurons to form association strings, which in turn form neural networks. A dynamic historical event is now represented in the static physical form of a neural pattern. How does this take place?

In the 1940s, Donald Hebb discovered that neural connections were made by the simultaneous firing of a pattern of neurons or neural networks triggered by events of apperception or cognition. The more often this simultaneous firing occurred, the more likely this pattern of neurons would fire in the future: memory was being encoded. But there is much more to this simple formula. The encoding process is affected by *focus*, *emotion* (which I suspect triggers multiple firings at the initial point of exposure, like pressing hard with a pencil on paper, leaving a deep mark), and *rehearsal* (like going over a mark with a pencil many times, emphasizing the mark). This encoding activity happens throughout the brain, and perhaps beyond – clinical reports relating to heart transplants, for example, suggest organs such as the heart also carry memory traces.

While the *physical basis* of the encoding of different memories appears largely the same, the *type* of memory varies according to the location within the neural system, and its *endurance* varies according to other factors.

Short-term or *working* memories are held in temporary associative processes typically governed by software in the frontal and parietal cortices. While the computer is activated, it has the capacity to 'hold' information, allowing it to process the material: the resulting information is not stored until I activate the *save* icon. As many an annoyed user has found, unless 'saved', the information is lost when the power fails. Similarly, there exists a working memory where material appears to be 'held' by the interaction of I^2 with an activated neural system (that is, an activated readiness potential), allowing the processing of initial matches, associations, and the applications of various algorithms. Interruption in that holding pattern causes loss of information – whether the interruption is authored by *I* (by focusing elsewhere) or results from failure in the integrity of the neural activation itself (such as occurs in epilepsy, concussion, or electric shock therapy).

This memory system is different from the *long-term* memories that are mostly processed by hippocampal software, which transfers material from the temporary holding pattern into longer-term storage by isolating the material to be remembered and establishing and consolidating the relevant connections. Some of this work is done in the later stages of REM sleep. Should hippocampal software be corrupted, I would no longer be able to integrate and store new information. Long-term memories can be found throughout the brain, their location determined by their nature. Software in the hippocampus can locate existing weak connections when I am re-exposed to an event in the weeks and months after the initial connections are made, and repeat the firing pattern (as Hebb discovered), so consolidating the trace. We might distinguish memory traces on the basis of content between *motor* memory, *visual* memory, *semantic* memory, *auditory* memory, *kinetic* memory, and so on: each is stored in brain regions dedicated to such functions, although each memory trace is potentially associated with memory traces of other modalities.

Another distinction is frequently made between *explicit* and *implicit* memory. It distinguishes between memories in which *I* takes an active role, or at least *I* has *awareness* of having a role; and 'automatic memories', in which there is no apparent role for *I*, or at least, no apparent need for self-awareness. The latter involves an exposure to something that creates a sense of familiarity without the capacity to consciously access the stored representation of the event, which involves *I*. Explicit or conscious memory necessarily involves the hippocampus and higher cortical structures such as the medial temporal cortex. Software in the hippocampal region, which also houses language software, knits things together into meaningful sequences, establishing the relevant connections with time, location, and context, allowing efficient search and retrieval. This is done deliberately through focused attention. It is generally mediated verbally and has fewer capacity constraints than implicit memory processing (Cruwys and O'Kearney, 2008).

In contrast to explicit memory, many implicit memories involve the amygdala region activating a visceral reaction, although it may not be so much that the amygdala *stores* implicit memories as it becomes a *pathway* to their activation. Siegel (2009) notes three unique features of implicit memory: I do not need to use focal, conscious attention for its creation; when it is accessed, I do not have the sensation that something is being recalled from the past; and it does not require the involvement of the hippocampus in its creation. Typically, it functions in the areas of perception, emotion, bodily sensation, behaviour, and priming, and is located in the relevant neural regions. It is generally triggered involuntarily, activating emotions and physiological responses. For example, seeing a dog that frightened me as a young child can trigger a fear response, but may allow no conscious memory as to *why* I reacted this way. Implicit memories may be established even when the hippocampus is poorly developed, such as in very early development, or when it is damaged or corrupted.[3]

For the clinician, this distinction between explicit (or *declarative*) memory and implicit memory is important, as the former lends itself to inspection and therefore to challenge and change in insight therapies, while the latter is better dealt with using conditioning techniques. Explicit memory allows a re-creative process of intentional recall by involving *I*. It is a deliberate search process, a reconstructive effort accessing fragments of connected stored information. It involves an encoding that 'depends on the ability to focus attention and integrate elements of an experience into factual or autobiographical representations' (Siegel, 2009: 153). It is developed by the practice of (usually verbal) recall, allowing me to reflect on things *at will*: a conscious, deliberate, *I*-directed access to neural material, thinking *about* the material, and therefore capable of changing its neural representation. Yet by what manner does *I* access memory when *I* *chooses* to recall something? Does *I* have the capacity to direct the brain with instructions to locate targeted information or make matches of new information with stored material, or is *I* itself involved in the process?

Implicit memory, on the other hand, is an automatic process. A common form of implicit memory is *procedural* memory, a simple recurrence of an event, such as a habit of behaviour, thought, or perception normally required for daily orientation and performance, in which there is minimal involvement of *I*. Being generally below awareness, the associative components of that memory are hard to access on demand, and are therefore not nearly as malleable in the therapeutic change process. While both explicit and implicit memories affect daily living, it is explicit memory that we generally think of and experience as 'memory'; implicit memory operates as a subterranean force, the unconscious processes affecting questionable motivations and maintaining annoying habits. Implicit memories create a particular challenge for the clinician.

The various explicit and implicit memories are stored in different brain regions (Carter, 2010). While long-term explicit memories generally appear to be established in the temporal cortex, some – those of conscious past experience and semantic memories – are distributed throughout the cortical areas, relying on frontal cortex activity for conscious retrieval. The various implicit memories appear to be located elsewhere: procedural memories and deeply engrained habits like riding a bike are stored in the putamen; unconscious traumatic memories such as experienced in phobias and flashbacks relate to the amygdala; and genetically coded memories – instincts – relate to the caudate nucleus.

But the distinction between explicit and implicit memory is not always clear. While learning acquired below conscious awareness necessarily creates implicit memory, conscious learning can begin as explicit memory and later become implicit. Such procedural memory appears to follow a different mechanism from implicit memories created through traumatic events. Whatever task I engage in becomes more automatic with practice in the *exact* form of doing it, without the variations in the performance of the task that occurred initially. So, for example, after writing a word many times, its spelling becomes automatic. The transfer from explicit to implicit memory as mastery is attained reflects in brain *efficiency*. Yet a related task, articulating (as against writing) the spelling of that word, continues to depend on explicit memory until it has been practised in its own right to the point of automaticity. Until mastery is attained, I give it conscious attention. And so *I* is consciously involved in learning that may subsequently become implicit, increasingly independent of the involvement of *I*.

Learning a task to the point of automaticity frees the brain for alternative focus even while the task is being executed. Task complexity can be systematically increased as each sub-task becomes automatic. And so I find myself thinking in ideas, not in individual words or sounds. I focus on where I am going when riding a bike, not my balance or pedalling action. I read the music score when playing Mozart (I wish!), not thinking about where I place my fingers. And when I enter my home, I greet my wife without thinking about where the kitchen is, or noticing the pictures hanging on the wall. All these latter tasks were once explicit, noticed, involving decisions and awareness, engaging *I*. Now they are implicit and assumed, influencing body and brain without engaging *I*. What was explicit has become implicit so that it can be subsumed in more complex activity.

A troubling form of memory typically associated with PTSD is the *flashback*, which has features both of implicit memory, in that there are precise replays of the traumatic event like a short 'video-clip' that can be reactivated and that is not amenable to change,[4] and of explicit memory, in that there is normally no question as to the origin of the traumatic event itself, which can be recalled consciously, at will. It has a unique and troubling feature: the *reliving* of the event emotionally. Such reliving is typically associated with implicit procedural memories: for example, when I ride my bike, I 'relive' my remembered ability to keep my balance. But here, the reliving can occur in the absence of the cue of a current, physical event (the bike I am sitting on): it may be intrusive or reactive to an explicit memory. Importantly, the 'reliving' is not limited to the vivid replay of the remembered event; it also triggers an emotional response (normally intense fear), which is not so much a memory as it is a *current emotional event* triggered by the memory.

Generally emotions and pain are excluded from the memory event itself. The idea of *emotional* memory is conceptually confusing. Where, for example, someone has experienced childbirth pain or kidney stone pain, there is no stored pain in the neural system. The recall is 'factual' only – *that* pain was experienced, not a re-experiencing of the pain. Re-experiencing pain and emotions requires release of the relevant neurochemicals. Memory, on the other hand, is the accessing of established neural templates. Perhaps we need to distinguish between the neurotransmitter-releasing traffic of information through neural pathways from the information held in the patterned firing of neural templates. The latter has to do with memory, while the limbic system or any pathway between the frontal cortex and the amygdala implicated in pain or emotion responses represents activating events rather than memory events, even though memory events may trigger them.

This distinction between memory and the emotional processes memory can activate is an intriguing one for the clinician.[5] The brain seems sometimes unable to disconnect an association between a past event and present danger, confusing the memory status of certain information with a current situation, such as we see in PTSD or some phobic reactions. It is normally the distressing emotion that brings the client to the clinician rather than the memory itself. It is how the memory continues to affect *I*, not the history *per se*, that becomes the clinician's challenge.

The brain normally recognizes a memory *as* a memory, and distinguishes *remembering* being afraid, as against being afraid *now*. Chloe suffered a phobic reaction to dogs. When I began work with her, the sight of a dog triggered fear. The memory associated with dogs was processed as meaning *current danger*, not past danger. When I finished working with Chloe, the memory of being afraid of dogs became just that: a memory. She remembered once being afraid of dogs, but this memory no longer triggered the fear as she no longer perceived the danger as current. Somehow, new meanings had disabled the pathway connecting the remembered events to amygdala activation.

Disconnecting emotion – that is, my immediate bodily response to the experienced event – from sensory experience or remembered information helps to separate it from current reality and contributes to the experience of it being a *remembered* event, not a current one.[6] But when this disconnection is done retrospectively, it needs to be done through the reprocessing of the material and integrating it into the perceptual frameworks of an existing mind map – not dissociation without integration. Here is an interesting notion: the process of resolving a disturbing memory may require both *connection* and *disconnection* – the neural networks need to be activated (I need to reconnect), but a disconnection needs to occur between the memory cue and the emotional response.

The role of focus

If I, as clinician, have an interest in memory, then I must have an equal interest in focus and decision making, as these help create memories. Without wilful and conscious focus on something, I am unlikely to remember it. Such focus involves decisions upon *what* to focus, and again we encounter the interaction between *I* and the brain.

Because the brain receives continual streams of multiple signals from both internal and external sources, on any of which *I* can focus at any moment, the brain needs to simultaneously facilitate some and inhibit other signals so it accesses only desired information. It is *I* that normally chooses the focus, causing the inhibition of unwanted information streams.[7] The information stream entering the brain interacts with the vast store of remembered events, allowing for a wide possibility of experienced events and associations. Yet *I* does not experience all possibilities, but selects from the possibilities a steady focus that becomes its reality, both present and remembered. *I* experiences attending to external events, and this correlates to internal neural events – *I* effectively moulds the brain through its focus and decisions over the years, writing onto neural hardware receptive to the job.[8]

The focus *I* establishes is an interactive function of *I* with the brain. I can 'see' many things, but I do not 'take in', nor do I 'notice' the majority of what I see. In deciding upon what to focus, *I* authorizes activation of the neural receptors corresponding to the thing being attended – it is a targeted interaction between *I* and a specific neural network. For example, *I* might decide to look for a familiar face in the crowd. *I* instructs (as it were) its neural software to make a match between a remembered face and the faces in the crowd. There are many faces projected onto the screen of the visual receptors. But only the specific receptors that make the desired match become activated and provide the communication sought by *I*. Such is the interactive process.

But attention does not only relate to incoming sensory information – it is also involved in thinking, where specific memories and ideas are consciously and wilfully selected from the vast store available. This thinking process is of a different nature: it is slower as *I* traverses the web of inter-connected pathways in some sequential manner, 'reading' the meanings held there, though it has the capacity to jump from one pathway to an entirely different one. Unlike the broad palette of incoming sensory information, patterns of thinking tend to be linear and associative. I would expect to find a different neural dynamic for these different attention events, although *I* has the capacity to apprehend both seamlessly. What determines the choice and capacity of *I* to select its focus, and how is this represented at neural level?

Imagine a couple sitting at a table in a busy restaurant. The music is loud enough for patrons to have to raise their voices a little to be heard: as the evening progresses, they need to raise their voices more as they compete with the many conversations around them. Our couple needs to work hard to shut out the background conversations, interesting though the other conversations might be, so he can pick up the relevant signals and make sense of what his fellow gastronome is so keen to tell him. As the ambient sound increases, the task becomes more difficult: words are misunderstood and meanings get distorted. It becomes exhausting to maintain sufficient focus to decipher what she is saying. Now imagine a barrier is placed around our couple's table, absorbing much of the ambient sound. Suddenly, conversation is much more relaxed: the incoming signals are much clearer, and there is no difficulty understanding what she is saying. Imagine a further change: this time the barrier is placed around the diner himself. It is wonderfully quiet where he sits, but now the signals from his partner have become very faint. Again, he needs to work hard to decipher what is being said: often he gets it wrong. He misattributes some signals as coming from his partner when they actually come from the table next to them. He gets frustrated and exhausted.

Such, it seems to me, is the 'restaurant' in the brain, busy with many competing informational signals. *I* is normally capable of focus, selecting the signals of interest and making sense of those signals. This focus involves putting momentary barriers – perhaps the selective action of neurotransmitters at the relevant synaptic junctures

– to enhance the information flow of interest and reduce the signals that *I* regards as momentarily unimportant. The software it uses to manage the brain 'restaurant' is a given, used without questioning, just as I do not question how the engine powers my car, even though I drive my car where I want to go. If the neurotransmitters do the job well (assuming they are involved – the role of emotion in the attention process certainly implicates neurochemical involvement), messages are easily interpreted, and neural energy is conserved. If, on the other hand, competing signals interrupt the informational pathways *I* wishes to access, *I* will become confused, misattribute or distort meanings, and generally get stressed and exhausted – a process we see in some psychopathologies.

While *I* generally determines what is attended to in the incoming flood of sensory signals, some signals are capable of accessing *I* as surely as *I* accesses signals of choice. Pain, a sudden noise, a bright light, a cry for help, or visual novelty will demand attention from *I*. The strength of the signal gives them precedence, temporarily inhibiting other signals despite the apparent non-involvement of *I* in the selection process. This can also occur in thinking – certain thought circuits appear capable of intruding upon or resisting management by *I* (usually in small thought loops, as Charlie discovered), to the point where *I* has difficulty moving on to other thought pathways.

Whether *I* chooses the focus, or the focus chooses *I*, different hardware appears to be involved. Although the attention process has the capacity to engage the brain's multiple distributed systems at any point, brain research suggests that 'volition' or 'focus' is managed through the prefrontal cortex (Goldberg, 2001). That is, *I* directs attention by way of the prefrontal cortex. Conversely, the neural system can demand attention from *I* by way of another region, the parietal cortex (Cozolino, 2002; Carter, 2010). In the first instance, *I* makes the attentional decision ('wilful' concentration); in the second, the sensory signal demands *I* makes a decision. The latter is quicker and easier on *I* – it involves more automatic processing, with faster frequency of electrical pulses.

The potential effect of a person's emotional state on his remembering and forgetting things is commonly recognized but has received little research attention.[9] When I am depressed and feel 'flat', I become disinterested, and have difficulty concentrating. Does this reflect lack of neural energy required for focus, or is the activation of emotion itself (the desire to know, whether it is curiosity or fear driven) necessary for focus? What *is* the role of 'interest' in establishing focus and, conversely, how do emotions compete with a particular interest in something, preventing focus in that thing?

The capacity for *I* to focus in a decided and sustained manner can be affected when *I* is in distress, or when in despair *I* has become passive and disinterested. I might have before me a book: I can read it mechanically and take nothing in, because I lack 'interest' in the material, perhaps because of distress about an external matter, or lack of curiosity about the subject. My reading is no longer an interactive search for information, but a passive event. The establishing of effective memory may require active *interaction* of *I* and brain rather than passive receiving of information, and emotional factors may drive that process. One way of priming helpful emotion is in *I* making plans and goals which create interest and energy and a basis upon which to discriminate and make decisions regarding its focus.

There is an eternal struggle for what gets the focus. Multiple forces operate, including *I*, signals from the external environment, internal signals (drives, sensations, emotions), and memories. If multiple forces define the focus, then multiple forces also define each experience of reality. The strength of *I* in that struggle is dynamic, as is the strength of the other forces involved. Powerful and important though the role of attention (like consciousness) might be in neural processing, it is not simply a neural event, nor simply a function of *I*. Rather, it embodies an interaction between the two. *I* can be passive yet aware of that which neural networks bring to its attention as a result of its own automatic processing activity – *I* becomes a passive receiver of information. But *I* can also have active involvement directing attention, even bringing about the re-alignment of neural circuits (Schwartz and Begley, 2002) and acting as the driving force in brain plasticity (Doidge, 2010) – *I* is then the active source of the discriminative processes that define the information it will receive.

When I choose to attend to something, *I* activates software dedicated to do the job, which requires a broad neural readiness potential. When *I* is passive and the brain is on autopilot, only neural activation specific to the activity occurs, and the larger infrastructure relating to decisions and awareness remains on hold. The efficiency principle prefers autopilot, which demands less activation of the brain. Paying attention is hard work, incorporating especially the regions of the prefrontal cortex and anterior cingulate. It is easier to 'tune out'. Learning, which requires attention to convert incoming signals to memory, is hard work. The work is the work of the brain, not so much *I*; it is the brain that needs the energy to accommodate the demands of *I* and thus gets fatigued – not *I*.

Nevertheless, focus has its own efficiencies. Attention activates certain neural pathways and suppresses others, filtering out distractions. In this way, the brain's *processing of information* is guided by the attention governed by *I*, so it only processes information necessary to create meaningfulness. When I attend to something, the act of focus causes all else to lose focus; and when I decide something, saying 'yes' to one thing means saying 'no' to the other. Just as the agency of focus helps in the remembering of one thing, it simultaneously *prevents* the remembering of another. In this sense, it is possible for *I* to actively *suppress* the creation of memories: here the prefrontal cortex is activated while the hippocampal function is momentarily suppressed and the wave of electrical activity in the parietal cortex is diminished.[10]

Remembering and forgetting

We revisit Geraldine's problem. Although, on the one hand, she wishes to remember what happened to cause her to react in apprehension towards her husband, she actually wants to remember *in order to forget*. More accurately, she wishes to activate the stored material at a conscious level to rework the associations causing her problems. She judges that her reaction must be based on a 'lost' memory – more accurately, an implicit memory. Her challenge is to convert implicit memory into an explicit one. Is this possible? Can the clinician dismantle hidden connections to help Geraldine 'unlearn' implicit memory? Can a boy 'unlearn' how to ride a bike? Can a woman 'unlearn' the fear that she might be raped again? Can *I* deconstruct or 'decommission' targeted neural pathways? That *I* can continue creating new neural pathways is one thing; to rid myself of established ones is another. Is this what *I* needs to do to properly 'forget' a memory?

Yet forgetting does occur, usually uninvited. The mind map that I depend on is itself dependent on neural hardware, so that any lesion, atrophy, disease, or corruption in any small part of that neural hardware can create peculiar 'gaps' in the mind map – essentially gaps in memory, with the devastating effects that Sacks and Feinberg documented, gaps of which *I* may or may not have awareness. There are many common and not so common reports of such memory losses. Furthermore, I may forget that I have a memory which is still intact: I can be unaware that I have a memory of an event, but my body nevertheless reacts on implicit memory. If you ask me: do you know where the keys are? I might say 'no', yet I might pick them up without thinking. On the other hand, I can be aware of losing an explicit memory: if you ask me, do you know where the keys are? I might accurately say 'no' – I once knew, but cannot remember now. Then there are different forms of amnesia, where there appears to be a breach between *I* and the neural system with a complete loss of conscious memory in relation to a particular time period. But can I deliberately bring about the targeted forgetting of long-term implicit or explicit memories?

If it is true that the apprehension of meaning by *I* brings about neural connections that hold that meaning in memory, can the reverse be true? We may find that not only does neural disconnection dissolve meanings, but dissolved meanings bring about neural disconnections – that is, real forgetting initiated by *I*, who decides the information is meaningless.

Forgetting does not depend on loss of memory trace alone – on the disintegration of neurons or neural connections. In the 'tip of the tongue' phenomenon, *access* to existing memories can be temporarily compromised, constituting another form of forgetting. We have noted the complexities of various memory systems. I suspect the conditions and neural parameters prevailing for the *establishment* of a memory (whether it is of visual, auditory, or somatic origin) may also be the conditions necessary for later *access* to that memory, and such access is a prerequisite for making changes to that memory. Recreating the environmental and neural conditions prevailing at the time of the establishment of a memory may be necessary to work with the memory. Therapeutic intervention would then need to activate the relevant sensory modalities to access such memories. Equally, ensuring those conditions are not repeated may enable the 'forgetting' of the event by making access to the memory difficult.

Chapter 13

I disengages

Unconscious states

While I am awake, *I* manages a stream of information, a 'train of thought' comprising a sequence of sometimes loosely, sometimes strongly, connected thoughts or ideas. James Joyce captured the idea of 'stream of consciousness' in his novel *Ulysses*, and psychiatrist Sigmund Freud hoped that capturing fragments of this stream in his free association techniques might give clues to the unconscious. Certainly, I believe it might give clues to the patterns of associations (and therefore neural connections) established over time; and I suspect that Freud's *unconscious* in this respect comprises fragments of difficult-to-access network connections that played a role in the development of behaviour patterns and belief systems. I follow this stream in conversation, creating a sense of 'connection' with the other; in trying to solve problems; when writing a book; or when daydreaming. But I also follow this stream into sleep. Interrupting that stream – 'losing my train of thought' – can disturb *I*, which seeks to re-establish the interrupted stream. If it cannot, a new stream is started. While the stream runs, *I* runs with it, like a boat on a current. The stream follows established neural connections: it is not determined by *I*. Yet at any point, *I* can interrupt the flow, or choose to re-enter it. Staying within this stream allows entry into the sleep state: just as a boat at rest drifts with the current, so *I* at rest drifts along a stream of associations into sleep.

Sleep is a mystery we all encounter – an act I at the same time control yet do not control. Who has not experienced a time when they want to sleep but cannot; or conversely, want to stay alert, but drift off? Does *I* have a say in this? Or is it an event where *I* needs to submit to the brain's demands? Sleep disturbance features in various psychological conditions; sleep deprivation can even contribute to temporary psychosis; but what *is* sleep? In sleep, the relationship of *I* with the brain changes. Does *I* disengage from the brain, or does *I* at rest remain engaged with the brain? Does the brain 'down tools', compromising the capacity of *I* to steer the neural ship? If I 'fall' asleep, what do I 'fall' from, and where does my 'fall' end? And how do I climb back out again? What happens to *I* in sleep? Importantly, I discover that whether I am dreaming or hallucinating – states of altered consciousness – I continue to be able to distinguish between *I* and not-*I* mental events.

This chapter explores disconnections corresponding to the attenuation of the relationship of *I* with the brain reflected in various states of reduced consciousness, of which sleep is one. It also provides glimpses into how *I* might relate to the brain, and how consciousness is not a simple on/off event, but a graduated one.

The disengagement of *I* in sleep

I begin with the proposal that, in sleep, *I* may be largely disengaged from the brain, but *I* does not cease to exist. I lose consciousness, but I do not lose *I*. Although 'conscious awareness' involves the activation of certain neural regions, this regional activation is not the same as *I*, as this would mean the cessation of *I* when these regions ceased to be active. Instead, I propose consciousness reflects the *engagement* of *I* with these activated neural regions. Both *I* and the brain remain extant in various states of consciousness, but the level of brain activation determines the state of consciousness. When I am unconscious, *I* is largely disengaged from its neural host, although it will continue to have some minimal functional capacity outside awareness, just as neural networks do.[1] The possible activity of *I* in the unconscious state is, unlike brain activity, impossible to measure and comment on.

As far as we can deduce, it is only in a state of awareness that *I* exercises authority over its body, making decisions that animate the body, and it is in this state that *I* serves as the endpoint of the communications received by the brain. If I should be unconscious, my brain would still function, although *I* would be disconnected to a large degree, affecting communication and volition. Piaget's principle of object permanence (just because I cannot see it does not mean it has disappeared) may also apply to the permanence of *I* when it re-appears intact after a period of unconsciousness. How does this disconnection between *I* and the brain take place in sleep, and how are things reconnected?

When I sleep, there appears to be a cooperative disengagement between *I* and the brain. Sleep accompanies the shutting down of awareness of environmental and bodily signals. This may be aided by habituation to incoming signals (for example, sounds and sights) which are familiar and repetitive so that they no longer require processing, allowing shut-down.[2] Unusual signals – novel sights and sounds – require processing and prevent or delay shut-down. Yet such signals, especially sound, kinaesthetic, and pain signals, may still be picked up by the senses and registered by the brain in sleep and are capable of waking me, re-engaging *I*. Before *I* is engaged, the brain can pick up signals. Does *I* enter a timeless zone, largely detached from the neural processing that memory and the sense of time requires, but become re-engaged *by the brain* as necessary? This is an extraordinary idea – that *I* should depend on its neural host to initiate a recommencement of awareness and activity. Yet in another unconscious state – coma – signals to the brain appear to be insufficient to re-engage *I*. Here another form of disconnection takes place.

With sleep, we know the disconnection process is regulated, at least in part, by an internal clock involving the neurotransmitters adenosine, melatonin, and neuropeptide Y. It is set by the twenty-four-hour day operating in the external world, governing a circadian rhythm which controls enzyme flow and body temperature.

Adenosine also plays a role in brain shut-down: its levels build up during the day, putting increasing pressure on the brain to shut down, causing sleepiness. Yet *I* can have input into this neural regulatory system by 'setting' some of the temporal parameters – 'I need to be up by 6am to get to work' – and ordinarily the brain clock obliges. But what is it apart from the readiness function of the circadian rhythm that disengages in sleep?

First, I shut my eyes. It may be that the brain finds it harder to disengage *I* from visual signals, which bring about immediate engagement, though visual signals are clearly not a prerequisite for *I* to function (the blind man is still self-aware). Darkness helps activate melatonin, implicated in the sleep cycle. Yet a tired man driving in daylight can enter into a trance state which we would call sleep while his eyes remain open, and the sleep walker may have his eyes open and see nothing, being, in fact, fast asleep. This suggests that if *I* does not help my brain shut down by causing my eyes to close, my brain can disengage the visual system without the involvement of *I*, so that even though my eyes are looking, I see nothing.

Second, sleep accompanies a shutting down of interactive analytical activity in favour of passive free association: that is, *I* needs to relinquish active control of focusing. The processing of information to deliver meaningful information to *I* – including focusing, analysis, decoding, 'search engines', and so on – requires considerable energy. The brain regulates the energy levels sustaining these (perhaps adenosine plays a role here): when the level is low (perhaps as a ratio of existing-to-required energy levels), a signal is sent to *I* to prepare for disengagement or, more accurately, a partial shut-down of systems (sleep), so that energy may be regenerated.

Third, sleep requires minimization of arousal levels such as from emotional responses and pain sensations.[3] Engagement with emotional systems, such as the neural pathways implicated in amygdala activation, needs to be inhibited. Nevertheless, these can be reactivated once I am in the sleep state, as I can dream dreams with emotional content. Perhaps the different levels of sleep may correspond to the number and type of pathways temporarily shut down by neurotransmitter activity, and to the partial reopening of pathways as shallower levels of sleep are entered into.

Finally, the brain is sensitive to the pattern of pre-sleep routines it has learned that contributes to arousal reduction and provides cues preparing the brain for shut-down.

At neurological level, the regions governing general arousal and the regulation of heart, lungs, and body temperature, the RAS and hypothalamus, play an important role in sleep.[4] The RAS also deals with psychomotor balance: perhaps this is why we sometimes experience the sensation of falling as we 'fall sleep' or the floating sensation that occasionally accompanies a dream. An area within the RAS called the *mesencephalic* region seems to be the brain's 'on' switch for consciousness, keeping me awake, although it acts more like a dimmer switch as it controls *degrees* of wakefulness and attentiveness. It is sensitive to a variety of sensory signals: pain, loud sounds, touch, and movement are all capable of throwing the switch to 'on' (Lindsay and Norman, 1972). This switch needs to be on for *I* to engage in attention processes.

While such neurological processes play a role in the activation of sleep, experience tells me that I can cooperate with these neural predispositions or resist them (to a point). The decision of *I* to sleep or not to sleep seems to set its own neural imperative. Here is an interplay any soldier on night-watch can attest to: the battle between *I*, who is determined to stay awake, and a neural system responding to other signals, determined to enter into sleep, a battle between *I* and the brain of epic proportions. One *I* generally wins at first, but which the brain always wins in the end: a necessary victory for the brain, as this regular disengagement of *I* from the brain allows restorative processes to take place. The brain is acting as it was designed to do – to protect and preserve the body so that it can once again engage in its other function, the expression of *I*.

Falling asleep is but the beginning of the nocturnal adventure. Once *I* has acquiesced to the brain's demands (or seduced the brain into sleep), the brain enters into an adventure unhindered by the controlling designs of *I*. Sleep is not a single event – there are layers of sleep; these reflect different levels of shut-down of interactive neural fields and are reflected in different brainwave patterns. Some neural regions operate throughout sleep, while others are shut down and reactivated during the course of the night. At least three neurotransmitters appear to be involved in this process: serotonin, adenosine, and melatonin, each in different pathways reflecting different aspects and levels of sleep, at times acting in concert, each performing different tasks.[5] Incoming signals – visual, auditory, kinaesthetic, tactile, and so on – are largely shut down, although the brain eventually activates alternate signals in the absence of incoming ones, sustaining the dream experience. We see again how the capacity to block information flow is as important as the capacity to enable it.

An example of this alternating inhibition and activation of neural pathways during sleep may be seen in the phenomenon of sleepwalking and talking. Howard recounted to me sleepwalking as a child: he was told that he had talked with his mother and *even answered her questions*, yet he had no memory of it; presumably, his *I* had no involvement. Was Howard 'asleep'? It seems that, even though his neural system was largely shut down, certain aspects had reactivated without engaging his *I*, which consciousness requires. He could sleepwalk, 'seeing' at an automatic level to prevent his body bumping into things (perhaps utilizing kinaesthetic memory), but not enough to process incoming visual information for meaning, engaging his *I*. He talked but did not process new material in his speaking, giving voice to material governed by neural signals in the absence of consciousness. In dream states, neural pathways are activated so emotions might find expression, although *I* has diminished control, finding itself at once active and helpless.

This level of disengagement between *I* and the brain in different levels of consciousness can be measured in brainwave activity. Little is known about these, and their relationship with the activity of neural software is a mystery. But what we *do* know is that there are different types of brainwaves reflecting different states of neural activity that vary between sleep and wake states. As I move from being fully awake to deeply asleep, different waves predominate, although at all times traces of the non-dominant waves remain.

When I enter sleep, I typically move from beta to alpha to theta to delta waves, and back again as I re-emerge from sleep. As each wave predominates, a different level of consciousness occurs. In the normal wake state, *beta* waves predominate. This associates with activity and busyness, anxiety and concentration, being agitated, tense, and afraid. When I am awake and my *attention is directed to some specific type of mental activity* (including visual sensation), beta waves pick up (Guyton, 1981). Beta waves are found mostly in the parietal and frontal regions of the brain and are associated with increased endorphin, noradrenaline, and dopamine levels, and help with associations, visualizations, pleasure, and good humour. Perhaps beta waves associate with active engagement of *I*.

As I get ready for sleep, *alpha* waves emerge. These are associated with being mentally and physically relaxed. They occur mostly in the occipital region (to a lesser extent, in the parietal and frontal regions) and require the activation of thalamic-cortical pathways. Alpha waves give way to *theta* waves, corresponding to entry into a dream-like state. Consciousness is reduced as I get drowsy, body processes become automatic, and there is a free-flow of ideas and associations. It associates with daydreaming, but also the dream-like state I experience as I awaken. Finally, in deep sleep, *delta* waves are elicited[6]: these waves appear to be produced by the self-managing systems of the cortical region when RAS activity is minimal – they represent non-conscious brain activity (Guyton, 1981).

In the course of sleep, the brain typically oscillates every ninety minutes or so between delta and theta activity, between deep sleep and, for periods of between five to twenty minutes, REM or 'active dreaming' sleep. Most sleep is delta sleep: it is restful and largely dreamless. Dream sleep is a state where general brain activity is no longer depressed, although signals are limited to certain channels. It is a peculiar state where the body is rendered paralysed while the brain increases its activity – it is more difficult to be aroused from this than from deep sleep; heart rate and respiration reflects dream material, and the eyes move as if corresponding to what is being 'seen' in the dream. Yet with all this activity, there is no environmental awareness, no controlled focus, no memory being created – *I* remains disengaged. Then, as the wake state is entered, I can linger some ten or fifteen minutes in the theta state as *I* enters into a dance of re-connectedness. This state is associated with out-of-body experiences, an awareness of *I* being separate from a still paralysed body.

Whether we study fMRI maps of neural activity or EEG graphs of brainwave activity, we find that the brain remains active in all states of consciousness, but varying both in the neural regions activated and in the brainwaves produced. I propose that these varying states of consciousness define the level of engagement of *I* with the brain.

Dreams: brain events or *I* revealed?

The interpretation of dreams has represented a romantic side of the clinician's work, given its more creative and mysterious origins, possible hidden and symbolic meanings, and long association with claimed supernatural revelations. And which clinician has not been presented with a client's dream at some point? Some readily dismiss such material: 'It is just the meaningless flotsam of your neural clearing house and not to be taken seriously.' Others take a different view, consulting encyclopaedias of dream symbols and exciting books on dream interpretation, looking to explain hidden messages of the subconscious. What are we to make of this; and what exactly *is* a dream?

Reporting a dream, I say: I *had* a dream, or I *was dreaming*. That is, it is something I was recipient of, or an activity I undertook. But what is the role of *I* in the dream process? I generally find myself an onlooker in my dreams – interaction is limited, although interaction can occur. I can become aware of being in a dream and finding myself temporarily trapped in it. Nevertheless, I am not always helpless: there are times I find myself acting upon decisions in my dream state that I continue to own in my subsequent wake state. It seems *I* can interact in a limited way with fragments of its mind map, allowing some recognition but poor orientation for *I* in a wider sense. It seems *I* can 'know' that the mind-map information it accesses in the dream state is somehow incomplete, just as its capacity to interact with that material is hampered.

If *I* is the origin and destination of information transfer and if my neural software acts as a mediating system through which *I* obtains information about the world, and conversely through which *I* expresses itself in the world, then how am I to understand dreaming? What is the origin of dream material? Is it *I*? Is it possible for my neural system to feed back to *I* material originating from *I* like some internal mirror? Certainly, dreams appear to be rich in symbolic material, a stream of meaningful ideas emerging from the mind map *I* helped create. Can I gain knowledge of *I* through the agency of my neural system during a dream? In this state, *I* seems unable to access memory *voluntarily*, although the brain seems to access stored material without authorization of *I* – *I* no longer voluntarily *inhibits* access to memories while dreaming. By what mechanism is voluntary access to (or inhibition of) memory, or voluntary control of other functions such as motor activity, established?

The mind map comprises the context in which meanings are imputed. The meanings of *I* are normally expressed through language and action. However, sequences of visual images may also be used to express meanings. Generally, the brain processes incoming visual signals to create meanings *I* subsequently apprehends. But in dream states, the reverse appears to occur: the flow of meanings (perhaps initiated by *I*) finds expression in mostly visual images whose sequence may be uninterpretable apart from the meanings they carry. The images the brain selects to convey those meanings are sometimes bemusing. It may not always be *I* that is the origin of the dream sequences. But for whom does the brain express these meanings in dreaming? Why this process? Does it work towards the integration of material comprising the mind map?

Whatever view we take, we face a peculiar conundrum in the relationship of *I* with the brain. Although I might understand dreaming as neural activity in the absence of an empowered *I*, and I do not remember most of my dreams, those I *do* remember may have the quality of *I* reacting to events created in my dream-world, situations *I* may or may not desire, which trigger emotions in me. Heidi described a 'lucid dream'[7] in which her *I* appeared to have the capacity to shape dream events. As she found herself flying in her dream, she chose the direction and movements of her flying, her choice reflected in her unfolding dream experience. Was this a remembered illusion of empowerment of her *I* within the dream context, or had her *I* actually become engaged? I can remember moments when in a dream I believed myself to be interacting with the real world: I had no cues alerting me that it might be otherwise. Further, there are dreams so vivid I judge they *have* to be 'real'. How am I to understand this? What cues have I to discriminate between these different states, and how does the *I*–brain relationship change in them? Has *I* the capacity to make judgements about the integrity of a mind map that becomes temporarily distorted in different states of consciousness?

The opposite also occurs: I may experience a threatening event so different from ordinary experience that it 'feels like a dream'. The threatening experience makes little match to my mind map so that I cannot make sense of it nor cope with it, and partial (emotional) disengagement occurs. This disengagement appears similar to that which operates during dreaming, so that *I* concludes the *origin* of the experienced event is the brain (that is, a dream), as against the brain mediating sensory material from the 'real' world. In either state, *I* appears to make judgements about the extent of neural engagement. *I* may feel my dream to be real, or my reality to be a dream. Mostly, *I* can discern the difference. But not always.

Peter explained that he had difficulty remembering whether an incident had happened. He had been having vivid night dreams – 'serotonin' dreams, his doctor had said (he was on amitriptyline). He had a clear memory of a woman he knew: what she wore, where she was, what she had said. But had she *really* said it, or was it a dream? He could no longer tell. He admitted that he had daydreams wherein he replayed conversations he had had with others. The same confusion occurred: had he *really* had that discussion, or had it occurred in a daydream? He would need to check to be sure. Peter was not hallucinating, but there was confusion between remembered reality and remembered dream or daydream. As he tried to reconstruct events, his brain would transpose one source of remembered information onto another. The resulting reconstruction was experienced as an accurate representation of a past reality. Only when he checked it with somebody, it turned out not to be so. Even *real* events, like the social event he had attended the Saturday before, became blended in the uncertain mix: had this event *really* taken place, or was it also part of a daydream? It was very confusing.

Why could Peter no longer make confident discrimination between what he dreamed and what had really happened? Had his *I* become so passive that it had become difficult to discriminate between its normally active interaction with Peter's neural system in 'reality' and its more passive role in a dream state? How was this reflected in neural disengagement processes? When daydreaming, was Peter unwittingly entering a trance-like state, triggering a partial shutting down of 'reality' by shutting down incoming sensory signals in favour of his flow of imagination? Yet *I* can play an active and leading role in the imaginative process, even though it relies heavily on freedom from the constrictions of external signals for this to happen. Are sleep dreams and daydreams similar neural processes, one prompted by unconscious neural signals, the other by fiat of *I*?

As with sleep, dreams and daydreams appear to some extent to be a function of selective disconnection of neural pathways.[8] Fewer contextual cues resulting from such disconnection lessen the ability of the cortico-hippocampal systems to utilize past learning to make sense of current experience. The breadth of dream experience may reflect the particular disengaged pathways. This event is not static: neural pathways are differentially engaged and disengaged in the course of dreaming so that I move between reality and imagination and back again. A night-time dream can incorporate information received through auditory pathways into the dream sequence as easily as it might exclude such information. Similarly, *I* might experience fluctuating engagement in the dream, sometimes defining events (as in Heidi's lucid dream), other times being defined by them (as in the helplessness typically experienced in nightmares).

There may also be lingering activity of neural networks that have been activated by the day's events. These networks retain connections, even if in a limited way, allowing some of the day's events to find expression in dreams. The fluctuations in connections between neural regions result in corresponding temporary reconstitutions and fluctuations of the mind map in dreams. Meanings are created from the limited connections allowed by the islands of information being activated.

Another conundrum is the role of memory in the dream experience. Is it only as I remember a dream that I come to recognize it as a dream? Is it possible to be aware of being in a dream state even as I undergo it? And why is it that I do not remember dreams unless I awaken while having the dream? It is as though *I* lies largely passive while neural software 'takes over', directing a complex informational flow and accessing stored material in memory. The lack of interaction of *I* with neural activity (which requires a certain level of neural arousal) and the absence of intentional focus seems to prevent dream material being encoded into memory. Does it require a critical level of neural connectedness and overall arousal – an emerging consciousness and re-engagement of *I* at some minimal level – for dreams to be remembered? Dream material is often accessed and encoded into memory as I begin to wake. Perhaps the emergent arousal level is strong enough for working memory to function, allowing it a birth in long-term memory. No doubt nightmares stimulate sufficient arousal to activate the waking state.

Does all this nocturnal activity have a purpose? It seems incongruous that during sleep the brain should waste energy on random and purposeless dreams that are simply a by-product of nocturnal fluctuations of engagement and disengagement of various neural circuits. Siegel offers that

> dreams are the work of sleep, during which we integrate emotion and memory. They occur when cortical inhibition is released enough to allow our subcortical limbic and brainstem regions to have a heyday with imagination and

feeling. They are an amalgam of memories in search of resolution, with left over elements of the day's events, and sensory inputs while we're asleep.

(Siegel, 2009: 141)

This certainly seems likely.

Dreaming allows processing – finding solutions to problems – in a context where neither incoming sensory signals nor alternative focus of *I* provides distraction. The visual and action symbolism found in dreams (the form in which memory is likely to be stored) form fragments of sequences of meaningful associations in the process of being integrated and resolved. Does dream expression provide fragments of deeper truths about *I*, truths I am afraid to confront, as Freud proposed? Or do dreams simply give expression to what *is* – as the articulation of experience might do in my conscious state, so visual pictures and sequences might do in the unconscious state? Either way, such expression being key to resolution, the binding and integrating of disparate bits of experience into 'meaningful' neural patterns allows these to be 'put to rest'. Siegel offers that such processes may be the purpose of dreaming. If so, dreaming is driven by a neurological need for resolution or homeostasis rather than by *I*.

I and other states of consciousness

Sleep and dreaming are not the only states of altered conscious. Other states bear witness to the graduated nature of consciousness, and the varying levels of engagement of *I* in those states.

Justin was in great pain post-operatively and given morphine. He subsequently described to me his hallucinatory 'morphine experience':

> It appeared as a vision: I felt I was on a curved slide, I was going round and round, a whirlpool action, gradually being sucked down. Then a 'guide' appeared, dressed like a twelfth century Roman peasant in a monk's cloak and fez hat. He said to me: 'You'll be OK. You'll have trials and tribulations, but you'll be OK.' The experience was very real: I remember it in great clarity. During the vision I always knew who I was, and I was able to make decisions – I knew the place to come back to was through me. My values stayed intact, my sense of self remained; I felt the integrity of self was secure. I was able to think about the vision as it happened, as though it were a movie. My first reaction was to fight what was happening, but then I learned not to do so.

This account has some important features. First, it describes an altered state of consciousness created by a drug disabling certain neural pathways to inhibit Justin's pain,[9] but also affecting his sensory processes. Second, the account underscores the integrity of Justin's *I* in conditions where his compromised neural functioning created temporary changes in his mind map. Third, the experience is different from a dream experience in both its vividness and its capacity for memory.

The capacity of many recreational drugs to selectively disable neural pathways has long provided users with the various experiential adventures they are seeking. But how can *disabling* neural pathways give rise to vivid and rich, albeit 'unreal', experiences? Yet there is generally a dual action: the inhibition of some pathways coincides with activation of others. These effects compete with the capacity of *I* to manage and direct the flow of neural information, which may be the intended effect, although accompanying hallucinations may also be unintended.

A question remains as to the *origin* of the material experienced in an altered state of consciousness, whether we call it a vision, dream, or hallucination. What might be the *source* of Justin's images? It does not appear to be *I* – *I* neither sought nor authored them (although *I* may have a role in its generation). Nor does it appear to be activation of material stored in memory: certainly, Justin did not recognize the images. It did not originate in the immediate external world – the experience was not shared by anyone. And it was hardly 'random' neural firing – the images were sequential, integrated, and to an extent meaningful. Justin understood what he saw.

Carter (2010) reports research suggesting that, whether someone actually sees a bed or imagines seeing it, the same brain region is activated. By the 1990s, Kosslyn and others found that mental imagery

> activated many of the same areas of the visual cortex as perception itself, show-ing that visual imagery was a physiological reality as well as a psychological one, and used at least some of the same neural pathways as visual perception.
>
> (Sacks, 2010: 228)

Whether I actually see my wife, dream about her, deliberately and creatively visual-ize her in a waking state, have a vision of her ghostly presence, have a flashback of an intense emotional experience I had with her, or have hallucinations of her after ingesting a drug, the same neural region is activated – the one representing my wife in my head. Although neural activation generally corresponds to the outside world, my experiences are not always of that world. When *I* apprehends the experience of my wife, dedicated neurons mediate the information for *I*. Nevertheless, what triggered the firing of those neurons and what is the *origin* of the experience held in that neural pattern? These are not necessarily the same.

Some suggest that hallucinations result from the brain misreading incoming information, or perhaps when it generates its own stimulus, interpreting it as com-ing from outside.[10] Yet the activation of neurons giving rise to hallucinations could conceivably result from any number of events, including misinterpreted signals from sensory (visual) pathways; drug-induced (or electrically stimulated) activation; activation by *I* choosing to recreate a picture in the mind; activation by neighbour-ing neural pathways as part of a memory-based dream sequence; or perhaps even from some poorly understood external source. The task of judging what is 'real' is a vexing one, as *I* apprehends the same neural territory regardless of the origin of the perceived event: can *I* determine the source by the quality of the experience?

That is, can *I* make judgements about the agent activating the neural networks it relies on? It appears sometimes it can, and sometimes it cannot: when I experience a flashback, it can; the one suffering schizophrenia often cannot.

Judging the source of experience is helped by context: the experience I have of my wife does not exist in isolation – there are many cues to which *I* has access to decide whether the experience is a dream, visualization, or an actual encounter. Tononi suggests that

> consciousness is the brain's ability to be in a complex state, even in response to a simple stimulus like a tone. The vast number of states our brains can enter when we are aware gives consciousness its marvellously rich feeling. In order to produce these states, the brain needs lots of neural elements that are active and able to respond, as well as a mass transit system that links them altogether.
>
> (Tononi, 2010: 79)

The experience of consciousness that *I* apprehends involves the simultaneous activation of many brain regions – that is, multiple information paths operating simultaneously. The brain normally has access to a wide range of cues to help *I* determine the nature of the conscious state. It is only when access to some of these cues are prevented through pathway disconnection that confusion about the nature of the experience results.

The ingestion of drugs is not the only context in which neural pathways are compromised, creating an altered state of consciousness. The compromise of any brain activity has immediate repercussions for the experiences of *I*. Yet the reverse is also true: when *I* is deeply distressed, brain changes are triggered by its distress that can result in altered states of consciousness, as might happen when someone undergoes a traumatic event. After Janet's rape experience, for example, she remained for many months in a 'disconnected' emotional state wherein she remembered little of the trauma. Her body functioned in 'automatic', which she explained involved no conscious decision making. She explained that she (her *I*) appeared briefly to separate from her body during the rape and subsequently remained in a semi-detached state for some time.

Such dissociative experiences can occur in varying degrees in relation to trauma, where everything might seem 'as in a dream', or as though it 'were a movie' during and immediately after the event. Typically called 'shock', such dissociation is more than emotional detachment as it paralyses volition. It seems there is a certain disengagement of *I* from neural processes, as if *I* is being protected from the threat of events in the natural world. Conversely (and perversely), dissociation can also result in self-harm, which may be seen as an attempt to 'feel' again. Here, some degree of depersonalization might be experienced: a feeling of estrangement, as if an outside observer of mental process and body. Again, the person might feel as if in a dream, or to lack emotional capacity, or as if they were not in control of actions or speech. The relationship between *I* and brain and body again becomes attenuated.

Other disruptions to consciousness may occur which are neither drug nor trauma induced. Dissociative states might occur in various psychiatric conditions and manifest at different levels of severity. These, too, reflect disconnection of important neural pathways. The dissociative process is generally experienced as a disruption of the usually integrated functions of consciousness, memory, identity, or perception of the environment – one in such circumstance might appear 'spacey', having trouble talking or understanding what is said; they might have a feeling or image without being able to link it to any other aspect of memory; they might report 'lost time' when they were not aware of what they were was doing; they might receive feedback that they did things they do not remember doing; or they might report feeling 'unreal', or that the environment seems unreal. The apparent disconnection of the neural networks in question compromises the avenues of access *I* has to its mind map, both to its memory systems and to its interface with the stream of incoming sensory signals.

A person may take advantage of the dissociations connected with the state of altered consciousness in choosing to enter a hypnotic state – to minimize pain, for example. Here an uninterrupted 'flow' of suggestion allows entry into a hypnotic state: other sounds, thoughts, or visual images would cut across the process and bring *I* into full functioning again, re-establishing heightened arousal and widespread neural activation. It takes time to 'disconnect' *I* from those aspects of neural functioning and to determine an internal focus. Hypnosis represents a process where *I* allows the disengagement of particular neural pathways for pain relief or to dissociate from certain memories or problematic urges.

Although dissociation is a common theme in different states of consciousness, *what* is dissociated varies greatly. Brain scans show that different neural regions are activated (or deactivated) in these various states (Carter, 2010). In slow wave sleep, for example, the limbic system becomes quiet. In hypnosis, the motor and sensory areas are activated and the right anterior cingulate region remains busy mediating a focus on internal events. In schizophrenia, the frontal cortex (particularly the dorsolateral prefrontal region) and the anterior cingulate region is far too quiet, suggesting multiple disconnections (the former may relate to reduction in planned or spontaneous behaviour, attention, and general social withdrawal, while the latter may play a role in distinguishing internal from external signals). With dreaming, brain activity is variable and can be widespread with alternating connections and disconnections, corresponding to the nature of the dream: commonly the brainstem and the visual, auditory, and motor areas are involved, although, as in schizophrenia, activity in the dorsolateral prefrontal cortex remains quiet.

Neural disengagement and the supernatural

There is another kind of experience, arguably reflecting another state of consciousness: the experience attributed to supernatural events. Although not normally discussed in clinical literature (many would argue it is better left to theologians), the issue nevertheless sometimes requires judgement and interpretation by the clinician. Researchers generally distance themselves from notions of the supernatural – and perhaps they are right to do so, given the nature of the 'evidence' we are dealing with. Yet it has not always been this way: science was born on the understanding that order in the natural world reflected natural laws established by divine intention. In the study of the natural, the supernatural was not dismissed.

But for many scientists, the word 'supernatural' creates an immediate scepticism: it is a word that associates with 'gullible' and 'unscientific'. For others, however, the word relates to remembered events and extraordinary experiences they may have had: for them it associates with 'spiritual', 'non-natural', an unseen reality. Whatever view we take, some people report experiences in such terms, for whom there may be a need to make a clinical judgement as to what these experiences might mean. In this respect, the clinician cannot altogether avoid the question of the supernatural as a researcher might.

The *Diagnostic and Statistical Manual of Mental Disorders* makes an interesting qualification in the interpretation of hallucinations when determining whether pathology is present:

> Clinicians assessing the symptoms of schizophrenia in socioeconomic or cultural situations that are different from their own must take cultural differences into account. Ideas that may appear to be delusional in one culture may be commonly held in another. In some cultures, visual or auditory hallucinations with a religious content may be a normal part of religious experience.
>
> (American Psychiatric Association, 2000: 281)

And so 'cultural' or 'religious' (read 'supernatural') meanings need to be considered when making the diagnosis and interpreting the symptoms: there is recognition a clinician may need to make judgement in these matters.

A surprising number of people report 'hearing from God' or seeing visions attributed to the supernatural – most do not end up in a locked ward, nor are they prescribed olanzapine, clozapine, or risperidone. Why? Is the experience of the supernatural different from psychosis? The brain is constantly processing incoming signals to which it attributes meaning: *I* is primed to send and receive communication through its neural medium. And so 'false signals' can easily occur. In the *absence* of communication, the brain searches for any sign that might constitute communication, creating meanings from such signals. Desire for and expectancy about certain forms of communication can result in false interpretation of incoming signals, distorting incomplete signals in the direction of expectancy and desire. This error may occur in psychosis, but also in the context of religious experience.

Yet there remains a long history of credible people who report experiences they unhesitatingly interpret as supernatural. And so the clinician may need to make a judgement about these reported experiences: are they indications of someone under severe stress or someone experiencing a psychotic episode; might they represent a simple misapprehension someone has resulting from some perceptual confabulation; or indeed, have they experienced a 'genuine' supernatural event?[11]

I need to decide the origin of material of which *I* takes no ownership and attribute appropriate meanings.

To be sure, when I consider the mystery of *I*, I wonder just how 'natural' *that* entity is when compared to the natural physical body in which it dwells. Although the body and brain operate in the natural world mediating the presence of *I*, *I* may be of a different order. If *I* is an entity separate from the brain, it may be unable to interact with the natural world without the mediating role of the brain. If *I* is of a different order, I need to allow for the possibility that *I* also has the potential to communicate with a supernatural (as against 'natural') world. However, in this domain, the neural system may be more hindrance than help because it ties me intimately to my memories, incoming sensory signals, and orienting mind map. It would make sense that when *I* is partially disengaged from the neural system it might better apprehend information from a supernatural source.

In dreams and states of deprivation, in near-death and when overwhelmed in trauma – these are the states where people commonly report having 'spiritual' experiences. Yet these are also the very states where neural functioning is compromised, so I might reasonably interpret the experiences as hallucinatory. And so both possibilities need to be considered, although I would argue that the quality of experience of a spiritual nature and the context of such experience compared to that of, for example, psychosis, is generally different.

Certainly I hesitate to attribute supernatural interpretations to events apprehended by the sensory system, given that this system is designed to give information about the natural world. But I do not share the conclusions of researchers like Persinger (2001), who reports artificially creating supernatural or 'spiritual' experiences, such as feelings of disembodiment, of timelessness, and even the feeling of being in the presence of an invisible but sentient being, by experimental stimulation of certain brain regions, implying that these experiences are 'nothing but' the activation of these neural networks. I have no doubt that supernatural experiences might be imitated through the stimulation of specific neurons, but the question remains as to the *source* of the experience: was it supernatural or experimentally induced? If an artificially stimulated neural pathway should give me a visual experience of my wife, this does not mean that the activated pathway is the *source* of the picture I have of her, nor does it negate her reality or the capacity of her presence to stimulate that same pathway. A supernatural source always remains a possibility: the question is the judged source of the meanings *I* apprehends.

Chapter 14

I feels

Complex emotions

Some years ago, serial murderers Catherine Birnie and her husband horrified the citizens of Perth by torturing and killing a number of young women. Catherine subsequently claimed she felt no guilt, remorse, or shame: it seems she felt no emotions at all. Yet how is it possible *not* to have emotions? Do not emotions form a natural and automatic response to life experiences? Is it possible to selectively or completely disengage from emotions? What is the *mechanism* of emotional response? Are different neural sites or neurochemicals associated with different emotions? Was Freud right about emotional repression, wherein emotions exist at some level, but of which there may be no awareness?

These are the vexing questions I now consider. I will also consider how *I* sometimes seems to apprehend emotions created by the neural system, while at other times *I* appears to be the source of emotions expressed through its neural system and body. It seems that the relationship of *I* with emotions can be consonant or dissonant – the ownership of the neural processes appears to fluctuate, and so we revisit the dance of *I* with the brain. I will review the apparent temporal nature of emotions, their purpose, how one might 'hold onto' an emotion over time, and explore what it might mean to 'resolve' an emotion. I will touch on why an emotion might sometimes powerfully imprint memories, yet at other times inhibit them. But I begin with the surprisingly difficult question: what *is* an emotion?

Definitional problems

Defining emotion is like grasping hold of a slippery soap in a bathtub. And just as slippery are the associated ideas. Is there such a thing as 'emotional memory'? How many emotions *are* there? Do they require connecting thoughts or ideas to be defined as emotions? Does there need to be some form of expression before an emotion is considered such? Is emotion necessarily a transient and current event, or can it be maintained in an ongoing state or linger after a past event? Perhaps we might get a better grip on that slippery soap by considering a specific emotion, such as anger. Anger relates to the belief that a situation is not what it should be – a response to a situation where the experienced restraint, interference, or criticism is perceived to be illegitimate (Reeve, 2005).

Rachel confides she is angry with her mother. What does she mean? To say she is 'angry' may be an *experiential* statement or a *positional* statement. Rachel may say: 'I am angry with my mother' in a sharp exasperated tone with fire in her eyes, heart pounding, and fists clenched. She means:

> I'm feeling roused and combative – I want to fight mum. She interferes in how I manage my little Sarah, telling me what I ought to be doing. As it happens, I didn't have much sleep last night and I've been feeling tired. I know I'll get over my anger soon, and I'll get a perspective on things.

This state is *experienced* as anger, by which we mean certain neural changes have taken place – amygdaloidal activation and the release of corticoid hormones and neurotransmitters (acetycholine, noradrenaline, and serotonin) corresponding with Rachel's feeling state. This is consistent with Rachel's *position* of anger towards her mother because of perceived injustice in the things her mother has said, although we see from her account there may be other unrelated factors. Once her arousal level drops after she has gone for a walk, breathed calmly, and can think straight, Rachel may properly address the cause of her anger. In this case, it would appear that Rachel's *I* and her body are responding as one in the emotion anger.

Alternatively, Rachel might say: 'I am angry with my mother' in a calm manner, showing no sign of arousal, no anger in the tone of her voice, nor bodily tension. She means:

> I feel distant from mum because she's wronged me. She frequently tells me my failings in my management of Sarah, although she hasn't made such criticisms recently. I haven't seen much of her, and she doesn't know how I feel. I've had a good night's sleep, and I'm feeling relaxed. Nevertheless, I'm angry with mum for her interference, and I've decided to keep our contact minimal.

Here Rachel has taken a *position* of anger towards her mother but is not *experiencing* bodily signs of anger. Her anger will remain indefinitely unless Rachel chooses to change her position in relation to her mother. This may happen if her mother apologizes for being over-enthusiastic with her critical advice; if Rachel decides she misinterpreted what her mother said and she does respect her ability as a mother after all; or if Rachel forgives her. Failing this, she is likely to negatively interpret her mother's communications to maintain consistency between the anger position her *I* has taken and the signals from mother. Her neural processes – the action of her amygdala and neurochemicals – are different from before: there is no arousal and she is breathing normally. Yet we would agree she is angry with her mother.

Other circumstances might arise where Rachel does not recognize being angry, but the conditions normally leading to anger are present; conversely, she might admit to feeling angry in the *absence* of the conditions defining anger, at least following Reeve's definition. Consider the following. Perhaps it is not Rachel who admits to being angry with her mother, but her *clinician* believes she is angry with her mother. Rachel might reply:

> I'm not aware of being angry towards mum. She's been generous to me and I love her. Sure, she tells me how I should raise Sarah and this infuriates my husband, but I ignore it. It causes tension between us, and I guess mum really shouldn't say such things, but I try to smooth things over.

But Rachel admits that some of the things her mother has said pass through her mind at night so that she does not sleep and she avoids inviting mother over when her husband is home. She feels a bit distant from her mother and she is not sure why. Sometimes she suffers headaches and becomes impatient with Sarah when mother comes around to give her a hand.

In this case, to say Rachel is angry with her mother is based on *indirect* evidence interpreted by her clinician, both of an *experiential* (she is tense) and a *positional* (she feels distant from her mother) nature. Yet when pushed, Rachel insists: 'No. I'm not angry – I just feel a bit down and tense when mum is around.' For her, her mother and the emotion anger are not connected. There is no recognition of anger, yet the *motivation* of her actions and her bodily responses suggest anger. We have made a distinction between self-awareness and *I*, so that Rachel's denial does not necessarily preclude this being an *I*-event: it is possible for her *I* to transact something of which she is unaware.

Finally, Rachel might say to her clinician, mouth tight-lipped and fists clenched:

> I'm irritable and impatient when mum is around: I'm getting into arguments with her although I know she's done nothing wrong. I'm over-sensitive whenever she encourages me as a mum, and I find myself wondering whether she's indirectly criticizing my parenting ability. I feel bad about my reactions, but I haven't slept well as Sarah kept me awake, and I'm worrying about our finances. Come to think of it, I wake up spoiling for a fight – with anyone. I don't know why I'm feeling angry.

Here Rachel admits to being angry and she displays the bodily symptoms, but there is no *cause* to be angry with mother: she does not attribute any wrongdoing to her mother. It appears she has anger *looking for a cause*. She has yet to fulfil the condition of Reeve's definition of anger: the belief that a situation is not what it should be – the restraint, interference, or criticism that is perceived to be illegitimate. Nothing illegitimate has occurred here. There is evidence of neural and bodily involvement suggestive of anger, yet Rachel's *I* seems dissonant to it; her *I* is not the source.

How are we to understand 'anger'? In the first example, there is evidence of bodily expression consistent with perceptions relating to unjustified interference and criticism: this surely describes the emotion anger. In the second example, perceptions relating to unjustified interference and criticism are voiced, the state of anger is freely admitted to, but there is no evidence of bodily expression of anger. If Rachel had said nothing, I would not have known she was angry. Should we distinguish between emotion and *attitude*? In the third example, the conditions of anger appear to be satisfied, but there is no awareness or admission of such. Is this the emotion anger, or should we distinguish between emotion and the *motivation* of latent or subconscious anger? Finally, we have an example of bodily expression consistent with anger, with admission to the fact. Rachel freely interprets her experience as anger, yet this does not reflect in her position towards her mother, nor is it consciously connected with any triggering event. Should we distinguish between emotion and *mood*?

If anger which is commonly regarded as an emotion is not always an emotion, but can be an attitude, a source of motivation, or a mood, then what *is* an emotion, and what *is* 'anger'? How are we to distinguish between these? Does it require for the one *experiencing* emotion to interpret internal signals as such? Is it possible to mislabel an emotion or have an emotion I do not recognize? Can the same label be given to different experiences with different triggers: the anger I feel when I perceive an injustice compared to the anger I feel when I stub my toe? For that matter, can the latter reflex be regarded as an emotion, though I call it anger?

If the emotion anger is reflected in a particular neural pathway signature, can this be triggered in ways apart from the conditions that normally give rise to the emotion? Perhaps anger, whether as emotion, attitude, or mood, can be defined as an active distancing or differentiation of *I* from the object of anger: the opposite of embrace and identification. Yet a similar process occurs with fear. If 'anger' is the term we use for the distancing position of *I* from an external event or other person, is *I* necessarily involved as the entity creating the distance? Or does 'emotion' require certain neural and bodily manifestations of a response of *I* to an event, although it is expressed in different forms between different people in different situations?

There is ongoing debate as to what emotions actually *are*, and for good reason. Aspects of the complex interaction of cognitive, perceptual, physiological, and behavioural events that contribute to emotional experience are also implicated in attitudes and mood. And then there is the relationship of *I* with emotion. It is hardly surprising that the discussion between clinician and client might be difficult: what do you *really* feel? What are you *supposed* to feel? Are you talking about how you feel *right now*, or about some 'underlying' attitude? Are your feelings telling you something about *yourself*, or about your relationship with others?

Reeve offers the following definitions: 'Emotions are short lived, feeling-arousal-purposive-expressive phenomena that help us adapt to the opportunities and challenges we face during important life events' (Reeve, 2005: 294); and: 'Emotion is that which choreographs the feeling, arousal, purposive and expressive components into a coherent reaction to an eliciting event'; and: 'Emotions energise and direct behaviour, and they serve as an ongoing "readout" system to indicate how well or how poorly personal adaptation is going' (Reeve, 2005: 296). Yet definitional problems remain. Closer inspection suggests anger, guilt, sadness, pleasure, jealousy, and so on may not meet the definition of 'emotion' outlined. Either they are not short-lived or accompanying arousal is minimal, or their purpose is unclear, or their expression is inhibited, or they are not adaptive.

Nevertheless, Reeve's definition remains useful, although I would wish to include the *I*–brain dynamic. I suggest that emotions act as a neural or bodily feedback system tied to the intercourse of *I* with the external world and my physical and cognitive self. They communicate meanings regarding *I*'s fluctuating relationship with the external world and with brain and body, finding expression in neurochemical release, facial shape, tone of voice, heart activity, bodily posture, and so on. They communicate to others the *position* of *I* in relation to an event or person – a position of embrace or distancing, of inclusion or exclusion and so on. They also constitute multifaceted *experiences* with many nuances of which *I* has awareness and seeks to interpret. Nevertheless, the distinction between emotion, drive, and impulse remains cloudy: consider greed, the desire for control or power, aggression, laziness, lust, curiosity, self-stimulation (getting a 'buzz'), and so on. Are these emotions or do underlying emotions energize these drives and impulses?

Various *appraisal* theories seek to explain key features of emotion. Their basic premise is that 'emotions are elicited and differentiated by the subjective interpretation of the personal significance of events'. They seek to explain 'emotional response patterns as a direct consequence of appraisals', and apply a conceptual framework to 'all instances of emotion, including automatic unconscious processing' (Scherer and Ellsworth, in Sander and Scherer, 2009: 45). These theories raise questions about the criteria people use to evaluate the significance of events, how causal attributions are made, how meaningfulness of events is established in the appraisal process, and the mechanisms of appraisal. These make significant contributions to our understanding of emotions and are well-articulated elsewhere.[1]

But I make one observation relevant to our purpose. Scherer and Ellsworth note:

> In many cases emotions are produced by unconscious, non-deliberate, non-voluntary factors . . . It should be noted that appraisal theorists . . . use the words appraisal or evaluation to cover a continuum of information processing from conscious, deliberative processes all the way down to unconscious, automatic processes.
>
> (Scherer and Ellsworth, in Sander and Scherer, 2009: 48)

Given the role *I* plays, both within and below awareness, the contextual role the mind map plays, again both within and below consciousness, and the role of other physiological predispositions (some DNA based), I believe Scherer and Ellsworth's notion of a *continuum* of information processing encompassing both conscious and unconscious factors is a necessary and important aspect. Importantly, emotions are not always the result of *conscious thoughts*, which is sometimes implied in intervention approaches. The origin of (or contributions to) emotions can be surprising.

If *I* and the body function in harmony, emotions would reflect the simple inter-course between *I* and the world. But as we saw with Rachel, they do not always do so. I can become aware of emotions of which I say: where do these emotions come from? Perhaps they do not even belong to me, but resonate with the emotions of one I love. The neural system is capable of creating emotion whose source is not *I*, which can lead to confusion and many interesting novels. Or *I* can be disengaged and be unaware of the emotions finding bodily expression, yet whose origin remains *I*. Although *I* normally plays an integral part in the creation of emotion through its role in appraisals, emotion may also be triggered by memory, dreams, hallucinations, or neural dysfunction (though I am tempted to argue emotion in these contexts represents the reaction of *I* to these events). The difficulty in articulating a definition is the complex nature of the emotion event itself, which may be designed to accomplish one thing but where things can go wrong (perhaps due to neural disruption), and so create an event more difficult to interpret. This is where clinicians really begin to earn their money.

Emotions and the brain

Are there dedicated neural pathways or 'signatures' releasing unique combinations of neurochemicals and connecting key neural regions which we might identify with particular emotions? The multifaceted nature of emotions warns us that trying to identify particular neural addresses for various emotions is likely to fail. While the limbic system is typically referenced, emotion sweeps across the neural land-scape, reaching into practically every facet of the mind map, whose components are scattered throughout the brain, in the frontal, temporal, parietal, and occipital cortices, in both right and left hemispheres. Emotions typically also involve appraisal by *I*, which we suspect is of no fixed neural address.

Emotion then energizes a response: the ANS becomes aroused, flooding information down the brainstem by way of the RAS, changing the patterns of breathing and heart expression. Selected neural networks are activated (simultaneously inhibiting others), favouring the right or the left hemisphere depending on the emotion, which releases a unique pattern of neurochemicals which *I* can both author and apprehend, and which translates into the colouration of the particular feeling experienced by *I*. Many muscle systems, whose ambassadors live in the somato-sensory region of the parietal cortex, also receive instructions, especially those relating to the face and hands, as the emotion finds bodily expression. Meanwhile, software in the frontal cortex processes information necessary for *I* to respond to the circumstances giving rise to the emotion.

We saw how Rachel's anger might mean different things: these differences are reflected in her neural activation patterns. There are several components to her anger that may be activated at once, or one at a time, or in some combination or in varying sequences. These components include the following. First, her appraisal of a situation relayed by a complex of incoming sensory signals, a *cognitive* event processed in the frontal cortex: she judges something to be unfair. This becomes the basis of her anger *attitude*, which may or may not trigger a cascade of neural activity. Second, her *I* takes a position based on that thought, a primarily *relational* event which can remain indefinitely: 'I don't want to be close to that person anymore.' This remains stored in memory.

Third, her body responds, triggering a surprisingly complex set of events, including *physical* events (her clenched fists, the anger in her eyes, the furrows in her brow processed in her parietal cortex), and transitory *visceral* and *respiratory* events (her tight stomach, pounding heart, and rapid breathing) processed in her brainstem, fuelled by her activated amygdala, perhaps releasing adrenaline, yet modulated by software in her hypothalamus by way of dopamine pathways. These pathways are activated by her *I* (mediated in her frontal cortex), and relate to her *feeling* or *mood* of anger. This neural activity creates brainwaves of a stress-related theta pattern, perhaps apprehended by *I*. Fourth, her *I* becomes *aware* and takes *ownership* of the process: 'I am conscious that anger in me is causing me to be distanced in my relationship and is creating my bodily reactions.' This makes possible management of the situation by her *I*, largely through frontal cortex software.

Yet the question remains: although Rachel's anger may activate many neural regions, is there a unique neural signature that allows her to recognize anger, a pathway that releases a unique neurochemical combination distinct from the perceptual event triggering the anger and which is always activated in anger, whatever its trigger or physical expression? And do the various nuances of anger – frustration, irritation, aggression, sulking, rage and fury, passive-aggressive behaviour, and so on – share the same neural pattern? It seems neural 'loops' can sustain an emotion: heightened arousal lingers after the initial emotion trigger, as neurochemical releases take time to wash out. A certain perception might activate Rachel's anger circuits, but her brain then scans for new problems unrelated to the original trigger to create meaning from the lingering arousal, so that she expresses anger about unrelated events. Do these also have a common neural pattern?

Rachel might displace the *object* of her anger: angry with her mother, she yells at her husband or daughter, while the relevant neurochemicals flood her brain. This may reflect appraisal confusion, or a reaction to her arousal state. Equally, Rachel might choose *not* to be angry about an event judged to be unjust, inhibiting such neurochemical release. Sometimes anger appears to be an event that happens *to* her, and sometimes her anger might cause such neural momentum that her *I* seems momentarily 'out of control'. Rachel also has 'mirror' cells – the basis for empathy – which can resonate with another's anger, and become a trigger for her own. Perhaps her anger becomes generalized, like fear and anxiety, by simple association of her aroused and vigilant state with otherwise unrelated events. Do all these events share a neural 'anger' signature?

We have considered the complexities of anger and its corresponding neural involvement. Many of these issues are true for other emotions, although each has unique aspects, activating different neural territory. The external event that normally triggers emotion involves *perception*: it is *I* that perceives. Such perception might be of loss, injustice, frustration, threat or rejection; of exposure or inadequacy; of being overwhelmed or being in error; of experiencing success or being denied success; and so on. The emotion event itself I refer to as *synaptic*, not only because it involves neural synapses, but also because it occurs in the gap between an initiating event and the response it energizes. Like the neurochemical release itself, the *experience* of emotion is relatively short term, though it may have lingering effects. The emotion orients *I* to the external event, placing it to the centre of focus.

I would expect to find differences in the neural structures supporting different emotion events, as well as differences in such structures from one person to another, whether in the propensity to neurochemical activation (neural reactivity) or in the pattern of neural networks. Certainly, we observe some people are more quickly afraid, others more quickly angry, embarrassed, guilty, or happy. Although the emotional and perceptual history incorporated into a person's mind map will play its part, these propensities may also be influenced by genetic factors. Let us consider the neural structures that might support different emotion events.

Guilt, shame, and embarrassment have been associated with the regions of the medial prefrontal cortex, the left posterior temporal sulcus, and the visual cortex, areas associated with processes of social cognition involving the capacity to 'read' others' mental and emotional states; and also with the insula, which plays a role in 'social' emotions such as disgust, pride, shame, humiliation, lust, and guilt (Cozolino, 2006). Because guilt and shame (or embarrassment) involves the judgement of self as having failed morally or socially, the medial prefrontal cortex is involved.[2] Other neural regions are also involved, although it is unclear which are responsible for the actual *feelings* of guilt (which has to do with an awareness of having done something wrong towards another) or shame (which has to do with feeling exposed as small, worthless, and intrinsically deficient) apprehended by *I*. We might expect to find differences in their neural signature: indeed, it seems that embarrassment fires up more neural territory than guilt, activating neurons in the right temporal cortex, the hippocampus, and the visual cortex to a greater extent (Takahashi *et al.*, 2004). But a unique pattern of neurotransmitter involvement defining either emotion is yet to be identified.

Grief, the reaction to the loss of a significant object or other, can trigger powerful and indeed painful feelings. The complexities of the grief reaction are seen in the *mix* of feelings that often accompany the process – sadness, anger, guilt, anxiety, and so on – so that clear differentiation of emotion becomes a problem. It seems that grief responses are linked to regions in the anterior cingulate and the orbito-frontal cortex, thus involving parts of the frontal cortex. Recent loss where the bereaved is suffering intrusive thoughts (the emotion having become relatively dysregulated) appears to activate parts of the amygdala (matching the intensity of sadness) and the anterior cingulate cortex; whilst those in denial show a decrease in activation in another part of the amygdala and the dorsolateral prefrontal cortex. More generally, sadness seems to activate the limbic and paralimbic structures in the cingulate, the medial prefrontal cortex, and temporal cortex; as well as the brainstem, the thalamus, the caudate, and putamen regions (the left prefrontal cortex is more affected by sadness than the right) (Freed *et al.*, 2009).

Such widespread neural activity is hardly surprising. When a significant loss takes place, a person's mind map may need to make many changes. Neural networks relating to the lost object need to be reformulated – many disconnections need to take place and new networks forged. There may be many specific 'losses' bound in the loss of a significant other. This involves considerable work for the brain, depending on the role the object or person of loss had in a person's life, and exhaustion may result. The grief process reflects the many changes that take place: changes in expectancy, in behaviour patterns, and so on. There may also be a fundamental change in the orientation of *I* reflecting the changes wrought by the loss of the significant other, an important counterpoint to the communication process.

The brain regions relating to happiness are different from those relating to sadness: these are not opposite, but different events. Little is known about the relevant neurotransmitter activity that defines these feelings, although it is well-documented that pleasant events – an aspect of happiness – release dopamine, which stimulates limbic structures, leading to 'feeling good', that is, pleasure.

While some emotions may coexist to create a state of mixed emotions (like sadness and happiness: the 'bittersweet' experience), in other instances the expression of one emotion inhibits another. The emotions *fear* and *love*[3], for example, appear to be mutually exclusive – neurologically, the systems activated with fear inhibit the systems activated in love. Love relates to social connection and the reward it embraces. When the neural areas relevant to love (the insula, anterior cingulate, caudate nucleus, and putamen) are activated, the fear networks centred on the amygdala, which prompt avoidance behaviours, are inhibited (Cozolino, 2006). In love, there is no scanning of the external world for threat, no autonomic arousal orienting the body for defensive action. While it is said that 'perfect love casts out fear', fear 'outranks and outwits' love in a number of ways at neural level: fear is faster, it is automatic, it is unconscious, it spontaneously generalizes to other stimuli, it is multisensory, and it is resistant to extinction (Cozolino, 2006: 318). That fear outwits and outranks love is not good news for clinician or politician, for marriage or friendship.

Although *I* might generally be the source of many emotions, *I* needs the body to generate the sensations and actions associated with those emotions. And while the brain releases different neurochemicals for different emotions, it does not *experience* anything – it is *I* that apprehends emotion experiences. Do feelings require expressive behaviours? Do I need to laugh to enjoy, or to cry to feel sad? Or the reverse: if my body 'acts happy', will *I* experience happiness? And are these expressive behaviours energized by neurotransmitter release? How can a feeling originate in *I*, when the actual experience relies on the neural system? Sometimes the fear experience results directly from a perception of *I* that then finds neural expression; sometimes *I* interprets neural activity reacting automatically to incoming sensory signals as 'fear'. Again we encounter the dance between *I* and the neural system: sometimes *I* leads; sometimes the neural system.

I is not passive in emotional experience, despite emotion being embedded in the brain and body. In the emotion literature, an underlying dynamic linked to the neural landscape is the *approach* versus *avoidance* orientation, with pleasure-seeking impulses grouped under approach orientation, and fear, anger, and disgust grouped under avoidance orientation (Reeve, 2005). The former is seen to associate with neural regions to the front and left of the brain; the latter to neural regions at the bottom rear of the brain and the right prefrontal cortex. But this formulation does not allow for the active role of *I*. Independent of the neural correlates of approach versus avoidance orientation, *I* can make a *decision* to approach or avoid. Generally, *I* will decide to 'approach' that associated with positive feelings and 'avoid' that associated with negative feelings. But *I* can also choose to 'approach' the scary situation, *despite* feeling fear: we call this 'brave'. Alternatively, *I* can choose to 'avoid' that food, *despite* the anticipated feeling of pleasure: we call this 'self-control'. The brain can mediate an emotion activated by environmental events or the memory of such events, a feeling that *I* apprehends, yet *I* retains the capacity (moderated by strength of *I*) to make a decision based on an *idea* not consistent with the emotional orientation activated neurally.

What happens when *I* experiences fear, but still makes a decision to 'approach'? The neural pathways mediating fear eventually fatigue and the fear gradually dissipates. And what happens when *I* experiences an enjoyable feeling of anticipation, but chooses not to indulge, avoiding the potential source of pleasure? Again, the neural pathways mediating pleasurable feelings eventually fatigue, and the pleasure experience gradually dissipates. *I* is able to regulate the brain response – to 'feed' or to 'starve' the feelings the brain presents to *I*.

The purpose of emotions

What is the purpose of emotion?[4] What is the reason a thought, memory, or experience should be coloured by this experience called emotion? Are envy, shame, and guilt adaptive, and how does grief help me? Yet how could I survive without love and what would life be without pleasure? Is there any avenue of communication (film, theatre, novel, music, or art) that does not find depth and connectivity through arousing emotion?

Emotions add their own dimension of meaningfulness and play a role in motivation, but where do they come from? Do neural events motivate me: are the decisions *I* makes governed by neural imperative? Yet it is not the brain that experiences emotion, but *I*; and while neural processing grants me perceptual frameworks, it is *I* that attributes values and makes moral judgements that inform emotional responses. There are circumstances where neural dysfunction results in reduced emotion experienced by *I*, such as anhedonia in depression ('I feel flat or dead inside'), or in some psychotic states ('I can't experience pleasure in my body'): what are the implications for the sufferer?

We encounter the familiar dance (or struggle) between the brain and *I*: *I* needs the brain to feel emotion, yet without *I*, no experience is apprehended. Sometimes *I* is overruled by emotional events in the body; other times *I* shuts down the emotional signals it receives. Sometimes the body flows freely with the emotions *I* wants to express; other times the body resists such intent. The emotion event, like consciousness, exists in the interaction of *I* with activated neural regions mediating the emotion, making sensation possible. It can originate in *I*, or *I* can become the destination. It is an encounter that releases energy for action of one sort or another, which, when it finds no expression, creates internal tension. Emotions communicate things about me to others as much as the emotions I discover within me communicate to me about the world in which I live. The purpose of emotion, like the communication dynamic, is bidirectional – it fulfils a purpose for me as well as for the other.

Let us first consider emotion as an expression of *I*. Where *I* is the source of an emotion, it is generally the outcome of a *perception* that creates guilt, shame, envy, anger, fear, or love. There is an element of *choice* (I *choose* to think about the person or incident in anger or love), or a perception of *personal culpability* (I recognize my guilt – I did wrong; my inappropriate behaviour is uncovered – I feel shame). The *purpose* of the subsequent expression of such emotion is to reveal to another my intent or circumstance.

Not that this is without hazard: the accurate interpretation of another's emotion signals requires capacity to make meanings in the context of one's own mind map. The look in my eyes, the pattern of wrinkles in my brow, the words that I speak and the tone of my voice, the movement of my hands and arms, and the beat of my heart – all these can communicate to the other my position in relation to them and my intent towards them, provided they know how to make accurate meanings. The rhythm of my breathing, the tension in my stomach, the flow of my tears, the tone of my laugh, and even the nature of my smile can communicate different things to the other, enhancing their understanding of me.[5]

Although it is *I* that decides, experiences, judges, and initiates things, I gain insight into *I* through interpreting my own physical responses: '. . . we see emotions derive ultimately from the physical self, we learn to access our bodily grid to locate ourselves within the world, and we ground the idea of our unique self within it' (Cozolino, 2006: 74). This is a second purpose of emotions: a source of self-knowledge. Even if I have limited awareness of decisions *I* makes, they nevertheless set the cognitive parameters for emotions, which can tell me about what I believe in and identify with, what is important to me, and what I have personally invested in, and so on.

But this, too, is not without hazard. Not only might I have difficulty deciding whether a *thought* belongs to me, as Charlie discovered: a similar problem can emerge with *emotions*. Recent research relating to mirror neurons, also termed resonance circuits,[6] suggests that when I experience the intentional activity or emotion of another, my own neurons can be activated in sympathy – the same neural signatures are activated as should the act or emotion be my own. Attributional confusion – did that feeling belong to me, or does it belong to another? – is a problem clinicians have long understood: in emotional contagion (as in crowd behaviour), symbiotic relationships, empathic responses, and transference processes.

Joshua explained: 'When I see a movie wherein the underdog eventually overcomes and is rewarded in his victory, I find myself crying freely.' How can Joshua cry about an event that does not belong to him, or about a person he cares nothing about? Is it simply an automatic neural response to the movie content and that he cries 'in spite of himself' – his *I* is not engaged, but neurons resonate to another *I*? Or is there identification with the other, so that the information that passes through his mind map matches some memory triggering the emotional response? Or has the movie engaged his *I*, so that his weeping is a bodily expression of an event with which his *I* is actually involved? Emotional entanglement and misattribution is a relationship hazard parents and children, lovers, and clinicians negotiate: what belongs to me, and what belongs to the other? It is about maintaining *I*–thou separation, seeking alignment and closeness while remaining distinct and separate. My brain might resonate with the emotional signals of the other, but the source of these emotions remains the other – the source is not *I*.

A third purpose, inherent in both the first and the second yet separate in function, is that emotion acts as a *motivator* or *drive* energizing action: whether it is a bodily process that energizes *I* or *I* that activates bodily processes. Emotions typically energize a response, often towards restoration: in grief, to recover the object of grief;[7] in anger, to restore justice; in compassion, to restore the fortunes of another; in shame, to cover defect or weakness; in guilt, to make atonement or restitution; and in fear, to overcome threat. Sometimes the object of the energized natural response cannot be accomplished, and *I* begins to suffer. Alternatively, the body is prevented from actioning the response so the energy builds up, creating tension or stress, and in the course of time, possible disease. There is energy expended in any change or transaction. The form of energy in the neural system appears largely to be electrical, in the change of ion potential, but it is also in the form of chemical events such as neurochemical release. Once the energy is expended, the change is completed, the transaction done, and things come again to rest, to a state of equilibrium.

The body is in a constant state of dynamism, both in its physical activities and in its chemical processes. Perhaps the biggest draw on energy is in emotional processes: in the activation of significant bodily responses, in ANS arousal, and in the subsequent work of lungs and heart. But the making of a decision, the maintenance of attention and focus, and the exertion of will over the body also draw energy. *I* itself may not create or consume energy – *I* makes transactions that draw on bodily sources for energy the neural system requires to do the bidding of *I*. When the available energy supply is depleted and a system fatigued, its performance is compromised. The production of energy is largely through metabolic processes (glutamate, an excitatory neurochemical, is a key source of neural energy), although *I* can generate energy in other ways, such as in the creation of a plan which creates internal tension, stimulating energy production until its realization.

We have argued that the purpose of emotions is to communicate to others my circumstance, to gain self-knowledge, and to energize action. But *I* may prefer not to take ownership of emotions that originate in me; *I* may want to suppress such communication or self-awareness. Nevertheless, Siegel (2009) argues that, even if

I blocks awareness of feelings, they would find bodily expression – through facial expressions of which I might not be aware, or in changes of heart rhythm that I do not notice. The body might even communicate emotional distress through physical pain, as found in somatoform disorder. When the body communicates in this manner, the destination of the communication is *I*. The body generates a message difficult for *I* to ignore, even though its interpretation is uncertain as it concerns matters *I* wishes to suppress. Such suppression would require neural disconnections authored by *I*, which might be difficult as *I* can communicate through the neural system *in spite of itself*, given the neural system's sensitivity to matters of *I*.

Yet success at disconnection of some sort can be attained. Neural disconnection to prevent emotional expression may form the basis of *hysteria* (now conversion disorder) where emotional disconnections can result in inhibition of sensory input or motor activity – which was not necessarily the intent of *I*. For example, my not wanting to 'hear' certain things might result in temporary non-intentional functional deafness. The intent of *I* translates into disconnection of a different order, reflecting distortion in the interchange between *I* and the brain. Nevertheless, the motivation for disconnection is communicated: the brain will not be denied its fundamental role of mediating the communications emanating from *I*.

One issue remains: if an emotion is short-lived (Reeve, 2005), and a purpose of emotion is to create energy and momentum towards the rapid resolution of that emotion, how are we to understand alleged long-term 'unresolved' emotions that originated in events of weeks, months, or even years ago? Should we think of these as *attitudes* or *motivations*? Is it possible, for example, to be in denial about grief, for it to be 'held in' for a lengthy period ('he hasn't grieved properly yet')? Or do perceptions and memories remain that create the ongoing preconditions for re-emergence of grief, ready to energize the incomplete transactions? These preconditions are not the emotion, but without them the emotion may not be re-experienced. It seems *I* can suppress the purpose of emotions being realized in the short term, but eventually such purpose finds expression. We now consider the issue of emotional resolution.

Emotional resolution and a moral conundrum

How often have we suggested to someone that they should *deal* with their issues or *resolve* their emotional problems? But what does this mean? Let us revisit the issue of anger and see what challenges it might raise for the clinician.

Rachel presents with an anger problem she says she wants to resolve. I ask her what the purpose of her anger might be – what is it telling her, or what is she trying to communicate to others? Might it reveal to Rachel that she perceives herself as having been unjustly treated, that she has unmet expectations, or might it serve the function of keeping others at a safe distance? I build a picture of Rachel's circumstances – that is, her perceptions – to understand what her anger is communicating. The evidence I use is what Rachel tells me: however 'scientific' I wish to be, I rely on her subjective report. It is my only avenue to the mind map that provides the context of her judgements.

Should Rachel agree that she perceives being unjustly treated, how might she 'resolve' the issue? Should her faulty perception be corrected: 'what happened here isn't *really* unjust – you misread the situation'; or: 'you made an unhelpful assumption about what you expected of the other'? Should she engage in discussion with the alleged wrong-doer to negotiate a just solution – seek their admission of wrong-doing? Should she forgive the wrong-doer – choose to release them from what she believes is owed her? Would success at one of these activities 'resolve' the issue and stem the flow of energy sustaining her anger and energizing the drive towards resolution? Alternatively, if Rachel agrees her motive in being angry is to keep others at a distance, what might be her avenues of resolution? Should she begin to dismantle expectations she might have of others being a source of threat, betrayal, or disappointment? Or should she begin to build a stronger sense of self, capable of withstanding other opinions and views?[8] Would success 'resolve' the issue for Rachel, and restore her energy?

It may well do so. The matter seems straightforward. Rachel might agree on the purpose of her anger and proceed to resolution. Yet what if I seek to adjust Rachel's perceptions ('Rachel, you need to think differently'), but Rachel is committed to her perceptions: she will not budge from what she believes the other ought to have done, and she is in no mood to forgive? Or what if Rachel suggests that the issue is that she has been wronged, but I believe she is seeking to distance herself from others (the triggering events actually took place some time ago), but she does not want to embrace such self-knowledge and change how she chooses to respond to events? The mind map that constitutes the patterns of meaning for me may not match that of Rachel. Should I bring her around to *my* way of thinking? Should I seek to convince her that her judgements about how she believes things 'ought to be' are wrong ('unhelpful')? What is the *goal*: to resolve the discomfort of Rachel's emotion, or to resolve the problematic circumstances her emotions bear witness to?

And so clinicians get drawn into moral issues – issues of the judgements a client's *I* makes that are expressed in emotional responses. Issues of guilt, shame, anger, and distress grounded in perceptions of right and wrong. The clinician makes judgements about the client's judgements and enters the moral arena. How is this to be managed? Ever pragmatic, many clinicians avoid the complexities of moral judgement by centring their judgements on how 'adaptive' or 'functional' Rachel's response is, or on the extent that her emotion might become a 'health problem' for her and those around her (Ellis, 1988). But moral issues cannot always be reduced to issues of adaptability, functionality, or logic; nor can they always be excised from what underlies an emotional response. The difficulty is that the basis for judging right or wrong may vary from person to person, grounded in their different perceptions of the world and of what 'ought to be'. The potential lack of common ground between clinician and client complicates the resolution process.

For now, let us propose that I encourage Rachel to move towards resolution by arguing that a 'should' should no longer be a 'should': remove the moral imperative, the perception of wrong-doing, the expectation of what 'ought' to happen, the dissonance between what is and what she thinks ought to be, and the problem is removed. Rachel no longer needs to feel angry (or guilty or anxious). I imply that Rachel's anger as an expression of perceived injustice should not be used to motivate the cause of justice – rather, she should question her perceptions of what *ought to be*. Once she has jettisoned what *ought to be*, her anger will be ameliorated, and her discomfort resolved.[9]

Perceptual processes (how I see things and what I believe ought to be) play a large role in emotional responses. The corollary is that changing those perceptions can ameliorate emotions. Yet consider the following: when I am running late, winding my watch back an hour appears to give me an extra hour's time, provided my only source of reference is that watch. My perception of lateness has changed. But my watch is *not* my only reference point, and an assumption becomes apparent: changing a perception assumes that perception does not accurately represent an external reality. I need to allow that a 'problem' emotion may be a valid reaction to an external problem: it is not necessarily due to faulty thinking.

A 'problem' emotion, according to rational emotive therapy (RET) founder Albert Ellis, is one that is unnecessary and unethical to live with because it acts against me ('I am miserable') and subsequently negatively affects those around me, who are not happy with my misery. The emotion becomes a social problem (Ellis, 1988). While there may be some truth to this, a new morality emerges centred on the idea it is morally wrong to experience a negative emotion because it adversely affects those around me. What is stated explicitly here can also be implicit in the thinking of some CBT practitioners, who are similarly in the business of replacing faulty thoughts with 'rational' ones through the process of logical disputation, in order that their client might feel better.[10] Even subtle terminology shifts – 'don't call it anger – the situation is just "annoying"' – dilute the moral aspect, reinforcing the idea we are simply dealing with an unnecessary experience which should be replaced by happiness.

This amoral position, however, fails to allow that emotion might have *meaning*. The purpose of emotion is not just to make life miserable (or enjoyable, as the case might be), but to motivate action in relation to life goals. Emotional experiences are interwoven with those life goals. The experience of one or other emotion does not constitute the goal – it simply gives information about where I am relative to that goal. Ellis's formulation sacrifices the inherent meaning for the more immediate amelioration of discomfort. In so doing, he runs the risk of *I* acquiescing to bodily comforts at the expense of life direction. Furthermore, the logic – 'emotion is the result of perception; change the perception and the emotion changes' – appeals to the efficient brain, but as cognitive therapists such as Young and Klosko (1993) discovered, changing perception is not as straightforward as it seems. Perceptions are rooted in the complex framework of remembered history (the mind map), a framework that creates its own meanings over many years. To change such perceptions entails revisiting this framework and making many adjustments to retain internal consistency.

What happens if an emotion is not 'resolved'? What happens to the emotional energy generated? Does it get channelled into other activities that bring no resolution or does it gradually dissipate? Or does energy keep being produced until suitable resolution is made? If so, might the constant generation of such energy eventually create neural fatigue? Or is the process attenuated (thus saving neural resources) but reactivated every time there is a reminder of the external event that remains unresolved?

I suspect that the neural networks relating to unresolved emotions get repeatedly activated on account of the lack of resolution, creating a strong memory of the activating event. Strong and recurring emotion creates the memory; later the memory recreates the emotion. Lack of resolution leaves a powerful trace of complex perceptions and memories which contribute to the ongoing preconditions for renewed emotional expression, so that transactional tasks not yet completed may be energized. On the other hand, the early resolution of emotion dissipates the emotional energy, the event is no longer revisited, and the neural trace quickly fades. A quickly resolved emotion leaves little memory.

Chapter 15

I suffers

Anxiety and pain

Not all sensations apprehended by *I* are always referred to as emotions. Anxiety is sometimes referred to as an emotion, sometimes a disorder. Pain can sometimes mediate the expression of an emotion, but more frequently signals a problem in bodily functioning. But like emotions, both become powerful sources of motivation that can compete with *I* in influencing behaviour. Both are also sources of suffering for *I*.

The illogic of anxiety

If the purpose of emotion is to communicate my circumstance, to gain self-knowledge, and to energize action relevant to the emotion, then what of anxiety – what does it communicate about my circumstance, what self-knowledge does it provide, and towards what useful action does it energize me? Is it an emotion like any other, or a psychological disorder that does not have the productive functions of an emotion? If both, when does it move from one to the other? To the extent anxiety motivates self-protective behaviours, it may be functional, but does it always do so? There frequently appears an illogic in anxiety: it may mediate fear in the absence of the thing feared, or in the absence of conscious awareness of what the threat actually *is*. The neural alarm provides self-protection, but protection from *what*?

When Margaret is asked to give a talk to a group of strangers, she notices her heart rate increases, her breathing becomes shallower, and thoughts present themselves that the talk will go badly, or that she will make a fool of herself. Why does this happen? Her *I* did not invite these unwelcome thoughts. Why does her ANS arousal increase? She is no danger right now. It appears her brain is engaged in a function without her choosing: in a rapid neural calculation which, I suspect, is genetically pre-programmed. Anxiety becomes a function of judged internal resources minus perceived demands (a negative balance sends an alarm). Or following Beck's (1976) formulation, a function of perceived threat proportional to the perceived probability and severity of the threat (or demand) divided by the ability to cope with the threat in conjunction with other external supports (rescue factors). When the balance drops below a certain value, an alarm is sent in the form of noradrenaline release, with immediate increase in ANS arousal. Margaret, however, is unaware of this neural calculation. She does not know her brain has measured her inner resources to be inadequate to meet the anticipated demands or perceived threat: all she notices is anxiety, a crisis in the strength of her *I*.

Margaret must now find meaning in the neural alarm, so she begins to scan for possible reasons. Not necessarily a 'correct' fit – just the best fit with the mind-map data available. Here comes an answer: 'I don't know the subject well enough'; or: 'I won't have enough time to prepare'; or: 'People are not interested in what I have to say.' The 'answer' may fit with certain memories or self-beliefs, and the interpretation is accepted as valid. The only thing is, the interpretation may *not* be valid: it may not reflect accurate information about Margaret or her circumstance. Further, it may not energize her to a productive response: a likely non-productive response is to avoid doing the talk altogether. So we move from a productive emotion to one that becomes dysfunctional and inherently illogical:[1] a psychological disorder.

The many faces of anxiety share this illogicality: worry, phobias, procrastination, panic attacks, and generalized anxiety. Why does she feel anxious about the harmless mouse? Why did he experience a panic attack as he was relaxing, watching TV? Why does she continue to worry about her health after her doctor assures her she is fine? Why does he wake anxious every morning, even though he is safe, there is food on the table, and he has a job to go to? Why does she avoid making the phone call that will potentially solve her problem? Why does he feel afraid to drive again after the accident – the road is no less safe than it was before his accident? Why is a neural alarm triggered in the absence of danger; why is the brain scanning for danger?

The measure of self-efficacy, a person's perceived ability to cope in a situation (Reeve, 2005), may be calculated below awareness. There are specific signals to which the brain is attuned that orient it to anxiety. When I avoid a matter, my brain *assumes* the reason for the avoidance is an inability to cope, and so anxiety develops. The brain may also interpret the lack of resolution of an emotion event as non-coping, so unresolved emotion may transform into anxiety. Alternatively, anxiety may result from avoidance of the expression of emotions – a fear, perhaps, of losing control, or of rejection, or of vulnerability. The brain weighs the possibility of excessive demand on coping capacity in any unknown circumstance, calculating a negative balance. Any failure of *I* in managing its neural inclinations may likewise be interpreted as not coping – including the non-management of the alarm signals (the anxiety symptoms) themselves. Conversely, any deficiency in neural functioning (for example, neural depletion, or the slowing physical and cognitive responses in the aged) will translate into neural resources being perceived as inadequate to anticipated demands. The problem for *I* is that these anxiety processes are automatic.[2]

At neural level, we have some understanding of the circuits activated in anxiety. The amygdala activates pathways linked to the ANS (responsible for the classic symptoms of racing heart, perspiration, shallow breathing, and so on), the thalamus, the hypothalamus, the hippocampus, and the orbital area of prefrontal cortex. Connections are made in the amygdala region between arousal (associated with anxiety and fear) and experienced or remembered events, people, thoughts, and sensations

(Cozolino, 2002). Those with panic disorder have particularly busy amygdala (and right temporal cortex). Disabling the amygdala would eliminate the anxiety experience, resting the ANS. Importantly, the fear or anxiety reaction is not limited to one neural circuit. LeDoux (1994, in Cozolino, 2002) proposed at least *two* circuits: the *fast* circuit and the *slow* circuit. In the fast circuit, a more reflexive one, signals move from sensory organs by way of the thalamus to the amygdala, bypassing hippocampal and cortical circuits – that is, bypassing the critical and more reflective faculties before firing up the ANS fight-or-flight reactions. The slow circuit, on the other hand, includes the hippocampal and cortical circuits, allowing a more considered judgement before the ANS is activated. Perhaps the illogical anxiety responses utilize the fast neural circuit so that the ANS is activated before *I* can register what is going on and deal with the unnecessary arousal.

The fast circuit notwithstanding, other authors suggest the septo-hippocampal circuit (this circuit involves the integrated action of the septal area, the hippocampus, the cingulate gyrus, the fornix, the thalamus, the hypothalamus, and the mammillary bodies) governs anxiety (Reeve, 2005). The hippocampal software compares incoming sensory information with expected events. Where there is a poor match (or non-match – that is, the events are experienced as unfamiliar), the hippocampus activates the septo-hippocampal circuit, generating anxiety. Disappointment, failure, punishment, and novel situations can stimulate the hippocampus, instigating anxiety-ridden behavioural inhibition (Reeve, 2005). On the other hand, the perception of coping and success can release endorphins, which shut down the septo-hippocampal circuit, giving relief from anxiety.

Hippocampal activation and release of noradrenaline facilitates the creation of new memories. And indeed, important memories *are* created in anxiety, but typically memories related to anxiety itself – memories that play a role in the subsequent dysfunction. This occurs independent of considered judgements of *I*, yet associative processes are incorporated. Nevertheless, this inside information on possible neural correlates of anxiety does not satisfy our puzzlement as to the capacity for anxiety to disable someone in a benign environment.[3] Matters are proving more complex than we want.

More so than other emotions, anxiety has a capacity to spiral. It does this in various ways. First, anxiety tends to associate with specific memories, not necessarily of unsafe events, but of events connected with earlier experiences of anxiety. The noradrenaline alarm wires to events associated with earlier alarm signals – that is, not logically, but associatively, by time or place. Second, when *I* discovers it is not easily able to disable the alarm system, *I* experiences not being in control of its neural domain – this sends a further alarm signal. The awareness of having little control reinforces the idea that *I* cannot, or will not, cope, creating further anxiety. The truth, of course, is that there really *are* limitations in what *I* can know or have control over. And so the saying: 'Don't be anxious about tomorrow – let tomorrow worry about itself!' The third prompt to spiral is anxiety about the anxiety symptoms themselves – both the factor of their discomfort and the perplexity about what the symptoms mean. This, of course, is a classic feature in panic attacks.

Intervening in the anxiety spiral may require identification of subtle avoidance behaviours (replacing these with an embrace motive), or the 'letting go' of attachments and expectations regarding things *I* does not control. It may necessitate becoming familiar with the unknown, or regulating arousal processes to help quell anxiety symptoms. There may be a need to acknowledge suppressed emotions, or desensitize neural reactivity to benign stimuli. It may require the explication of implicit memories of threatening events, or the development of a perception that the environment is, after all, safe. Or intervention may be as basic as ensuring enough rest for neurons to be up to the task demanded of them, or practising skills so that the performances required are within a person's capacity to manage. Some of these interventions involve addressing the position of *I* with regard to the environment – its perception of competence and awareness of performance capacity (or incapacity); other interventions deal directly with automatic neural processes – with associations and neural capacities (or incapacities) below awareness.

I finish with a note on what seems the most illogical of all – anxiety related to death. This might make sense if death was considered an unknown. Yet death is frequently not considered unknown: for some, it is understood as entry into nothing. But the awareness of *I* that it might one day cease can cause deep existential crisis. Colin admitted he had begun to drink – too much – because of a fear of death and descent into oblivion. Once his body was dead, Colin believed his *I* would cease. Why should his conclusion elicit anxiety? That it might elicit grief, one could understand: he had given up a faith that had provided him a very different outlook. But why anxiety? In every respect, he was comfortable and secure – he had nothing to fear. And fear of eventual 'oblivion', literally 'fear of nothing', seemed somehow inherently illogical. Perhaps the self-preserving response of his nervous system was triggered not by the idea of its cessation, but by the idea of possible loss of control of *I*. Although there was no immediate threat, Colin's *I* was considering oblivion, and anxiety resulted. Although his body might go, his *I* appeared attached to the idea of eternity, despite Colin's logic.

The logic of pain

'. . . And you had better not tell me it's all in my head,' Robyn said threateningly upon explaining the suffering she had experienced after her back injury, clearly suspicious about her referral to a clinical psychologist.

> I can tell you the pain is very real. I can hardly sleep, I can't enjoy the dancing I loved, and doing housework has become pretty much impossible. I am becoming increasingly frustrated and despondent. I would do *anything* to be rid of this pain.

I reassure her that her pain is real, and have no doubt it causes her great suffering. Working in a pain management clinic, I have been confronted by possibly the most desperate people, some willing even to take their own lives because of their debilitating, exhausting, and apparently permanent state of pain. Nevertheless, the question needs to be asked: what *is* pain? *Was* it in Robyn's head, after all? And how does it relate to her *I*? It appears that not only was her back in bad shape, but also – perhaps especially – her *I* was suffering. The signals that carried the pain message along the neural pathways from her spine to her brain were simply electrical signals: they were not pain sensations travelling to her brain. So what did the message *do* for her to experience pain? The signal travelled to a point in the somato-sensory region of Robyn's parietal cortex corresponding to her back injury – is this where the pain signal was transformed into a neural event causing suffering to her *I*? These questions we now consider: how the body communicates with *I* using pain sensations and, conversely, how *I* expresses suffering through its body.

Unlike anxiety, and unwelcome though it may be, pain has intrinsic logic and purpose. It creates a signal that something is wrong; and the intensity of suffering it creates for *I* demands a response. In this sense, pain represents the body's most powerful self-protective mechanism, at the same time creating a signal difficult for *I* to ignore, and mobilizing the body's own protective measures. When *I* receives a pain signal, the immediate question it considers is: *Why? What is causing this pain?* The signal needs to be interpreted, although misinterpretations pose a hazard. Without sensation and pain signals, the body would inevitably fall victim both to external and to internal assaults that would ultimately destroy it. Such was the experience of prominent hand surgeon Paul Brand, who worked with leprosy patients who had lost sensation generally in their hands and feet, resulting in repeated and unnoticed injuries that led eventually to the destruction of those body parts (Brand and Yancy, 1993). He was one of very few who promoted research into the *re-establishment of pain circuits* as against research into its amelioration. Yet we might reasonably ask: why such suffering for *I*, rather than a less intense sensation?

There are two distinct, though related, aspects to pain: certain pain-related brain regions are activated by signals from both proximal and distal parts of the body; and it is a distressing sensation for *I*. Pain signals are triggered by a noxious event somewhere in the body, and travel along two types of nerve fibres to the brain: one a 'fast' system, which results in sharp pain, the other a 'slow' system, which results in deep, burning pain. These systems tend to be mutually exclusive (Carter, 2010). Some come from peripheral nerve fibres (sometimes termed *nociceptive* pain) that are typically activated by temperature extremes, physical pressure, or chemical reactions; some come from disease or damage affecting the nervous system itself (sometimes called *neuropathic* pain), which results in different kinds of pain sensations.

The destination of these signals, however, does not appear to be a specialized neural 'pain centre'. Rather, travelling through the thalamus, we see activation of the relevant somato-sensory region in the parietal cortex, providing orienting information about the sensation. On the other hand, we see activation of the insula (which has to do with language and the 'social emotions') and the anterior cingulate cortex, which is primarily associated with attention and emotion, and essential for the conscious experience of pain, whether of physical or emotional origin. Pain shares attributes with emotions as it activates similar brain regions. However, apart perhaps from the release of the neuropeptide substance P, most of the activity in the anterior cingulate appears to be a *response* to the pain sensation. The brain releases natural pain-killers, endorphins and enkephalins, to ameliorate the suffering of *I*.

The effect of this neural activity is twofold: it provides orienting information to *I* by way of the mind map about the possible *source* of the pain, and it motivates *I* to do something through the suffering created – to protect the damaged area and to avoid the circumstances that gave rise to it. This, however, does not mean the body cannot react to the situation independent of conscious response governed by *I*. Reactive and restorative activity can take place in the neural system below conscious awareness, often more quickly than the actions initiated by *I* due to *awareness* of pain. Nor does it mean that bodily trauma always results in pain sensations – the neural system can inhibit signals, usually because competing neural events can take precedence both in neural resources and in the attention of *I*. Less commonly, signals normally giving rise to pain sensation may be apprehended by *I* but without creating suffering and therefore not generating the motivation to effectively deal with the situation.

The parallel activity of neural messages creating a subconscious neural response on the one hand, and pain sensations apprehended by *I* on the other, is evident in Barry's story. Barry suffered Parkinson's disease as well as a heart condition. He noticed that, under certain stressful conditions, he would suffer angina, and the numbing and shaking in his hands would be greatly exacerbated. But he also observed:

> My shaking serves as a precursor for my chest-pains. My pain always comes some seconds *after* my shaking has begun. When I exert myself, whether I am digging or lifting something, or even when I get excited about something, I get chest pains, but not before my hands begin to shake.

It seems that there was initial neural acknowledgement of cardiac stress in Barry's hand shaking, a Parkinsonian signal, while conscious awareness of his cardiac problem as mediated by pain sensation (that is, the activation of his anterior cingulate) was momentarily delayed. His neural distress signals appeared to operate independently from his pain experience. In Barry's case, the pain event created a cycle: the first response of Barry's *I* to his acute chest pain were the thoughts: 'What's going to happen now? Who will help me? I'm about to lose control.' Whereupon panic would begin whose source was *I*, and the bodily expression of this, his shaking, would greatly increase. What began as Barry's *I* suffering as a result of a body event became a body event expressing the suffering of Barry's *I*.

There is another possible aspect to the pain event for Barry, which some hypothesize is present in chronic and complex pain conditions. Over time, changes may take place in the body-map representations in the mind map where there is ongoing activation of pain signals because of *remembered* pain events, not current body-induced pain nor *I*-initiated pain. What started as a problem in the body may eventually be represented as functional changes in the mind map, which endure after the physical problem has ceased to exist.[4]

We have proposed that a purpose of pain sensation is to motivate *I* to a protective response. For the body to create urgent awareness in *I* of the problematic body event suggests *I* has executive control of the body. Nevertheless, *I* can find itself powerless to control the events creating the pain experience. This can result in a cascade of secondary problems, prolonging the suffering in *I*. Logical as the pain response appears to be, closer study shows complex interaction with other systems involving both *I* and various neural and bodily responses. Turk and colleagues observe:

> Anxiety, tension, depression, and perceived incontrollability appear to exacerbate a variety of somatic symptoms and the perception of pain. These psychological variables have been shown to modulate the production of stress hormones, neurotransmitters, and autonomic arousal, including increased muscle tension. Consequently, modification of anxiety, depression, tension, and perceived lack of control may lead to decreased production of ACTH, catecholamines, decreased muscle tension, and increased availability of neurotransmitters (e.g., serotonin), thereby modifying pain perception, pain response, and suffering.
>
> (Turk *et al.*, 1983: 351)

Suffering and *I*

We have seen how the body can alert and motivate *I* through the pain experience to deal with problems besetting the body. But the reverse occurs too, where *I* creates pain in a healthy body as a physical expression of its suffering. Barry's experience suggests this process may sometimes begin a cycle where body signals create pain sensations *I* is helpless to deal with, and then *I* finds expression for this subsequent suffering in physical symptoms.

In the pain experience, it is *I* that 'suffers' – not the body. The body can be injured or decay; but it does not 'suffer'. Should, for example, my foot be injured, nerve endings immediately send signals along nerve pathways telling of the problem, stimulating neurochemical responses which *I* apprehends, whereupon *I* experiences suffering that it interprets: 'I have injured my foot – I must now attend to it and protect it.' However, it is possible for a body to be injured, to be dysfunctional, or to decay, and for *I not* to experience suffering. It is equally possible for *I* to experience suffering in the absence of bodily injury, dysfunction, or decay. Although neural activity may be necessary for *I* to experience suffering irrespective of the health of the body, it is possible for *I* to be the *origin* of the suffering, and for neural activity to mediate its expression. The same neural activation experienced as pain may have different sources. Let us return to Una's story.

In the days before the discovery of her daughter Ciara's murdered body, Una writes:

My body is tense with pain. It is a searing physical ache as if every nerve end-ing is exposed and it stretches from the very core of my being to the tips of my fingers and toes. My heart is in continual spasms of pain.

(Glennon, 2010: 21)

and: 'I am still tense with shock and pain continues to rack my body with the feroc-ity of physical suffering' (Glennon, 2010: 24). Una's body had been untouched – it was suffering no physical trauma, no disease nor injury. Yet her *I* was in great suf-fering, not least because of her helplessness. This suffering found expression in her body *even though there was no reason for her body to send pain signals to her brain*. Neural chemicals normally released by bodily signals to be apprehended by *I* as pain are here released with *I* as source. While one might point to intervening variables, such as the emotional stress of preceding days resulting in release of cortisol and other neurochemicals, and while Una's pain sensation was mediated by her neural system to make it a *conscious* experience, the *origin* appears to be her *I*, not her body.[5]

Despite the origin of Una's suffering being her *I*, normally the drive is for *I* to *reduce* suffering, not *create* it. Is it possible that when *I* suffers without bodily reason for such suffering, it experiences helplessness? It then projects the suffering *onto the body*, giving the impression of injury or dysfunction, perhaps empowering it to address or indirectly reduce the suffering by releasing the body's natural opiates. Is this the reason for somatization of emotional distress? When *I* fails to do this indi-rectly through internal neural pathways, might its alternative be self-harm?

Deliberately stimulating pain in acts of self-harm as if to initiate suffering in *I* is curious indeed, when most are driven by the opposite desire – to avoid pain and to experience pleasure. More puzzling is why someone in a healthy body should seek to bring about such destruction: what existential pain or dysfunction could cause this? There may be a clue in the old adage to pinch oneself to see if something is really true. The deliberately inflicted pain might act as the ultimate test that I am properly conscious, receiving signals in my natural body that I *ought to experience* when *I* is suffering. Perhaps it is the response of *I* where *I* is in a state of disorienting disconnection and unreality in relation to its own state of suffering. Perhaps self-harm acts to confirm the reality of suffering through bodily manifestation, at the same time providing an avenue for amelioration through endorphin release.

The capacity to suffer is an attribute of *I* which may originate in body, but also in other sources. The body in turn may carry symptoms of suffering in *I*. What causes *I* to 'suffer'? Generally, it appears to take place when *I* is aware things are not in order, whether in its body, in relationships, or more generally in interac-tion with the external world. *I* gets disturbed with the perception that something is 'wrong', and it normally addresses such disturbance to reduce suffering. This, of course, assumes that there *is* a 'right order', a way 'things should be' in the body, in relationships, and in the world.

Part V

Clinical applications

Chapter 16

Depression

I and neural fatigue

Helen's complaint is not unfamiliar to the clinician.

> I don't feel myself these days – I can't be bothered doing anything. I've lost interest in others and in my future – I've lost my "zest" for life. I feel heavy, sad, worried, and a kind of foreboding. Everything is black. What's wrong with me? I don't want to go to work – I'm too tired to do anything – I'd rather stay in bed and sleep. I can't even concentrate reading the books I used to enjoy. I put off doing things, making decisions, and seeing friends. I'm a pain to live with: the smallest things make me irritable. I don't want to be with my husband and I'm not coping with my children: I just want to run away. What's the point of living anymore? Life doesn't make sense. I feel I'm a burden on everyone.

This is a strange thing. Who is this 'myself' Helen no longer feels? What happens for her *I* to 'lose interest'? Why doesn't Helen get energized after a good night's sleep? How is it possible to 'lose' the point, the reason for living she once had – where did she lose it? What is happening?

I will argue that there are two aspects to depression: a depleted neural system and a weakened *I*. I will present bipolar disorder as a different manifestation of a depleted and dysregulated neural system. We will discover an interactive dynamic between *I* and the brain which sees a brain fatigued because of chronic issues distressing *I*, and *I* reacting to a fatigued brain, creating secondary symptoms.

Defining a complex condition

The many and varied presentations of the phenomenon called depression have long been recognized, but it remains an elusive concept with variation in symptoms, aetiology, and prognosis.[1] Controversy surrounds attempts to categorize depression.

Yet clinicians recognize its symptoms: fatigue, loss of motivation, social withdrawal, low mood, disinterest, loss of pleasure, poor concentration and memory, abnormal patterns in sleep and appetite, slowed motor activity, and low frustration tolerance. It is associated with 'negative' thinking – 'I'm useless, worthless, unattractive, and I don't deserve your interest and concern in me'; and with 'negative' feelings, such as guilt, sadness, and shame. It emerges in the context of chronically stressful *external* events, such as financial problems, trauma, personal loss, and rejection or hostility by a significant other at home or work; or of chronically stressful *internal* events, such as painful memories or physical pain, unrelenting anxiety and insecurity, disempowerment, alienation, and ongoing frustrations and resentments. Certain predisposing circumstances are also well known: adolescence; having babies; other family members suffering depression; and some physical illnesses. It affects body chemistry, depletes biochemical resources, and affects neurochemicals and the pathways they service. But what *is* depression?

Theorists point to the vicissitudes of past experience creating self-defeating thought and behaviour patterns. They argue that a pessimistic outlook on life and a person's belief that they are helpless and ineffectual is likely to result in depression. They point to epidemiological studies linking stressful life circumstances with depression risk. Others of a medical persuasion suggest depression is a 'disorder' of mood, an illness with a common aetiology, a 'disease' of the brain. They point to biochemical imbalances and reduced activation of certain brain areas. I will argue that each defines an aspect of the process, but that it is neither the past experiences per se, nor the brain's chemical troubles alone that define depression. Rather, it involves *all* these, each interacting with the other, creating a downward spiral and loss of balance in the dance of *I* with its neural mediator. Central to this downward spiral is a fatigue of neural systems.

To communicate concepts, clinicians commonly use analogies. An analogy I sometimes use to explain the idea of neural fatigue is that of a depleted car battery. Clients relate well to this analogy: 'Yes, that's *exactly* how I feel,' they say, 'run down like a flat car battery'. The battery powers many aspects of the car's functions, so a depleted battery can vary in its effect, just as the effect of depression varies depending on the amount of energy the function requires and the amount of stored energy available. Like the neural system, the car battery supplies electrical energy derived from chemical processes and needs to be continuously recharged. If the energy output is greater than the input, eventually we have a problem. Once the battery is depleted (I say to my client), it takes time to recharge. The car's energy output should be minimized: it takes a long time to recharge a battery while the headlights are on! And so it is with a depleted neural system: the demands that have been implicated in the depletion should be minimized or addressed so that effective recovery may be promoted.

A neural fatigue model

My computer does not get depressed, even when filled with negative ideas. Humans do. Why? I propose that *I* interacts with neural depletion and associated hardware malfunction to produce depression symptoms, and here the computer analogy fails. The *I*–brain interaction transforms one event into another – neural fatigue transforms into a depression spiral as *I* reacts to a brain that no longer performs as it should.

Both neurons and the synapses they support require energy to function. The chemical machinery supplying energy for neurotransmitter synthesis and release eventually disintegrates, so neurons need to resupply that chemical base, which they ordinarily do without difficulty.[2] When prolonged demands are made, the system becomes fatigued so that neurons have difficulty maintaining proper synaptic function: this may result in temporary disconnections, or whole systems may slow or shut down. A minor and short-term fatigue effect might be the temporary loss of meaning when specific patterns of synaptic connections become compromised, or when the strength of information carried by electrical pulses weakens (a process called *adaptation*).[3] The result of longer-term fatigue, however, can lead to depression. This longer-term fatigue is typically the sequelae of stressful life events,[4] which is accompanied by chronic cortisol release. The physiological results of stress-related cortisol release[5] and neural depletion can be widespread and varied, affecting neurochemical production and electrical potentials, and causing dysregulation, neural atrophy, and general systems failure.

When things are not in good order – either within or without – stress occurs. Someone might experience stress in chronic unemployment, physical pain, because of rejection by close family members, relationship breakdown, repeated personal failures, or surgery leading to a chronic state of anxiety, resentment, or helplessness. Stresses relating to the environment might range from a short-term traumatic experience to chronic inability to cope with daily demands, or the need for prolonged and rapid new learning. Stresses relating to *I* might result from alienation and disconnection because the world is seen as a punishing place, or from patterns of self-blame and self-rejection. There may be ongoing withdrawal or resistance because of a decision of *I* not to 'embrace' the external world. Equally, the conflict might be of *I* with the body itself: a rejection of the very body *I* has to express itself in, leading to chronic negative emotions.

In some people, these stresses are sufficient to lead to neural fatigue and trigger a depression spiral. Increased vulnerability to stress, the compromise of neural resilience, and subsequent depression may be genetic[6] or result from early life experiences.[7] In the spiralling nature of depression, neural stresses secondary to the initial fatigue event may contribute to the depletion process. These secondary stresses may relate to guilt, poor self-esteem, or lack of confidence, to an expectation that things will go wrong, to a sense of disempowerment, or to a lack of hope concerning the future.

In trauma-related stress, for example, noradrenaline – the neurotransmitter involved in the fight-or-flight response – is activated, increasing heart rate and creating energy. During and after the stressful event, it creates general neural arousal and sensory alertness, engaging *I*. *I* scans for danger, attending to every detail, evaluating potential threat. Meanwhile, the amygdala's fear circuits work hard. Such intense neural activity quickly depletes energy sources, and the neurons begin to shut down to allow recovery. Other neural demands relate to the need to find meaningfulness in the event and ways of resolving the emotional stresses created.

But there may be no relevant memories to help establish meanings, or the available options for emotional resolution may be limited. *I* works hard to integrate the foreign information into existing mind-map patterns. This ongoing demand and preoccupation with the event leads to repeated activation of the same pathways – looping as it were – contributing to neural depletion.

This takes a toll on neural networks and pathways, in the case of trauma because of intense activation over a small period, but it may also result from constancy of activation over a longer period. Typically, we might observe chronic over-activation of the reticular formation areas of the brainstem, of the hypothalamic-pituitary-adrenal pathways, and of the hypothalamic-pituitary-thyroid pathways (Weissenburger and Rush, 1996) and their respective neural regions, resulting in release of cortisol and other neurochemicals. Fatigue featuring partial shut-down of these systems and possible dysregulation or neural atrophy may follow.

The hippocampus is implicated in this process.[8] The functions of the hippocampus, a site of new cell growth, are generally attenuated in depression. A reduction in hippocampal volume may even occur,[9] affecting memory processes and dysregulation of hippocampal–amygdaloid circuits (Cozolino, 2002).[10] Arden and Linford (2009a) point to stress-related cortisol production inhibiting the production of *brain-derived neurotropic factor* (BDNF) as the reason for such degeneration in both the hippocampus and the amygdala.[11] The functions of the hypothalamus and the prefrontal cortex are also commonly attenuated in depression, reflected in the loss of appetite and libido and in difficulties in concentration and decision making, directly affecting *I*.

Although other emotions are also involved, depression is often related to sadness. Goleman reported that brain areas involved in ordinary sadness almost completely shut down when a person becomes clinically depressed:

> Sadness and depression seem to involve the same brain region, the left prefrontal cortex, in different ways. It gets more active during ordinary sadness, but shuts down in people with clinical depression. Perhaps the left prefrontal cortex somehow burns itself out when sadness persists for several months.
>
> (Goleman, 1995: 3)

Along a similar vein, Carter observes: 'The brains of people who are depressed are generally less active than normal – there is simply less going on than there should be' (Carter, 2010: 167). This lack of activity may be due to neural atrophy as much as to synaptic inactivity. Phelps makes a strong case for the atrophy process in depression:

> We now believe that mood disorders are produced when stress and other factors shift the normal balance between cell growth and cell shrinkage . . . mood problems can make neurons shrink and even die . . . This brain shrinkage is called *atrophy*, and the chemicals that cause it are called atrophic factors.
>
> (Phelps, 2006: 130)

Such atrophy has implications for the effective functioning of neural networks and the software they support.

The energy depletion of neurons affects their synaptic activity, both in their capacity to synthesize many neurochemicals (including serotonin and dopamine) and in the progressive inactivation of transmitter receptors (presumably to allow cellular recovery). This depletion affects the transmission of neural information relying on electrical pulses drawn from the electrical potential of sodium and potassium ions. Depletion can lead to a partial shut-down[12] or compromise the brain's engagement with *I*, resulting in loss of 'will-power', passivity, and a sense of helplessness. Such progressive and self-preserving shut-down (often over a period of months) allows restoration of the affected neural areas, and eventual spontaneous remission of symptoms normally occurs. But the shut-down can be over a protracted period and lead to neural atrophy. The fatigue effect is widespread as complex mechanisms are involved. But the problematic aspect of the depression process is its capacity to cycle – to act against its own recovery because of the *I*–brain interaction, maintaining a depressed state potentially indefinitely, with learned patterns of behaviour and thinking making it increasingly resistant to treatment.

Many different areas of the brain have been implicated in depression, but not all of these at the one time in the one person.[13] It is probably the unique group of neural networks involved in the difficult experiences and extended neurotransmitter excitation or neuropeptide release that risk fatigue. While the shut-down allows recovery of depleted neurons, the associated withdrawal can contribute to the depression cycle. Neural fatigue may also affect the neural regulatory functions[14] which maintain the excitation/inhibition balance. Over time, the depression process can alter the body's internal regulatory settings defining the extent of energy production, so re-establishing homeostasis. If in response to neural depletion I slow down, my energy requirements also decrease and my energy production is correspondingly reduced, and so I stay easily fatigued. To stimulate neural energy, neurons need to be progressively restimulated as much as the system allows, just as I would need to exercise as much as my muscles allow to build muscle strength after a period of atrophy. Disrupted neural regulatory functions may contribute to the mood fluctuations often seen in depression.

In the 1960s, Birkmayer proposed that excitation and exhaustion syndromes were two poles of inadequate adaptation or dysregulation of neural activity of the brainstem reticular formation (a central regulatory system communicating both up through the limbic system and down through the vagal system) found in depression. He attributed this dysfunction to 'any stream of afferent stimuli (i.e. stress), wherever they emanate [which] can cause this breakdown of the adaptive mechanism' (Birkmayer and Pilleri, 1966: 93).[15] Furthermore, he argued for other expressions of neural dysregulation from life stresses – the *excitation syndrome*, related to bipolar disorder, and the *dissociation syndrome*. In his thesis, all are disturbances linked to brainstem reticular formation, which has a critical role in general bodily regulation, although the effects are not limited to this region.

The neural fatigue model posits that depression may begin as a helpful regulatory process: a shutting down of systems to allow recovery of a depleted neural system.[16] In this sense, depression is not so much a disease or an 'imbalance of brain chemicals'[17] as it is an initially adaptive process that becomes maladaptive. It may have a protective function where apathy acts as a shield against ongoing emotional demands, despair, and distress (as seen in contexts such as concentration camps, orphanages, and other prolonged and hopeless situations). When poorly managed, this 'normal' regulatory function may trigger a depression spiral where continuing and unavoidable demands on a non-coping system lead to counterproductive reactions in *I*, to agitation, self-destructive tendencies, neural atrophy, and even death.[18]

A waning life force

Helen finds herself with greatly reduced energy, which she needs to be motivated, energy that translates into a 'zest for life'. Her fatigue causes a drop in her frustration tolerance and her personal resources to cope with life's daily challenges. Her low frustration tolerance causes her to become easily irritated, and her poor personal resources cause her to become quickly anxious – even the smallest of expectations and demands begin to overwhelm her. But Helen's reduced energy affects not only her physical capacity to do things. It also lowers the capacity of neurons to perform the functions normally required of them, especially in the timely release of neurochemicals governing emotions, regulating various body processes, and mediating the relationship of her *I* with her body.

Her neural fatigue affects the capacity of her *I* to focus and to make decisions. It is difficult for her to manage her neurotransmitter gate-keeping work, to navigate neural pathways, and to access neural networks, including those responsible for making and storing memories. Shopping requires decision making: that becomes a chore. Talking to friends requires focus: that becomes hard work. Moreover, the neurochemical activation allowing her *I* to experience anticipation and pleasure and wellbeing is now all but gone. Even a walk along the river or watching the flowers in her garden come to bloom, activities she once enjoyed, have become things to do and perceive, no longer to enjoy. And the work her neurochemicals did at the instigation of her brainstem reticular system and limbic system to regulate her body rhythms and functions are affected – her sleeping patterns are disrupted, her appetite gone, her sexual desire absent. She may even find her menstrual cycle disrupted, or stalled altogether.

Because of this state of affairs, Helen stays in bed in the morning. She sleeps without restoration, she eats without satisfaction, she exercises without being energized – the normal restorative processes seem disabled. She no longer wants to see her friends, go to work, or make love to her husband. She begins to disconnect from the world around her and withdraws into herself, no longer making plans to do anything because she knows she has no energy to do them. And as she disconnects, her world becomes increasingly meaningless.[19] The connections required for meaningfulness become increasingly fragmented. All of which causes her *I* to lose confidence in her capacities.

What began as neural fatigue now leads to self-criticism and guilt and growing despair. Not only are Helen's neural capacities depleted, her mind map has been undergoing a 'refit' – she interprets incoming messages in the context of her depressed state. Her *I* becomes increasingly distressed about her incapacity to manage life's demands. Her neural depletion is letting her down.[20] She feels guilty that she does not want to see her friends and that she does not cope with her children. She feels guilty about her sexual disinterest in her husband, about her short temper, and about not doing things around the house. She feels frustrated that she can no longer do what once came naturally, and she becomes increasingly frightened about what is happening to her because she does not understand. How will this end? What if it never goes away? What if her husband leaves her, and her friends move on? She frets and worries, but is paralysed by inertia. She is overwhelmed with sadness: for the joy she has lost, for the life she once had, for the self that no longer does what it should.

What Helen does not realize is that her distress, worry, frustration, fears, and self-criticisms make further demands on her fatigued neural system. Although her 'battery' is depleted and her neural system is shutting down to allow recharging of the system, she has 'left the headlights' on, and her recovery is going nowhere fast. She has entered into a depression cycle, where her *I* is reacting to her neural depletion, making more demands instead of cooperating with the recovery process. If she does not get out of the cycle, the increasing sense of trappedness and general despair could lead her *I* to make a radical decision: to take her own life, releasing her from her situation. She has nothing to look forward to, she feels she is a burden to herself and others, and life has lost meaning. Furthermore, her low activity levels signal a reduction in the energy required to function each day, so her brain restricts neural energy production.

Depression might begin with neural fatigue and its initial processes may be self-regulatory and self-protective, but it then enters a self-perpetuating cycle that maintains debilitating fatigue. In this cycle, Helen's *I* becomes increasingly helpless to change its neural incapacity and to interact effectively with her external world, to the point that her *I* feels trapped in a hopeless situation. Her *I* loses hope.[21] She may consider running away or escaping into sleep. But increasingly, as hopelessness feeds agitation, thoughts and images intrude that finishing life is the only way to escape. Where do these come from? Are they, like Charlie's perplexing thought, ones of which Helen's *I* takes no ownership at first? Indeed, her *I* may be disturbed that they have arisen. Perhaps they come as a result of the inherent neural drive to seek solutions to the pressing problem of not coping, a solution her brain presents to *I*? Perhaps they find origin in memories of others who have done similarly. Perhaps they are the natural outcome and extension of despising herself for being so ineffectual; or of guilt or anger at herself for being in such a mess. But the solution creates immediate conflict for Helen's *I*: while tempted by the possibility of release from torment, she is appalled at the finality of the solution and its likely impact on those around her. So it takes time to process the implications and justify to herself the validity of this option.

Helen's *I* enters a period of intense struggle with thoughts that at the same time promise release and signal annihilation. Should her *I* be strong, she may be better able to resist the suicidal impulse, but should her *I* be weak, her resistance fades. While her distress continues, the tempting thoughts and images keep intruding, creating confusion, conflict, and further distress, until she finds the remnants of neural energy to force a decision, taking a side in the internal debate. The decision is to embrace the intruding thoughts, to validate the suicidal thoughts as representing a viable and preferred solution. She rationalizes the new position: 'No-one will miss me anyway'; 'I'm a burden on my family and society'; 'I have no future, and have nothing to offer anyone.' And as is the case when *I* makes *any* clear decision, resolution is reached, a peace established, a plan formed that temporarily generates energy that will be seen by those around Helen as a sign of progress: she seems at peace now, happier than before, more focused and energized. The guard of those around is dropped, and the tragic outcome is inevitable.

Once Helen has adopted the position that suicide is a valid solution, this position remains until the solution has been activated, or until her *I* moves to a new position in relation to suicide. And so the idea of suicide, even though it may begin with thoughts alien to *I*, becomes a conscious act of *I* embracing the thought presented to it. It becomes a moral act for which *I* is responsible, even though it finds its origin in an ongoing state of subjectively unbearable despair or alienation.

Arresting a downward spiral

Helen's recovery will depend on several issues. What stresses brought about her neural fatigue? These need to be addressed. The downward spiral between Helen's increasingly distressed *I* and her fatigued and unresponsive neural system needs to be arrested. The possibility that her neural shut-down provided a protective function needs to be considered – she may need alternative forms of protection from the stresses giving rise to her neural shut-down. She needs to be given an energizing lifeline of hope, to commit to realistic plans which help to fire neural drives, and to experience the small successes that build strength in *I* once again. Her *I* needs to be released from unrealistic self-induced demands. Finally, the optimal conditions for neural recovery need to be ensured: conditions promoting the restoration of neural energy levels such as restorative rest, exercise, right diet, and planned rewarding activities.

Practitioners of CBT argue that the negative emotions characterizing depression, such as anger, guilt, and sadness, find their basis in negative thought patterns that need to be changed. Therapists such as Burns (1980) focus on targeted thoughts or 'internal verbalizations'. The questions a cognitive therapist might thus ask of Helen include: 'What dysfunctional thoughts and beliefs are associated with her problems; what reactions (emotional, physiological, and behavioural) are associated with her thinking?', and: 'What are her underlying beliefs (including her attitudes, expectations, and rules) and thoughts?' (Beck, 1995). Other CBT practitioners might include images mediating such beliefs as focus for intervention. Thoughts, schemas, and images, whatever their origin, become the target for change in the amelioration of depression. Nevertheless, Clark and Steer note 'the cognitive model does not postulate a sequential unidirectional relationship in which cognition always precedes emotion, but assumes that cognition, emotion, and behaviour are reciprocally determining and interactive constructs' (1996: 75). This point is well taken.

While CBT is an important component of the intervention process,[22] it does not address the complexities of the mind map or the *I*–brain dilemma. Nor does it make distinction between thoughts generated by *I* and those generated by the brain in spite of *I*. Beck recognized aspects of this dilemma:

> a number of psychological problems are not adequately addressed by the model of individual schemas . . . Among those problems are the following: the multiplicity of related symptoms encompassing the cognitive, affective, motivational, and behavioural domains in a psychopathological condition; . . . and the relationship among conscious and unconscious processing of information.
>
> (Beck, 1996: 1)

Just because Helen's brain can generate thoughts and images to match her negative feelings, it does not mean they created her mood, although they have the capacity to do so. Even if we could successfully change Helen's thoughts and images, whatever their origin, this may not change her underlying mood, the reasons for her mood, or the learned behaviours associated with that mood.

Helen's thought habits may elicit negative emotions on a chronic basis, leading to neural exhaustion. But equally, intense emotional experiences, trauma, and chronic exposure to other people's intense emotions can also lead to neural exhaustion. And although both physical and mental exhaustion (here I mean, because of much thinking and decision making) may lead to short-term depressive symptoms, generally depression is linked to stresses with an emotional origin. We have seen that a dimension of depression concerns how Helen's *I* responds to the fatigue – a response creating further stress and releasing cortisol in its own right. As Helen's *I* becomes distressed – by her state of exhaustion, about the guilt of disappointing others and herself, about failure, about possible financial implications, about relational loss, and so on – a cascading of problems results. These secondary reactions place further demands on her exhausted system. Attempting to change the pattern of her thoughts may be thus more difficult than it appears, given the complexities involved in the depressive process and the inherent stability of Helen's mind map.

It is sometimes said that CBT is employed to address the negative thoughts giving rise to negative emotions, while medication addresses the mood which gives rise to the negative thoughts. But things are not so simple, and I will later make some further observations regarding medication. For now, I note that the capacity of antidepressant medication to reduce the intensity of emotional experience can provide a helpful role in Helen's recovery, although there is little evidence that psychotropic medication is curative in the sense that they have a regenerative function in relation to neural depletion.[23] Whatever interventions are employed, their potential effectiveness largely depends on when the clinician enters Helen's depression cycle in order to disrupt it – the longer the cycle has been established, the more difficult it becomes, given the multiple factors that sustain it and the growing distortions her mind map suffers.

And so the clinician's challenge becomes a multiple one, especially when Helen comes to the point of considering suicide. On the one hand, the clinician seeks, through practical interventions, to contribute to the amelioration of the distress, the helplessness, and the existential hopelessness and meaninglessness suffered by Helen's *I*, which birthed her suicidal ideation. On the other hand, he may need to dialogue with Helen's *I* about a decision she grapples with – whether to end it all. Or the considerably greater challenge – the clinician may need to enter into dialogue with Helen to convince her to change her position *once the decision to end her life has been made*.

If Helen has decided to take her own life, the immediate expression of this decision may be the experience of some relief from inner conflict, with resulting energy to focus and to put her life in order, making specific plans for her anticipated suicide. She finally feels better, more in control. This convinces her that her decision is correct, making the clinician's job more difficult. Her decision to take her own life becomes an established position around which many subsequent decisions are made. Although it is only an 'idea' and not yet an event, the idea is as powerful as the event and gives rise to the event. And it is this idea that needs to be challenged. Helen's *I* needs to clearly and actively *change her position* for the threat to be lifted. Here Helen's family and friends and her clinician sweat it out as they have no control over the decision she ultimately makes.

The case of bipolar disorder

Unlike Helen, Stephen had plenty of energy, despite having hardly any sleep. If he thought something should happen, he had no problem confronting the issue – in fact, it just kept going around in his head, he could not let it go. He could not rest until he had done it. Instead of feeling bad, Stephen felt good, despite the relationship and financial shipwrecks he left behind. Instead of feeling helpless, he felt in control of everything and enthusiastic to the point of aggressiveness, his self-esteem positive to the point of grandiosity. He was creative, clever, and quick. The pain, fear, anger, and confusion of his adolescent past and the memories of his violent father appeared to have left no mark in his life. He remained positive about the demands and criticisms of those around him. In the face of stress, he remained optimistic, his mood upbeat, and his humour contagious. The more he committed himself to something, the more capable he felt. But increasingly, his actions became irrational, his judgement impaired, his actions spiralling out of control. His successes spurred him on: the more he did, the more he thought he could do.

If Stephen's neurons were fatigued, he felt anything *but* fatigued, until finally the crash came. He became increasingly agitated, his frustration tolerance increasingly poor, and his concentration and memory worsened. When the transition to exhaustion came, it was rapid, and his whole world collapsed around him. Was he exhausted because of his manic period, or was his mania a different expression of neural exhaustion, wherein his neurons had become dysregulated in favour of disinhibition?

The *Diagnostic and Statistical Manual of Mental Disorders* lists many 'types' of mood disorder. These categories are under constant review and source of ongoing argument as clinicians seek to make diagnoses where symptoms might vary from formalized categories. The many problems such categorization has created are leading to a new conceptualization of disorders: the idea of 'continua' or 'spectrums'. Such conceptualization allows for the many shades of difference that are seen clinically, although questions about the appropriate labelling of such continua and where to place individual conditions on each continua still create challenges.

And so, for example, different bipolar conditions might be identified on a continuum, with labels such as Type I, Type II, soft bipolar, and so on. However helpful such continua may be, finding meaning in different symptom patterns of mood disorder may be misleading: roses come in many shapes and colours, but all are roses. How do we place these on a meaningful continuum? Likewise, the dysregulation resulting from a fatigued neural system may have different expressions which we might observe in different symptom patterns, yet these patterns may ultimately speak of similar origins – a neural system under stress.

Siegel (2009) suggests bipolar disorder is a problem with the coordination and balance of the brain's mood-regulating circuits. But why should this happen? It is a mood disorder defined by a symptom constellation that, on the face of it, differs radically from what we might expect to find in depression. In Birkmayer's model of a stressed neural network, 'excitation syndrome'[24] is seen as the opposite pole to 'exhaustion syndrome'. He sees both as inadequate adaptation or dysfunction of a brainstem reticular formation under stress. The exhaustion syndrome has self-protective features, while the excitation syndrome finds the brain's self-protective impulse attenuated. This provides more empowering features for *I* and an inclination towards more rapid connection and intimacy with others, yet the associated high-risk behaviours and poor interpersonal boundaries leave *I* vulnerable and exposed to suffering.

Birkmayer gives this account of the 'excitation syndrome': the patient's

> autonomic and affective state is highly tense and is rendered more so by each new stimulus. He thus can find no rest. The persistency of the abnormal behaviour is an indication that the compensatory mechanism of the reticular formation is not able to provide a smooth, silent balance. The threshold of reticular stimulation is lowered . . . with the result that all stimuli, under normal circumstances subliminal, elicit an excessive reaction and via reticular connections a permanent arousal in related regions.
>
> (Birkmayer and Pilleri, 1966: 92)

Here the fatigued neural system, instead of shutting down, displays its loss of regulatory capacity and fatigue by no longer being able to *inhibit* responses, which can require more energy than the *activation* of a response. This pattern is typically seen in people who have a longer history of neural stress, often finding its origin in adolescent years or before.

This suggests a pattern of neural failure and regulatory dysfunction that is more severe than is typically the case in depression, a pattern that appears to go beyond any protective function.[25] It also suggests that the developmental tasks of adolescence relating to the individuation process may have been affected and the relevant neural templates and corresponding mind map has been compromised, contributing to poor interpersonal boundaries and compromised judgement, leaving *I* vulnerable. Yet the other pole of dysfunction – 'exhaustion syndrome' – is normally also observed in those suffering 'excitation syndrome', as they move from one pole to another, hence the label 'bipolar disorder'.

While Stephen experiences the 'excitation syndrome' commonly known as 'mania', he is generally happier about his state of affairs than when in the 'exhaustion' phase. Yet the cyclical nature that draws his *I* into a dance in which it loses some authority over his brain is not unlike that seen in the 'exhaustion' phase – in depression. Although the brainstem reticular formation appears to be the powerhouse that energizes and regulates the neural system activating Stephen's mind and body, it is nevertheless normally moderated and managed by his *I* through his 'higher' prefrontal circuits. The reticular formation houses as it were the accelerator pedal that brings about action where emotions are energized, muscles tensed, and heart rhythm accelerated. But when the accelerator pedal gets 'stuck', the drive for action can outstrip the capacity for his *I* to modulate the activity and to make good judgement, so that it may lose control of the process.

Yet Stephen's *I* may allow its momentum, *invite* it even, because of its enjoyable and reinforcing aspects. His *I* may be unwittingly drawn into a cycle that allows increasing neural dysregulation, maintaining the excitation state of an already fatigued system. This further lowers his frustration tolerance and concentration ability and increases his agitation. It is an arousal that loops back onto itself, prompting physical activity, fast-flowing thoughts, and the search for stimulation, all of which further arouses his body, while his *I* increasingly loses control and his judgement is lost.

We observe this process not only in those with bipolar disorder, but also as a feature after trauma experience; I suspect similar neural mechanisms. Thus a trauma does not immediately lead to classic depression symptoms – these typically come later. Rather, excitation symptoms are seen first. We see this with Janet, who, after the rape, went through a period of high ANS arousal that can be described as a manic state over many months before 'crashing' into depression. An important difference between Janet's experience and Stephen's bipolar is that, with Janet, the initiating event, the trauma, was clearly delineated and the specific associations between aspects of the traumatic event and her subsequent avoidance and anxiety reactions could be readily traced.

Chapter 17

Battle for the mind

Psychosis and *I*

While Charlie battled unwanted thoughts, he still experienced thoughts as thoughts. David, on the other hand, reported:

> I heard voices in the night speaking to me. It was hard to make out what they were saying, but they were definitely voices, not thoughts. I had a strong sense the voices were accusing me: I think they were evil spirits.

David was diagnosed with schizophrenia. What he heard in his head that night were not thoughts, but 'voices'. Voices of which he took no ownership, ones that did not appear to find origin in his *I*, yet were somehow expressed in his neural system so he had conscious awareness of them. The content was not always discernible, but he attributed malice to them. He was the passive and unwilling recipient of the experience, one he could not escape because the voices did not respond to his protestations, and, being in his own head, there was nowhere for David to escape. How was this possible? Was there another *I* involved, or was David's neural system playing tricks on him? In session, David would experience sudden breaks in his stream of thought, losing his way in conversation, and asking me to repeat what had just been said. Sometimes his thinking would fragment altogether, so that he would jump from one idea to an unrelated one. He was often lost in daydreams, disconnected from the world of others. It was a world generally without pleasure: a demanding, alienating world that fuelled guilt and loneliness and hopelessness. A world in which his *I* battled to gain ascendency.

   In this chapter, I will argue that psychotic disorders, like mood disorders, are better understood as dynamic processes with various manifestations that fluctuate in the course of neural breakdown, rather than a stable 'condition' that can be clearly categorized. I will review neural correlates of schizophrenia, explore the developmental aspect, and consider the role of a weakened *I*.

A struggle with schizophrenia

David, diagnosed variously with OCD, bipolar affective disorder, schizo-affective disorder, and schizophrenia (depending on what he told his psychiatrist), suffered psychotic episodes. It had been a problem since his late teens. He was lonely and unhappy, yet he tended to stay alone to minimize stress. He sometimes felt a psychotic episode emerging and would become frightened: he no longer felt 'normal' in his body, but somehow separated. Although he might experience panic at the onset of an episode, he became exhausted fighting the invisible threat, so 'I eventually give into it'. He would 'relax into' the psychosis, and begin to enjoy a sense of grandiosity, becoming courageous, and believe in 'anything', losing his critical faculty.

The voices he heard were variously attributed to 'evil spirits', 'angels', and 'God' – 'up there', he said, his eyes rolling upwards. The 'voices' were continually present, 'disturbances' or 'impressions' in his head – indistinct auditory signals – that his brain sought to interpret. Sometimes he would describe these voices as accusatory, so that he needed to confess sins – on a better day, he would say the voices were 'telling lies', although it was difficult not to believe them. But there were also times when he welcomed the voices – a source of companionship, the encouraging and intimate presence of God.

Where did the voices come from? Was their origin his brain, producing thoughts alien yet sometimes comforting to his *I*, formulated from his own history and circumstances? The voices (or were they thoughts?) appeared to have a compelling quality to them and were difficult to resist, but they were clearly not *I*: 'The scariest thing is the voices taking over and controlling my behaviour and thoughts. I live in constant fear of doing something I don't want to do.'

There was no sense of ownership of these voices and the impulses they motivated. Was their origin another entity within him, its presence made possible by frequent 'acceptance' of their entry by his *I*, to which he subsequently attributed various identities in seeking to create meaningfulness of the experience? Was it a presence that required a priest rather than a clinician? It seemed that David was trapped in narrow interpretive regimes, in limited associative networks with limited flexibility to cope with external demands: 'I can concentrate well within certain limits [specific aspects of his own history and interests] – but I can't break free from this. My thoughts just go round and round.' His capacity to manage his neural resources and to maintain focus had been compromised – it was difficult to concentrate even for a few minutes at a time. He was unable to break free, to establish broader patterns of thinking and awareness, as though his *I* did not have the strength to do so.

David struggled not only with voices, but with difficulty making plans and decisions, with following through on decisions, with doing and thinking new things, with a loss of pleasure in small things, with a realization he was not in control of his life, with periods of frustration and agitation about his circumstances, and with suicidal despair. He desperately took hold of any sign of hope, but then came crashing down again when the voices took ascendancy again. And so he would give in, allowing himself to slip into daydreams or escaping into sleep.

Others share David's story, with the first signs of trouble typically emerging around adolescence. From the inception, there may be an awareness there is something wrong, something that cannot really be identified, something *I* is losing control over: 'Help me, mom, something is wrong in my head,' said one teenager; and another wrote: 'I don't know what's the matter. Things are not going well. I think there's something wrong with my head' (Torrey, 1988: 65). Such awareness heralds the dawn of hell on earth for some, where the life they had hoped to live is lost to a daily struggle to maintain control of their lives, to make sense of themselves and the world so that they might participate in the kind of life those around them understand and control so easily. Their helplessness and fear leads to despair, so that they withdraw, running from stress and responsibility, looking for elements in life they might predict and control.

What is happening for these people? How are we to understand David's distorted world? What might be happening in his brain, and how does his *I* manage its dysfunctions?

Limbic failure

Because of the dynamic nature of the brain, any theory of psychopathology should be dynamic at its heart. The finding of an excess or depletion of one or other brain chemical or the identification of activation or inhibition of one or other neural pathway or neural region will never suffice as explanation, although such findings need to be accounted for in a dynamic theory. The search for the neural key to schizophrenia or to psychosis in general has borne limited fruit to this point, although some neural correlates have been identified. This, of course, is bad news for the intervention process. Mostly, current intervention is about using psychotropic medication to ameliorate the most disturbing of the symptoms – of agitation and aggressive impulses. Some relief from hallucinations and delusions may also be provided, although the ameliorative mechanisms are unclear.

In his extensive review of neural correlates to schizophrenia, Torrey warned that looking for specific brain involvement is problematic because 'the brain is a functionally interdependent and intricate system, and abnormality within it can throw the whole system off: like an electrical system with a short circuit – it can occur anywhere, but the result is the same' (Torrey, 1988: 138). He lists as key suspect in schizophrenia a failure in some aspect of the limbic system, especially to the left of the brain, the region generally associated with language and conceptual thought.

The limbic system serves a central integrative function between the regulatory and interpretive activity of the frontal cortex, and the sensory and emotional signals coming up through the amygdala and thalamus: it is a system by which 'raw experience is harmonized into reality and coherent activity is organized' (Torrey 1988: 138). It connects the amygdala, hippocampus, hypothalamus, nucleus accumbens, ventral septum, mammillary bodies, stria terminalis, and olfactory area: in fact, it has direct connection to *all key areas of the brain*, including the upper brainstem and cerebellum. Essentially, it maintains the mind map. Abnormalities in the limbic system (for whatever reason, including epilepsy, brain damage, and brain disease) lead to distortions of perception, illusions and hallucinations, feelings of depersonalization, paranoia, and catatonic-like behaviour. At which point we have covered pretty much the range of schizophrenic symptoms. Nevertheless, any dysfunction or atrophy of a specific neural region contributing to the limbic system can disturb the whole system, so that the neurological origin of a psychotic experience could vary from one person to the next.

Yet what might have happened to David's limbic system for schizophrenia symptoms to emerge? It appears failures in the integrative functions of the high-level software are occurring – internal mental events seem to be confused with incoming sensory stimuli, erroneous associations are leading *I* to make idiosyncratic interpretations and meanings of events, and general fragmentation and distortion of higher-level abstract ideas are being encountered. Mind-map confusion is occurring. The issue, though, is not so much that limbic pathways are disrupted, but *which ones experience failure*, and *why these*?

How could such pathway failure cause David to become deluded? And why did he hallucinate, 'seeing' or 'hearing' things, as though parts of his brain were under-stimulated or highly expectant, the condition under which such experiences might occur naturally? Is his limbic system being cut off from some sources of information that it should create its own data, or does *I* oblige with introjected meanings? Is this what happens with chemically induced hallucinations – does the toxic nature of the chemicals interfere with natural communication pathways, so that the brain (or *I*) constructs a reality from fragments of information, as it might in dreams, or in circumstances of sensory deprivation? Is this also the reason for the psychosis sometimes induced in people in meditation retreats (Kuijpers *et al.*, 2007)? It is as if the psychotic state represents a failure or interference of communication systems so that the interactive brain seeks out information and meanings to satisfy *I*, who prompts the brain to supply the information (or perhaps supplies it itself), however inadequate it be? Certainly, interruptions have been identified in informational flow between the frontal and temporal cortex regions, and the frontal and hippocampal regions in the left hemisphere, pointing to disconnections between them.

There is a homeostatic principle whereby biological systems attempt to maintain internal stability in the face of external environmental changes so that the internal environment of any free-living organism is maintained constant, within limits. This is generally achieved through regulatory systems, incorporating on–off switches and feedback mechanisms – hormones play a role. A similar principle may operate at a higher limbic level to provide a stable environment for *I*. That is, *I* demands of the limbic system effective and reliable orienting data to maintain functional meaningfulness in relation to these inputs: a properly integrated mind map. Multiple sources of data are constantly processed and integrated, not all of which pass through awareness – when one information source is attenuated, pressure is placed on the remaining sources to compensate, ensuring an ongoing stable environment for *I*. The limbic system is primed to integrate information so the mind map remains up-to-date and meaningful.

Normally, there is a balance between external sensory inputs, memory inputs, and creative internal inputs that 'fill in the blanks' so that a 'best fit' in relation to meaningfulness of the data as a whole is provided – an integrated mind map. Where there is attenuation of one input source (such as external sensory inputs), *I* searches for compensatory data from other inputs (such as memory) to build a coherent picture. A dearth of data from memory or creative internal inputs creates greater demand for external sensory inputs: there is an ultimate homeostasis or balance in the system.[1] If the limbic system fails to adequately integrate and process external sensory information at the abstract level of meaning attribution, it may draw from other sources of information to provide 'stable' and 'meaningful' orientation for *I*, or *I* may simply impute meanings. David might 'see' things or 'hear' things that do not find their origin in external sensory inputs, but from other inputs. Meanings attributed to the events in David's awareness begin to reflect an idiosyncratic internal world, rather than the shared external world.

Neurological research has many potential biochemical targets, and certainly this is true with psychosis and schizophrenia. However, interpreting these findings outside a comprehensive dynamic model is unlikely to be productive. I suspect research findings represent various inter-related aspects of the limbic systems' software failure. One finding in those suffering schizophrenia is excessive dopamine levels (activated in parts of the limbic system).[2] It may be that, in their attempt to address critical neural pathway failures, neurons respond by releasing dopamine to enhance neural connectivity and creation of meanings. However, instead of activating desired pathways with their associated meanings, bogus pathways with distorted meanings may be activated: a pattern of hallucinations and delusions. Nevertheless, whether dopaminergic rivers are in flood or drought, other neurotransmitters will also be affected. And so noradrenaline changes have also been found, and there is possible GABA involvement in the prefrontal cortex and hippocampus (Torrey, 1988). Excess dopamine may also interact with neuropeptide activity, affecting the experience of pleasure.

In other research reported by Torrey, abnormalities of electrical potentials have been found in the frontal cortex and left hemisphere in schizophrenia sufferers (but also, to a lesser extent, in those suffering mania and depression) pointing to cellular dysfunction (Torrey, 1988). Structural changes have been found (such as the widening of the corpus callosum, presumably to allow greater informational traffic between left and right hemispheres; and abnormalities in the upper brainstem), as well as cerebral atrophy (also found in bipolar psychosis and 'other brain disease'), mostly in the prefrontal cortex. In other research, 'smaller brains', especially smaller frontal cortices, and shrinkage of the limbic medial temporal cortex structures (such as the hippocampal formation, amygdala, and parahippocampal gyrus) have been reported. These imply that limbic system failures correspond to physical degeneration of neural hardware supporting the system. Yet these features also occur in depression, which may well be secondary to schizophrenia.

Just as the symptom clusters we call depression and anxiety may result from different life events in different people yet represent similar neural processes, so it is feasible for schizophrenia (and psychosis in general) to result from different life events but have in common failures in the higher-order integrative functions of the limbic system. This being so, the relatively high incidence of people suffering schizophrenia symptoms (up to one per cent of the general population) suggests that the integrating limbic system is not particularly robust. Aspects of the system can break down as a result of both organic and functional events. Adolescence turns out to be a particularly vulnerable time.

The developmental factor

Parents can attest to the turmoil of adolescence as the teenager seeks individuation. A corresponding radical brain reorganization takes place around this time, so that the adolescent is confronted by both internal and external changes. Changes occur in relation to self-awareness, new freedoms and responsibilities in relationships, and in the loss of social protective frameworks and structures. For many, the changes can be overwhelming. They may fear the emerging realities and new responsibilities, not coping because of inadequate mind-map orientation, and making poor decisions with life-long consequences. They may struggle to make sense of new things, and lack the experience necessary to guide decisionmaking.

This can lead to escape into excessive daydreaming, introspection, and other altered states of consciousness, aided in some by drugs or alcohol to avoid or find protection from the overwhelming feelings. Frequent escape of this kind can limit opportunities for the adolescent brain to reformulate its mind map around new learning, associations, and growing familiarities. It is a tenuous time where *I* may go through a crisis of position in relation to others and at times lack the neural resources needed to manage the tasks it faces.

A major developmental task during David's adolescence was the establishment of self in the context of a whole new set of decisions, meanings, and relationships. But this process became overwhelming and stressful for David's *I*. As it struggled to reorder and realign neural networks, especially in the prefrontal cortex – key to focus and decision making – it escaped into selective dissociation. It became difficult to establish where his *I* fit into the wider world, one no longer defined by parental parameters. The range of possibilities was too great, the decisions were too onerous because the outcomes were difficult to predict, and there was too much new information to process. And so the process faltered. David's *I* withdrew, putting off decisions and losing its sense of position relative to the growing awareness of the world. David's *I* dissociated from aspects of his external world, so that the growing and complex structures of internal meaning became compromised.

David's brain continued its search for meaning. Only the full range of material was no longer available. The selective dissociation resulted in only partial information being available to his emergent self, and invalid associations were made as his brain searched for information that dissociative processes denied him. These invalid associations resulted in distorted and inaccurate meanings, contributing to general disorientation and fragmentation of his internal picture of the world and an inadequate sense of self relating to that world. There was a crisis of meaning – should his brain retain its own meaning structures, distorting the incoming information to fit these structures; or should it review its own structures to better fit the sensory signals that mediated the external world? To do the latter would require reversal of the dissociative procedures it embraced to minimize stress, general discomfort, and emotional pain. To do the former would be to enter a psychotic state. And so the vulnerability to emerging schizophrenia increased.

The idea of schizophrenia having a developmental aspect finds support in the timing and manner of its inception, and in the interactive nature of the symptoms that emerge over a period of months or even years, some symptoms being reactive to others. In this regard, a consideration of prodromal features (precursors) in schizophrenia is instructive (Yung and McGorry, 1996).

Prodromal symptoms such as preoccupation, daydreaming, and social withdrawal relate to the tendency to withdraw from external demands. Other symptoms relate to tasks involving the limbic system and associated neural regions: disturbance of attention and inability to concentrate; thought blocking; reduced abstraction; obsessive compulsive and dissociative tendencies; increased interpersonal sensitivity; change in sense of self, others, or the world; change in motility; speech and perceptual abnormalities; and increasing suspiciousness. Then there are symptoms that appear to be neural reactions or reactions of *I* to limbic failure: anxiety; restlessness; anger and irritability; deterioration in performance at school or work; aggressive and disruptive behaviour; and symptoms of depression – anhedonia, guilt feelings, suicidal ideation, mood swings, apathy and loss of drive, boredom and loss of interest, fatigue and loss of energy, somatic complaints, poor appetite, and sleep disturbance.

The early symptoms pointing to limbic failure with its associated emerging mind-map confusion relate ultimately to attentional problems. This reflects difficulties in the proper management of the multiple streams of incoming information – a task shared by *I* and its neural host. This view is also taken by Chapman:

> The chief abnormality in attention was the inability to filter out irrelevant stimuli, a disturbance of the ability to selectively attend to information. The patient is distracted by multiple events and feels overwhelmed, resulting in information overload and finally a total disruption in attention.
>
> (Chapman, 1966, in Yung and McGorry, 1996: 361)

And also:

> The patient is aware of intermittent 'blank spells' or 'trances', which also has been described by other investigators [that is, sudden disruptions in attention, thought, perception, memory, speech, and motility]. These blocking phenomena may be caused by defects in selective attention. As the patient becomes more and more distracted by multiple sensory experiences, he would then switch suddenly to being unable to attend at all. With increasing volumes of information that he is unable to process, the patient finally reaches a point where his consciousness is disturbed.
>
> (Chapman, 1966, in Yung and McGorry, 1996: 361)

But for the adolescent, the overwhelming volume of information is not only of 'multiple sensory experience'; it is also information relating to emerging new life realities. Could it be that schizophrenia represents the failure of neural pathways relating to the prefrontal cortex focusing, mediating, integrating, and making sense of the necessary information, so that it creates its *own counterfeit reality*? Perhaps it is during this time of adolescent reorganization that the compromise of some neural pathways leads to deprivation of important orienting information, putting pressure on other pathways. Dopamine changes may relate to the attenuation of limbic system pathways (due to informational overload), resulting in stimulus deprivation in pathways expectant of stimulation necessary for their ongoing function. When none is forthcoming, the pathways create their own stimulation (or *I* initiates this) from alternative data sources.

For some, there may be a vulnerability to limbic breakdown or poor prefrontal cortex integration because of genetic factors or earlier developmental events, such as prenatal conditions or birth complications, that create subtle neurological weaknesses not revealed until later.[3] For others, a mix of other internal and external stresses may contribute, such as unsatisfactory home and family relationships which are hostile and critical or, conversely, which are possessive or invasive; or families with disordered communication patterns, creating confused meanings.

I am suggesting that *informational deprivation and attentional disruption as a result of limbic failure* may account for psychosis in general. I am further suggesting that *neural reorganization during adolescence and information overload resulting in selective pathway shut-downs* contribute to that limbic failure in schizophrenia. The capacity for attention and decision making is invested in prefrontal cortex software, which undergoes overhaul in adolescence. This software plays a central role in the governance of overall neural functioning through the limbic system and is a primary avenue through which *I* is enabled to find expression. Failure in attentional software results not only in difficulties with focus, but also in problems inhibiting unwanted competing signals (perhaps contributing to the 'background noise' experienced as indeterminate voices and unusual visual sensations).

I falters

We have considered that David's schizophrenia may relate to limbic system software failures resulting from vulnerabilities and stresses during the neural changes of adolescence. But the psychosis experience fluctuates, suggesting neural connections and disconnections are a fluid affair. This fluctuation may reflect a dance between *I* and a neural system struggling to maintain a functional mind map.

What role might *I* play in schizophrenia? David's *I* encountered failures in making sense of things and it began to experience disorientation. There were lapses in his ability to concentrate and express himself. He became frustrated, confused, and afraid. Did his brain create these emotion signals as a result of internal communication breakdowns, or was his *I* reacting to poor matches between incoming signals and his mind map? Further, given that meanings are a function of *I* rather than brain, can it be that *I* is not only the *recipient* of distorted meanings, but also becomes the *source* of confused meanings? Importantly, was there any pre-existing 'weakness' in David's *I* contributing to his schizophrenia?

In adolescence, the relationship of *I* with the brain approaches maturity, changing position from dependency on others to a separateness preparing it for a healthy and mature *I*–thou relationship. Its network of meanings change, and it develops confidence in its neural capacities, allowing an emerging strength in *I* to manage demands and enter conflicts with confidence. But what if *I* did not find such strength or if meanings associated with *I* were dysfunctional? What if *I* had become self-critical and self-condemning, even alienated from its own mind map – perhaps reinforced by exposure to criticism, ridicule, or indifference by others?

Instead of 'flowing with the self' and taking pleasure in being *I*, *I* can become alienated from its sense of self, losing confidence to express itself robustly through the body, leading to passivity and diminished efficacy. Escape into fantasy and daydreaming becomes a way of coping, and a habit of dissociation can develop where *I* becomes increasingly tenuous in its expression in a hostile or confusing world. What happens to a weakened *I*'s management of incoming signals? Does a dissociation habit weaken neural traces, compromising the capacity to accurately create meaning from incoming signals? Or do confused meanings result in poorly laid neural networks?

It may be that dissociation habits contribute to conditions for psychosis: the ultimate expression of retreat from a reality that *I* could not manage, giving rise to a sense of the ineffectualness, worthlessness, and blameworthiness of *I*. Dissociation from incoming signals from the 'real world' might see these replaced with interpretations confirming the blameworthiness of *I*, or a reaction against these notions may result in grandiose delusions. New realities are created around fear and self-condemnation. Could a weak and ineffectual *I* predispose to paranoia where neural attributions match feelings of guilt and inadequacy? Can *I* now only escape the neural entrapment of a fantasy world of misattributions and pathway distortions with medication that disables aspects of neural functioning, taking pressure off *I*? Yet such intervention invariably also disables functional pathways.

It is possible that a weakened *I* failed to weave together major software systems contained in the limbic system during the critical period. Equally possible is the reverse: connection failures for organic reasons might weaken the capacity of *I* to find strong expression through integrated neural networks. But most likely, the process is bidirectional. Partial mind-map fragmentation creates dysfunctional neural connections and bogus meanings that contribute to disorientation and distress for *I* as it becomes aware of its poor control and limited authority of its neural host. Ego-boundaries become blurred, creating fear and insecurity. This feeds social withdrawal and isolation, further reducing normal inputs dissonant with the fragmenting mind map, reducing the stress associated with such dissonance, but disallowing corrective processes. A psychosis spiral is established.

Whatever role a weak *I* might play in limbic failure, it is likely that the partially disabled limbic system contributes to partial disablement of *I*. The mind map becomes a source of *disorientation* rather than orientation, and *I* begins to react with alarm. If the breakdown is sufficiently severe, we might expect a traumatic stress reaction leading to withdrawal or agitation, avoidance behaviours, or even regression (such regression presumably making less demand on higher-order limbic software). *I* becomes distressed because the neural information on which it relies to apprehend meanings is proving unreliable and inaccurate, and it has no way of correcting the inaccuracy. The distress of *I* is reflected in the neural system, which in turn expresses that distress in neurochemical and bodily responses. There is an interactive dynamic in the failure of the neural system to communicate accurate information to *I* and in the consequent distress of *I* finding expression in the body. The scene is set for emerging depression, so we can anticipate a complexity in symptoms that muddies the waters of diagnosis and categorization.

Not only is the neural system compromised in psychosis, but so, it appears, is *I*. Frankl observes that a common characteristic in schizophrenia is a weak sense of self – of *I*.[4] We have already considered the question: how can *I* be 'weak'? Yet it seems *I* can be weak in the sense it is ineffectual in decision making and in forming good judgement, in maintaining focus, and in following through on plans. It becomes ineffectual to the point it sees itself as being *acted upon*, rather than having the capacity to initiate and maintain action through its brain and body. This passivity and the alienation of *I* from its mediating mind map and supporting neural networks fluctuates, sometimes with jarring abruptness.

When David listens or talks to me, his concentration stream is regularly cut through so that he loses the thread: 'What was I saying?', or: 'Sorry, can you repeat the last bit again?' It is as though his *I* loses momentary contact with his brain – a neural disengagement. This is not a distraction through an *external* source, but a momentary *internal* disconnection. His *I* fights to stay engaged with his brain. When he makes a decision to do something, momentary disconnections disturb the enactment of the decision, so that automatic responses take over. The interruption in engagement of *I* with neural software has diverse outcomes: consciousness and attention is disrupted, as is accurate interpretation of incoming signals, and there is greatly reduced empowerment to enact the decisions of *I* – of 'free will'. This disruption compromises capacity for responsibility – the capacity to act on what *I* decides and wants. Judgement is also disrupted – *I* does not get the clear (properly interpreted) and complete information that it needs to effectively 'weigh' matters. *I* is disabled and becomes passive, and its passivity contributes to disconnection.

Passing acquaintance with psychosis

There is sufficient variation in schizophrenia symptoms that schizophrenia, too, will no doubt soon be awarded spectrum status. But more confusing is the overlap in the symptoms of many conditions given separate category status in the *Diagnostic and Statistical Manual of Mental Disorders* where psychosis is a feature. I suspect any event causing neural software to suffer major malfunction due to the partial breakdown of its supporting hardware (that is, neural pathway disconnections) would result in disorientation of *I*. This frequently leads to secondary anxiety and depression (though the reverse may also happen), creating diagnostic confusion.

I have suggested that schizophrenia has a developmental and perhaps organic aspect wherein psychosis symptoms may be evident over a protracted time, and vulnerability to psychotic breakdown may remain for years. But there are events of much shorter duration wherein psychotic symptoms may occur, never to return after recovery: a 'passing acquaintance'. Such events suggest functional problems resulting from temporary cellular failure or because of temporary chemical interference. And so it is feasible that in profound depression – that is, during severe neuron depletion – neural hardware cannot sustain the relevant limbic software activity, giving rise to temporary psychosis. Sleep deprivation could lead to neuron depletion with similar results. Indeed, psychosis may also result from severe trauma and stress experiences where protective dissociations take place.

I have described the interactive nature of neural processing where *I* imputes meaning and fills in 'gaps' of information based on what it predicts *should* be there. Many experiments have shown this effect: the perceptual 'completion' of information which is, in fact, incomplete (see, for example, Gregory, 1970). We also see this effect in induced and natural states of sensory deprivation where people begin to hallucinate[5] or in the sudden absence of a familiar pattern of experience (perhaps due to the death of a loved one), where, for example, the brain attributes sounds (hearing the voice of the loved one) to past realities. Even dreaming could be understood as the brain creating 'realities' where normal information flowing from the senses has been temporarily attenuated.

This dynamic also occurs in the event of chemically induced hallucinations – be they due to illegal drugs or legally administered pain killers. Chemical interference can shut down or distort neural pathways through the artificial activation of some neurotransmitters and the inhibition of others. Clearly, this is the intended effect of a pain killer – but this also may create an internal state of information deprivation. Those neural networks seeking activation by normal information streams now denied by the chemical block create a default reality resulting in hallucinations. However, the *source* of the material creating the default reality remains unclear.

For all the devastation the psychotic state creates for David's *I*, it remains the clinician's task to engage his *I*, which normally retains some minimal capacity to deal with the neural pathway failures associated with psychosis. David needs help to extract meaning from his experience, to understand the interactive relationship of his *I* with his brain. Perhaps a clinician might work to retrospectively establish the neural connections necessary to create functional meanings that make better approximation to the external world. David's experiences reflect brain dysfunction, not necessarily *I* dysfunction, although his *I* may be 'weak'. Somehow his *I*, which maintains its integrity in suffering, needs to deal with the uninvited thoughts and sensory experiences and the resulting interpretive confusion. Frankl wrote:

There is nothing conceivable which would so condition a man as to leave him without the slightest freedom. Therefore, a residue of freedom, however limited it may be, is left to man in neurotic and even psychiatric cases. Indeed, the innermost core of the patient's personality is not even touched by a psychosis. An incurably psychotic individual may lose his usefulness but yet retain the dignity of a human being.

(Frankl 2006: 133)

Chapter 18

When *I* loses control

Addictions and OCD

When I asserts control of the brain, it 'takes each thought captive' – it takes charge of its neural home. Frederick challenged me, saying: 'I'm addicted to sex – is there anything wrong with that?' Yet *anything* – *any* urge, addiction, or compulsion not regulated by *I* allows the brain ascendency over *I*, compromising the sense of self. Similarly, the habits learned to manage fear or guilt within me can take over, impinging on the essential freedom of *I*. I then need to be delivered from the impulses of my own brain.

In this chapter, I explore how what begins as decisions determined by *I* motivated perhaps by curiosity, perhaps by the search for pleasure, or perhaps as a coping strategy, have the capacity to create powerful neural pathways that paralyse *I*. These pathways create addictions or compulsions, causing *I* to lose efficacy and dignity. Here the problem is not about neural *disconnection* (except that *I* becomes partially disconnected) but unwanted neural *connection* – powerful associative networks built around drive reduction. These connections hold apparent meanings that are fleeting. In addictions, the lead position in the dance between automatic neural processes and the authority of *I* changes over time in favour of neural processes.

Addictions: *I* forfeits control

Rosemary was confident that she could make the change. In the past, she would open a bottle of wine before she started cooking and drink as she relaxed for the evening. The bottle would be empty by bed-time. She knew that she was drinking too much, and we agreed on some parameters she was to set in place to manage the problem. She left confident the problem had been addressed. Yet when I next saw her, she was bewildered. The strategy had seemed so straightforward: why had she failed? When last I saw her she had made a clear decision about what to do, but when next she was cooking her evening meal, her decision gave way to something within her that she could not control. Once again, the bottle had been opened as she began to cook; once again, it was empty by bed-time. It was as if her *I* had been disabled and put in temporary suspension. 'I do not do the things I want to do': how is this possible? Is it force of habit – the enactment of some procedural or implicit memory – or the development of a chemical dependency?

Rosemary is like many clients who present with a history of alcohol misuse that relates to a multitude of internal and external associations and triggers, and probably more than a few reinforcers.[1] Rosemary now needs to make the decision, not just once, but repeatedly, about whether she will resist or acquiesce to the predispositions her learning has created. She needs to ensure that her *I* is 'engaged' to carry out repeated decisions to resist the demands of her brain to drink again. I can help map out the various triggers and circumstances that prompt her brain to make those demands. I can understand the reinforcement schedules operating. I can prepare a plan to introduce alternative behaviours to those triggers and circumstances, or I can try to change the reinforcement schedule, so that what was rewarding becomes punishing. But as Rosemary found, despite the initial decision she had made and the plans put in place, her brain had a way of deceiving her and getting its own way.

In addiction, the authority of *I* over the brain is relinquished to an automatic process – one that also interferes with communication between *I* and another, because *I* is no longer at the helm. An impulse is generated by the brain to which *I* acquiesces because it 'feels good' and in such acquiescence there is a drive reduction. Any energy required to resist the impulse is preserved, but at the expense of disgust at *I*'s own 'decision' and a resulting sense of helplessness. The release of certain neurotransmitters (perhaps dopamine or noradrenaline) has become an end in itself, although I will argue for a more complex process involving changes in neural regulation and associative networks. Meaningfulness is replaced with sensation which is satisfying now, but loses its point upon satiation.

Why did I drink so much? How great the regret tomorrow! Yet also, what confusion today – the meaningless in what *I* am doing – how does *I* cope without entering despair? What counterfeit meaningfulness does it need to devise to make sense of things? Somehow, *I* has subjected itself to neural imperatives and given the brain authority over *I*, against the proper order of things. *I* becomes passive, no longer in control, and it is in danger of becoming indifferent relationally, losing capacity for love and intimacy.

How did such a state of affairs begin? Perhaps with a mind-map orientation of poorly recognized emotional needs comprising implicit memories of lack of nurturance, intimacy, or purpose; of not coping; of emptiness; of rejection, and so on, leading to a state of disquiet and unhappiness. This may trigger impulses that temporarily distract or pleasure. Once acquiesced to, the fleeting but highly reinforcing need satisfaction creates a learned pattern of behaviour, along with conditioned cues and links to external stimuli. Neural connections are quickly established because the strength of emotion, the sustained focus, and the repetitive nature of the associations ensure the required synaptic firings. The resulting drive state not only competes with *I*, but also the 'other'. But it also leads to guilt and disquiet towards the self, a loss of confidence and dignity and self-regard. Breaking the power of addiction is complex: the mind-map orientation has to be addressed. The resulting habit pattern and the complex network of social and environmental cues needs to be interrupted and replaced. The dignity and empowerment of *I* needs to be re-established, and relationships with significant others may need to be restored.

So we find that *I* sometimes struggles to be in control of the very brain it depends upon to interpret and relate to the natural world. Rosemary might make a decision with herself, her husband, or her clinician to make changes in relation to her drinking. But when the temptation comes, the efficacy of her *I* is suspended while her brain activates the familiar default responses. Learning connected with the emotion centres of the brain is powerful to overcome the capacity of *I* to manage and regulate the brain. Implicit memories drive Rosemary's behaviours. When addiction 'rules over me', *I* is no longer able to overcome the insistence of the neural prompts or to 'control' the decision-making process. How is it that *I* has lost its authority and power over the brain? Does this mean *I* is no longer responsible?

What we refer to as addiction is the process where an external event is experienced often enough to result in *neural adaptation*, so that neural regulatory mechanisms (governing neurochemical activity) come to require the ongoing experiencing of that external event for its own homeostasis. The regulation of the neural system has come to depend on the external activity – whatever its nature – to maintain internal neural balance. In effect, that activity becomes an *extension* of a neural process, a neural requirement, as it were, rather than an activity managed by the initiative of *I*, as it once was. In its drive for internal homeostasis, *I* is now compelled towards the activity maintaining that homeostasis, the acquired 'need' to maintain neurochemical balance. In the process, the frontal cortex involvement through which *I* maintains its regulatory functions becomes attenuated. In this sense, addiction is neither an 'illness' nor moral failure (though it can give rise to both), but an artificially created neurochemically based drive. The external events and activities that neural processes come to depend on are surprisingly varied. The power of the resulting compulsion is surprisingly strong.

Typically when we think of addiction, we think of substance misuse as the external event. In this context, the idea of neuro-adaptation following the repeated exposure to drugs or alcohol is well accepted:

> All known drugs of abuse have the common effect of elevating the level of dopamine in the nucleus accumbens . . . Continued use of drugs and alcohol will eventually result in the reward system reducing the amount of endogenous dopamine by causing a decrease in the number of dopamine receptors. Craving and withdrawal, two indicators of addiction, are directly related to reduction in dopamine receptors in the brain.
>
> (Marlatt and Witkiewitz, 2009: 3)

Yet neural adaptation relates not only to dopamine balance, nor only to neurochemical processes per se, but to all aspects of the software systems it maintains. This in turn obeys a homoeostasis of its own: the maintenance of the mind map. In this regard, Carter observes:

many other brain areas are also involved [in addiction] – frontal areas are involved in seeking behaviour, for instance, the septum is responsible for some of the pleasurable feelings associated with drug use, and the amygdala produces emotional responses. Each type of drug works in a slightly different way to produce its characteristic effect.

(Carter, 2010: 104)

Carter notes that ecstasy and hallucinogenic drugs stimulate serotonin-producing cells, activating areas in the prefrontal cortex and the temporal cortices; amphetamines release both dopamine and noradrenaline; opioids fit into receptors that normally take endorphins and enkephalins; smoking mimics dopamine release and releases acetylcholine; while alcohol and tranquilizers decrease neural activity through action on GABA neurons. Clearly much more than dopamine is implicated – and these are just the ones we know about. And, I would suggest, more than neurotransmitter activity is implicated in the compulsions *I* is left to deal with. On the back of these neural drivers is a value system and lifestyle represented in the mind map, which seeks its own stability, resisting change.

Food, drink, and sex that no longer satisfies

Esther looked in the mirror. The image her retina captured was of a wasted body, bones protruding, ribs that could easily be counted, arms and legs thin as pencils. Yet what she 'saw' reflected the position her *I* had taken, not what was reflected in the mirror: 'I am fat – I am unacceptable.' Whatever the original reason for such a decision and at whatever age it was made (the way her father and the boys at school teased her in her primary school years for being 'chubby'), her position remained. The decision her *I* made long ago over-ruled the sensory information her visual system now mediated, and it was this decision that determined her actions, not the image on her retina: she refused to eat. But the decision of her *I* had also had an impact on her neural regulatory system. It had affected the way her hunger signals were activated and interpreted, on the reward she felt for not eating, and on the guilt she felt if she did. Here another neural regulatory system – different from that involved in drug use – had adapted to external changes, creating an irresistible urge in Esther to *not* eat. No amount of reasoned argument by her clinician or impassioned pleading by her distraught family could convince Esther of the illogic of her ongoing actions. All this did was to create further internal conflict and distress.

Addiction as an expression of neural compulsion is not just about drug and alcohol misuse. Gambling and hoarding, video and computer games, internet and compulsive texting, compulsive sex and pornography, compulsive exercise and body building, binge eating and not eating – there is a host of expressions of neurally mediated compulsions that can hijack *I*. I suspect that, with these various addictions, even though they may not be chemically based in the way drug misuse is, many different neurochemicals are nevertheless activated or inhibited, including dopamine, serotonin, noradrenaline, oxytocins, and vasopressin in their varying proportions. These in turn are associated with a powerful network of neural pathways forged over time, associations and connections that resist change. Along with the development of these pathways, adjustments in the regulatory mechanisms governing these pathways create what becomes a dysfunctional system.

While Esther's difficulties began with a decision that she was not acceptable based on what she heard her father and the boys at school say, her subsequent behaviour (her negative self-talk, her sensitization to her weight, her changed eating patterns) created neural pathways so that these patterns become automatic. Eventually, changes were created in her hypothalamic regulatory system that processes incoming information about hormones, neuropeptides, glucose, and fat levels, and reports back to the frontal cortex. Now the necessary messages were no longer getting through, if indeed the same messages were still being sent. What was once experienced as a need to eat mediated by hunger signals was now replaced by the greater need to experience the reward of *not eating*.

Esther's 'addiction' was to weight loss, but there are many different addictions, each with its own neural pathway systems and regulatory mechanisms. Each will no doubt be reflected in a partial and transitory attenuation of limbic pathways, keeping involvement of *I* at bay. Just as it is possible for a neural problem (such as neural depletion in depression) to result in corresponding adverse decisions by *I* (for example, to take one's own life), so also the reverse is true: *I* can make an adverse decision based upon dysfunctional mind-map orientation ('I am unattractive – I am too fat') that eventually results in neural problems (dysregulation leading to loss of appetite, as in anorexia). In the latter, the clinician is faced with an almost impossible task. He needs to convince his client's *I* to adopt and enact a position different to one embedded in the mind map that finds expression in an extremely rewarding behaviour pattern;[2] and simultaneously, to work at lessening the capacity of the neural regulatory and reward systems that keep those behaviours in place, rendering *I* ineffectual.

The compulsion of addiction interferes with *I* connecting with others, whether family member, friend, or clinician: the power of the compulsion overcomes the capacity of another to properly communicate with *I* – the information from the other is blocked by a competing neural drive. *I* often turns to deception to hide the compulsive behaviours that generate guilt or shame. If *I* is not connecting with others, what *is* *I* connecting with? If *I* is defined as source and destination, sending and receiving information, what happens when it acquiesces to addiction? How does the brain interpret the addiction process – what meaning does it attribute to the controlling compulsions?

Yet the point of addiction is that it has no point: the action never satisfies the underlying need; it only satisfies the drive created through the misplaced activities to which the underlying need gave rise. There is no neural feedback loop announcing satiation, no sense of a task meaningfully completed. In the end, exhaustion takes over and depression looms. It is a body without *I* at the helm every time the compulsion is ascendant. How can the clinician empower the client's *I* to overcome the compulsion? Can chemical intervention help ameliorate the drive state?

Indeed, the power of a drive can be reduced chemically, but unless *I* chooses once again to take the helm with strength of conviction, the problem remains and the clinician is left to develop strategies to help the client keep out of trouble. This typically means controlling aspects of the environment that support the activities feeding the addiction, recognizing his client's *I* might never regain sufficient control over the relevant neural pathways. At neural level, the question becomes how to *disable* dysfunctional reward systems, how to *disconnect* what has been neurally connected, and how to *reset* the neural regulatory systems that now have faulty settings.

OCD: Rogue thoughts and impulses

Addiction is not the only context wherein compulsions assert themselves: obsessive compulsive disorder (OCD) is marked by debilitating obsessions and compulsions. But where the drive in addiction is to embrace an essentially rewarding activity, the compulsions in OCD are generally driven by the need to quell fear or guilt and avoid perceived danger or moral inadequacy – fear or guilt and avoidance feeding each other. Nevertheless, in both, *I* is rendered powerless by the neural imperative, by behaviour which *I* at one time authorized but which now torments. *I* becomes passive and helpless.[3] How can this happen? Let us consider Raymond.

Like Charlie, Raymond experienced intrusive thoughts, although his were not of stabbing, or indeed, of harming anyone. On the contrary, the thoughts that plagued him told him that his own life was in danger, that he would become ill and die. Raymond had lived in fear of his violent father and a punishing God for as long as he could remember – he was able to recount various traumatic events from childhood. He lived in fear of many other things too, especially of various undiagnosed illnesses that presented him with a large array of changing physical symptoms. As he lived through the conflicts of adolescence, the fears and protective compulsions worsened. He constantly washed his hands, avoided touching money, and withdrew from sport and other activities and public places that might result in wounding or contamination. But the more he withdrew, the more anxious he became and the more crazy thoughts would go round in his head, fuelling his fears. He became imprisoned by fear. Daily life became impossible, each day a battle for survival, and he became frustrated, ashamed, and severely depressed.

Raymond's psychiatrist tried various drugs – fluoxetine, citalopram, olanzapine, and paroxetine – but these resulted in somatic side effects providing further focus for his fears and his complaint 'I'm not myself any more.' He knew his fears were irrational – he found CBT of little value, as it told him what he already knew (that his thoughts were illogical). Yet he was unable to free himself from the intrusive refrain 'what if . . . ?' He had attempted exposure and response prevention (ERP) therapy but found it too distressing to follow through: it exacerbated his fear. He was embarrassed by his out-of-control thoughts and behaviours and his failure to address his problems, and he lived in constant torment of a dysfunctional life. Yet any momentary successes he *did* have he viewed with suspicion. When he did not 'listen to his thoughts,' he observed: 'I didn't feel right not worrying. To be me, I need to worry. When I start to feel good, it's too good to be true, so I look for reasons for it not to be true, and I quickly doubt the ideas that might help me feel better.'

Raymond lived in a state of chronic vigilance. His mind map was primed to match meanings to his pre-existing guilt and fear. Once an interpretation of danger was made about an innocuous event, powerful neural associations broadened his anxiety, even though he knew the associations were illogical. These associations resulted in looping obsessional thoughts: 'Touching this money will cause me to become ill.' His fear facilitated dysfunctional neural connections that created irrational thoughts. An anxiety cycle became established. What to do? The drive to resolution was as much a function of the discomfort of his *I* as it was a neural system under stress. Numerous 'solutions' presented themselves, both 'logical' and magical – washing hands, avoiding situations, avoiding contact with money, arranging furniture in particular ways, counting, and so on – solutions whose intensity matched that of his fears. Over time, depression reactive to anxiety and OCD left him with few emotional resources and a weakened and ambivalent *I*.

Initially, Raymond (that is, his *I*) was able to decide whether to action irrational solutions – but once actioned, the thought–response cycle became automatic. These actions provided temporary respite from both discomfort of *I* and neural demands for homeostasis. His actions became 'reinforcing events'. And so the irrational behaviours became powerfully imprinted, despite their illogic. But Raymond *had* to perform them – he had nothing else, and he was desperate for relief. This was a momentary solution to his fear. Unfortunately, these events took place during his adolescence, at which time his sense of self was being overhauled. But instead of establishing a strong sense of self, he was left with a weakened *I* wracked with doubt, having no confidence in his capacity to manage his own neural processes. Yet it was a way of functioning that, although distressing, had become familiar to him: any change held its own fear of the unknown.

Considerable research has been done to uncover the neural correlates of the OCD that tormented Raymond, with a view to possibly introducing a neurological solution. Research implicates the caudate nucleus: perhaps there is a problem regulating the transmission of information relating to worries between the thalamus and the orbito-frontal cortex. In any event, Cozolino (2002) notes that OCD symptoms correlate with heightened activation of the middle portions of the frontal cortex and the caudate nucleus. Another neural region implicated is the *striatum*, located in the basal ganglia, which is involved in the control of automatic behaviour generally, allowing us to multi-task (Lambert and Kinsley, 2011).

Schwartz and Begley (2002) hypothesize about potential mechanisms, introducing the idea of *brain lock*, arguing for an 'OCD circuit', similar to one activated in worrying:

> When [the OCD] circuit is working properly, the result is a finely tuned mechanism that can precisely modulate the orbital frontal cortex and anterior

cingulate by adjusting the degree to which the thalamus drives these areas. When that modulation is faulty, as it is when OCD acts up, the error detector centred in the orbital frontal cortex and anterior cingulate can be overactivated and thus locked into a pattern of repetitive firing. This triggers an overpowering feeling that something is wrong, accompanied by compulsive attempts somehow to make it right.

(Schwartz and Begley, 2002: 71)

They suggest that the caudate region houses gating mechanisms that modulate the fear circuits emanating from the amygdala region, as well as the circuit between the thoughts and judgements housed in the software of the anterior cingulate and the orbital frontal cortex. Somehow, the gate is jammed or the neural associative string is fused so that the full circuit gets activated outside of the control of *I*. Perhaps at the software level, basic 'if–then' algorithms become fused, creating irresistible neural pathways: 'If I don't do this (count in twos), then something bad will happen.' Whatever the mechanism might be, an activated caudate nucleus or a malfunctioning of the OFC–striatum–amygdala–thalamus neural loop does not necessarily identify the *cause* of OCD, but we can reasonably conclude that aspects of the neural software have become dysfunctional, especially in relation to its connective properties – as they are with addictive urges.

Exposure therapy: A necessary evil?

Raymond's resistance to ERP therapy is not atypical – the idea of embracing a feared thing understandably puts people off. Yet it is generally regarded as a necessary component to an overall intervention programme that normally includes components such as CBT and/or mindfulness therapy. And not only for OCD sufferers: exposure to a feared or distressing stimulus is used more generally in other contexts and with other therapeutic approaches, such as eye movement desensitization reprocessing (EMDR) for PTSD, or systematic desensitization for phobias. It is a process where the therapeutic intervention requires a client to do something about which he or she is in deep conflict: at the same time Raymond wants to be free of the tyranny of the compulsion, he is highly motivated to perform the compulsion to ameliorate his fear. It is a conflict between his *I* and neural processes that inform and motivate his *I*; a conflict between mind and body.

ERP therapy[4] is an approach wherein Raymond is expected to confront the presumed object of his fear (the stimulus triggering the compulsion) and so to choose to enter a distressing situation while the automatic 'protective' behaviour, the compulsion that keeps him 'safe', is prevented. The behaviour is prevented long enough for 'habituation' to occur – when there is a significant reduction in reported distress. To ease things a little, a hierarchy of feared objects or events might be created in cooperation with Raymond so that some confidence in the procedure and sense of empowerment might be built through the successful confrontation of lesser fears before more distressing ones are attempted. Yet the process is frequently resisted, and success not always assured.

At a neural level, such targeted exposure to a feared or distressing object activates and eventually fatigues the relevant neural pathway (the illogical thought and compulsive behaviour connection), at cost of suffering to *I*. The fatigue is intended to lead to atrophy of the particular pathway or neural association string – as it were, to 'burn out' or disconnect it. The difficulties are to contain the distress, to maintain focus on a specific object, and to restrain the particular compulsion so that the key neural pathways are activated and fatigued. Meantime, the entire neural system is drawn into a state of high alert, leading to arousal of many networks, including those specific to the targeted thought and behaviour, thereby exacerbating the problem. In its drive to homeostasis, the brain urgently seeks other safety behaviours to replace the one targeted for change;[5] and in the state of high arousal, other illogical thoughts are created and other problematic neural association strings can become fused. That is, replacement compulsions may be developed.

What to do? Often the use of an SSRI or other psychotropic medication is thought to help inhibit fear networks, lessening the degree of overall neural activation and therefore the suffering of *I*. But this, of course, does not disconnect the particular pathway of concern.

We are thus confronted with the complexity of the problem. Raymond's compulsions were secondary to his guilt and fears. The illogical obsessional thoughts which became the focus for his fears were not the *source* of his fear, but provided an expression for what had become a generalized fear state in a place that should have been his sanctuary – his home. Raymond's *I* knew distress because of his home situation. The compulsions were neural aberrations serving to re-establish homeostasis, a process not only largely independent of his *I*, but at odds with the integrity of his mind map. Schwartz notes:

> One of the most striking aspects of OCD urges is that, except in the most severe cases, they are what is called ego-dystonic; they seem apart from, and at odds with, one's intrinsic sense of self. They seem to rise from a part of the mind that is not you, as if a hijacker were taking over your brain's controls.
>
> (Schwartz and Begley, 2002: 55)

Yet, although OCD *urges* may be ego-dystonic (that is, they do not find their source in *I*), the underlying guilt and fear giving rise to these urges generally *do* relate to *I*, as we see in Raymond's history. Intervention needs to recognize this bilateral process – the initial involvement and decisions by Raymond's *I* in relation to his guilt and fears, and the subsequent 'high-jacking' by his brain's controls as it seeks its own solutions to the state of arousal. In OCD sufferers, mind-map orientations predisposing towards fear, guilt, responsibility, and perfectionism are typically found, and these need to be addressed.

Is it possible to overcome the scourge of obsessions and compulsions without exposing Raymond to more suffering? Schwartz argues in the affirmative and trains his patients in mindfulness techniques, increasing awareness of dysfunctional neural pathways and creating *bypass* neural pathways: that is, establishing new associations. His patients are instructed to develop these pathways through the practice of directed focus (in part, this means staying in control of the ideas engaging the mind). *I* is encouraged to retain control of a brain that wants to do its own thing: Schwartz's experiences suggest that his patients enjoy some success in consciously and deliberately bringing about the desired changes.

Nevertheless, the underlying issue remains to be addressed: *I* needs to *change position* regarding responsibility, guilt, or fear. *I* needs to be empowered to *choose to confront* underlying mind-map predispositions, which requires clarity as to what those predispositions might be. Where *I* remains passive and the clinician forces the issue, a fundamental tension remains between a disempowered *I* and the brain – this can be a potential problem with any therapy that involves exposure training, and I suspect often underlies the issue of client non-compliance. Reinforcing the helplessness of *I* only feeds anxiety and depression; strengthening the sense of self-efficacy, on the other hand, should improve outcome potential. Where one's attachment history predisposes towards poor self-efficacy, further challenges are presented.

Chapter 19

Dissociation and exile of *I*

After years of creating a vast network of neural connections, an adult emerges with many capacities. But these capacities are only as good as the integrity of the network connections, and there are many ways in which these connections can be attenuated or fail. Such failure can give rise to a wide range of unusual and disturbing symptoms, as Sacks and Feinberg testify in their fascinating case studies. We are probably most familiar with disconnections that occur as a result of hardware failure, perhaps due to dementia or brain injury. But disconnections also result from software failure, and perhaps most astonishing, from a deliberate attempt of *I* to bring about functional disconnections for self-protection. These are comprehensive disconnections relating to patterns of association strings; not just temporary disconnections related to information flow regulated by neurotransmitter activity.

We have looked at depletion of neural capacities in depression; on failures in limbic-system connections in psychosis; and on unwanted neural connections in addictions and OCD. In this chapter, we consider neural disconnections that occur in different contexts, some protective, some destructive, some initiated by *I* to manage suffering, some automatic neural responses to informational overload, but some also the result of hardware failure.

Dementia and brain injury: I exiled

Lifestyle factors and health knowledge have enabled us generally to live longer than our ancestors, but it has not protected us from brain diseases that cause *I* to be exiled in the latter years, trapped as it were by a neural system that no longer sustains an intact mind map. The gradual atrophy of brain hardware results in extensive breakdown of vital neural pathways with corresponding breakdown of software systems. This reduces access to memory, creating difficulties in recognition, affecting meaningfulness, familiarity, capacity for complexity, and the data needed for decision making. As the capacity of *I* to interact with its body and the external world is reduced, it experiences increasing frustration and distress to the extent *I* has awareness of what is happening.

Just as there is a clear sequence in the original development of neural capacities, building increasingly complex systems around a bank of supporting mid-level software, there is now a sequence that operates, roughly speaking, in the reverse. It is a fluctuating process. *I* fights to retain its neural capacities by accessing information through alternative pathways as neural failures interfere with the proper functioning of higher-level software. But over time, more pathways are affected, and this begins to fragment the higher-level systems sustaining the mind map and the capacities for processing new information before affecting more basic systems, underlying software, and earlier learning. It is not random disintegration, but a systematic failure of systems involved in recognizing, matching, and interpreting incoming information. Declarative memories go before implicit and procedural memories. And just as music is one of the first things an infant can remember (even before birth), music memory is among the last to go in patients with Alzheimer's. Music may be remembered long after the husband or wife of fifty years is forgotten (Sacks, 2008). Also among the last to go are aspects of self-awareness, especially the awareness of one's own capacities.

Yet, asks Sacks, does the eventual loss of one's self-awareness constitute a loss of self – is *I* no longer 'at home'? The evidence suggests not. Even as the brain deteriorates, that which helped define *I* (the aspects of *I* written into the brain) seems to linger, providing some minimal orientation for *I*. Explains Sacks:

> Someone with Alzheimer's may undergo a regression to a 'second childhood', but aspects of one's essential character, of personality and personhood, of self, survive – along with certain, almost indestructible forms of memory – even in very advanced dementia. It is as if identity has such a robust, widespread neural basis, as if personal style is so deeply ingrained in the nervous system, that it is never wholly lost, at least while there is still any mental life present at all.
>
> (Sacks, 2008: 372)

Progressive neural disconnection leads to fragmentation in the mind map, leaving *I* disoriented and failing to recognize incoming signals, and conversely, *I* finds it increasingly difficult to express itself through the collapsing neural networks – but *I* and aspects of its identity remain essentially intact.

Similar problems can result from other forms of hardware failure, whether from stroke, brain injury, or infectious processes such as meningitis or brain abscess (see, for example, Griffiths, 1997). In their celebrated case studies, Sacks and Feinberg record a range of unusual manifestations and experiences when neural disconnections occur in such conditions. The relationship between *I* and the body can become vexatious in brain injury – something has been lost, something difficult to see or conceptualize, but undeniably real. The sufferer has 'changed'. He or she may become partially or comprehensively amnesic, with severely restricted access to the mind map, or the mind map might cease to provide proper orientation for *I*: *I* appears changed, perhaps even 'absent' – as in a sleepwalker. Alternatively, *I* may no longer be able to engage the brain to express itself the way it once did: *I* is there, but disconnected, much to the frustration and despair of those around. However, unlike the progressive deterioration in neural connective systems found in dementia, here there is generally opportunity for the brain to restore some neu-ral connectivity to damaged and disconnected systems. Doidge (2010) argues that these processes of *brain plasticity* normally involve conscious focus, which I suggest involves *I*.

PTSD: *I* dissociates

It had been two months since the agitated balaclava-clad gunman entered the bank and demanded cash from teller Corrine. It was the moment she was convinced her life would end. And in a way, life as she knew it *did* end then. Although she had a year earlier been to a half-day 'training' session to learn what to do in such an event, she really did not expect it to happen to *her*. This sort of thing only happened to others. And so she felt guilty that she had frozen at his sudden appearance and in dream-like obedience had followed his instructions, and guilty that she had not remembered the procedures she had been taught.

Moreover, she no longer felt safe – not only in the bank, but also in shops, walk-ing down the street, and at home. She had become suspicious of strangers. She upgraded her home security and always wanted someone to be with her. Some-how, she imagined the robber would track her down, even though she knew this was ridiculous. Corrine just could not get the image of him out of her mind – try as she might to rid herself of the intrusive memories and periodic nightmares by refusing to discuss them, distracting herself, and avoiding reminders of the event. She even lost interest in the job she loved, and had resigned.

But the more Corrine tried to avoid, the worse her anxiety became. She could not stop the scene re-appearing in her mind, as though the whole thing was hap-pening to her all over again. Just as she had frozen initially, she froze each time the memory was replayed. Normally, memories change over time, but Corrine could not – she did not want to – connect with this memory, to engage with it and reshape it. It remained fixed and unchanged: a permanent threat loomed in her head months after the event. She became increasingly morose and depressed – her sleeping was poor, she could not concentrate, she became withdrawn and irritable, and she was altogether disinterested in the things that once held her attention. She had lost the life she once knew.

In recent years, post-traumatic stress disorder (PTSD) has received enormous attention, promoting awareness of the devastating impact trauma can have on individuals and families. Wars and natural disasters, motor vehicle accidents and rape, violent holdups and abductions: these and many other events can result in PTSD. But what *is* PTSD? Typically, it is defined by symptoms including the re-experiencing of the traumatic event through nightmares, flashbacks, and intrusive memories; the avoidance of thoughts, reminders, or localities associated with the trauma; general numbing and lack of responsiveness; and increased physiological arousal, including hyper-vigilance towards distressing cues, sleep difficulties, exag-gerated startle response, and increased anger and concentration difficulties. Yet no symptom exists outside dynamic neural processes interacting with *I*. Outlining symptoms may be useful in categorization, but understanding *processes* gives greater insight into the condition and clues towards clinical intervention.

PTSD presents a mixed picture of neural disconnections that need reconnection and connections that need to be ameliorated or disconnected in order to restore a functional mind map. It sees a neural response locked into self-protective patterns long after the trauma event. It results in repetition of thoughts, behaviours, emotions, or other physiological responses disconnected from current environmental events, and disengaged from *I*. As with addictions and OCD, the loss of control by *I* of these responses creates its own distress, and therapy typically seeks to enable *I* to reassert that control.

Before we consider the issues of *I* and mind map in PTSD, what is understood at neurological level about the trauma response? We have already touched on the neural correlates of fear and stress. The neurological effects are widespread. All parts of the neural landscape are affected, as they are with emotional responses in general. Cozolino notes that 'trauma produces a wide variety of homeostatic dysregulations that interfere with all realms of personal and interpersonal functioning' (Cozolino, 2002: 258). This is seen in the various neurochemicals that are activated. Noradrenaline stimulates fight-or-flight readiness by activating the relevant functional connections with the amygdalae and the ANS. Compensatory endogenous opioids ameliorate the emotional pain by functional *disconnections*, contributing to analgesic effects, dissociative reactions, depersonalization, and derealization. Dopamine release activates the frontal cortex and its cognitive controls, while increased glucocorticoid levels sacrifice long-term bodily conservation and homeostasis for short-term survival. Finally, a decrease in serotonin reduces capacity to cope with stress.

When Corrine was first confronted by the armed bandit, she froze – her *I* was temporarily disengaged from much of her neural software, minimizing exposure. She could not think, she could make no decision, she could take no action.[1] While noradrenaline and glucocorticoids flooded her neural system, she dissociated – as though she were in a dream – protecting her *I* from suffering. Her body was endangered and her brain overwhelmed, and so her *I* effected a large-scale disconnection both during and immediately after the event. Her brain was left to run automatically, as it were. But the disconnection protecting her *I* also led to poor integration of the event into her mind map, creating difficulties in making sense of things, in knowing what to do, and in establishing meaningfulness in a mind map with no place for the experience.

Meanwhile, powerful connections were made between the narrow range of her focus during the trauma, the disconnected fragments of what she had consciously seen and heard, and the alarm systems mediated by her amygdala. These connections were later re-experienced as flashbacks.[2] Each time her memory was activated (by both internal and external triggers), her emotions were experienced anew. The subsequent activation of fear created a new event wherein she was re-traumatized: cortisol was again released. The memory giving rise to renewed trauma acquired new elements connected with the prevailing circumstances of her flashbacks – the acquisition of these new associations fed her anxiety spiral.

And so she became preoccupied with 'what if' and 'if only' thoughts, attempting to re-establish connections and meanings while vigorously avoiding anything that might reactivate the alarm systems that were so easily triggered: What if the bandit had fired? What might she have done if she had had warning? Why did she do nothing – could she have done something differently? If only she had stayed home that day! This integrative process (managed by hippocampal software) also took place in her REM sleep – her dreaming. But the intensity of her holdup-related dreams woke her up. She was restless: something was not resolved. Her internal conflicts, the preoccupations that cut across her concentration and her constant scanning of her unsafe world, resulted in neural stress, in eventual exhaustion and depression.

Corrine's mind map had no adequate basis upon which to interpret and respond to the unexpected event and her *I* became disoriented. Her *I* was pressured to work on the mind-map reformulation every waking moment, to establish a network of new and more functional neural connections, perhaps creating new values and new ways of perceiving the world. But she also had to deal with the unpredictability of the threat – with her *I* not being in control, with being vulnerable to annihilation. She decided she was no longer safe in an unpredictable world and she subsequently interpreted ambiguous signals in this light, changing from a position of embrace to one of alienation and suspicion in regard to her world and those around her.

The re-integration of Corrine's mind map, the making sense of things and the weaving of the trauma experience into the tapestry of life memories while disabling the relevant alarm circuits, and the reviewing of the decision of her *I* in relation to her position in the world (that is, to once again believe she was safe and in control) became significant challenges for Corrine and for the clinician assisting her. While her memories remained poorly integrated, they could remain intact for many years (unlike normal memories that are modified through the retelling). Yet they remained disconnected from context – time or place – so that her *I* had difficulty placing these fragments into historical and social context, and inaccurate connections were retrospectively made.

Although her trauma memory was stored as implicit memory, a narrative needed to be developed to create declarative memories that allowed her *I* controlled access to the disturbing material. But the uniqueness of the trauma event required many new associations to be forged for integration to occur. Its uniqueness caused it to be differentiated from everything else in her neural landscape, and the unceasing rehearsing of this experiential aberration caused the memory fragment to be easily activated. Retelling of the narrative would grant Corrine's *I* much needed control of the remembered event, allowing her to better 'fit' the memory into her perceptual framework. On the one hand, the paucity of established pathways connecting the traumatic memory to other memories and cognitions allowed for repression or dissociation of that memory. On the other hand, when Corrine was 'stuck' on the memory, she had few neural exit pathways to move away from the disturbing material, to shift her focus onto related but non-disturbing material following the 'natural' associative flow of her brain activity, her *I* moving from one thought to a connected one. Could the development of appropriate narrative enhance the number of 'safe' connective networks in her brain?

Yet the retelling too easily results in re-traumatizing, and herein lays a clinical dilemma. Subsequent intrusive memories easily reactivate the dissociative state, a coping strategy protecting both *I* and Corrine's neural system. What to do? It is generally accepted that vicarious exposure to trauma, correctly managed, is necessary to deactivate the alarm system, just as exposure therapy does with OCD.[3] One of these exposure procedures, EMDR, originally employed the technique of focusing on a moving finger while simultaneously activating the traumatic memories (Shapiro, 2001). How this induced 'disconnection' (or memory integration?) works is unclear – some argue the controlled exposure or desensitization is the key element, although the focus of *I* on the 'neutral' and meaningless moving finger while the memory is activated may play an important role in preventing new and unhelpful connections to the traumatic material. The visual nature of this focus, given the visual nature of most trauma memories, may also be relevant.

We have seen that disconnections can result from neural hardware failure (relating to dementia or brain disease or trauma) affecting *I*. It can equally result from overwhelming pressures on *I* that result in the functional shut-down of certain neural pathways in relation to 'simple' emotional traumas, such as results in PTSD. 'Simple' trauma is complex enough. Complex trauma creates further challenges involving its own unique disconnection patterns, as we will now consider.

Other dissociative processes

Evelyn was distressed:

> my friend said that I saw her yesterday, and that I'd been very angry with her and had gone off my face and sworn at her and that I'd referred to myself as Hannah. But I don't remember this – I don't remember seeing her and it's just not like me to treat anyone like that. I feel like I missed the day: it's a blank. Yet I have lingering feelings this morning that don't belong to me. All I remember about yesterday is feeling unwell and wanting to hurt myself. But I did find some damage in my room – I don't know how it got there. It's freaky. It's happened before.

If her account is accurate, it appears Evelyn was suffering a dissociative episode in which she entered a role or personality unlike the self she knew, but of which she had no memory. How are we to explain this? We can understand her *I* might disconnect to protect against trauma. But why should Evelyn dissociate when she has no recollection of trauma? Perhaps dissociation can begin as a protective habit of *I* in relation to unremembered traumatic events of long ago, which continues to protect her when she encounters certain cues.

I has this quality: it is able to suffer. But *I* seeks to limit suffering where possible. What conditions bring suffering about? *I* can suffer if the body is diseased or injured. But *I* may also suffer when it is not treated as meaningful – when it is dismissed, ignored, or squashed down; when *I* is treated as 'non-*I*'. Here the essence of *I* – as source and origin of communication – is denied and disempowered, and its integrity is compromised or lost. It becomes a fight for its very existence. Under such threat, *I* may dissociate to protect it from loss of integrity or from annihilation. Dissociation may occur in different ways and different neural territory can be disconnected. A particularly disconcerting dissociative process is a condition called *dissociative identity disorder* (DID – earlier termed *multiple personality disorder*).

Severe and repeated physical or sexual abuse in early years of development may lead to complex PTSD, which generally manifests in self-regulation difficulties: affect dysregulation, impulsivity, and attentional problems. This in turn can lead to problems in self-definition (including self-harm and suicidal inclinations) and relationships, and is typically recognized as *borderline personality disorder*. Here *I* enters into serious conflict not only with the environment but with its own brain and body. For some, this conflict may lead to DID, where dissociative episodes are experienced as amnesic episodes that serve to protect *I*. DID reflects protective dissociation habits generally established before the development of an independent self during adolescence. These response patterns generally preserve fragments of the pre-adolescent mind map defining *I*, leading to a fragmented personality.

Connections are necessary to make sense of things and to develop a coherent self narrative – an internally consistent story of my relationship with the world and others. Dissociation can compromise those meaning and identity systems, leaving a fragmented 'self'. This does not mean *I* is fragmented; rather, the mind map has become fragmented. The relationship between *I* and the world no longer makes sense as a whole. If *I* tries to make sense of some fragments of experience, it needs to ignore information from unrelated fragments. This is disorienting for *I* and prevents comprehensive and functional relationships with others, which require an integrated identity. The small parcels of identity created by *I* in DID – packages of internally consistent perceptions and roles – only remain adaptive in limited settings.

The classic presentation of DID is the person who slips from one identity to other dissociated identities (called 'alter egos', or just 'alters'), as appeared to happen for Evelyn. While engaged in one identity, Evelyn was mystified as to what happened while she had entered another identity. If Evelyn's mind map was to be likened to a town, her alters would represent neighbourhoods cut off from the surrounding neighbourhood for safety reasons, except perhaps for one heavily guarded laneway. Within this isolated neighbourhood, life continues, oblivious to life outside its borders. From time to time, Evelyn (her *I*) finds herself in such a neighbourhood, cut off from the wider neighbourhood in the sense that she has no memory of it in her dissociated state. Her dissociation protects her from information linked to trauma memories. Complete dissociation occurs where no information of an emotional, cognitive, or behavioural nature is shared between her alters: however, partial dissociation may also occur where only part of the personality structure is disconnected, such as certain emotions or cognitive memories.

A sufficient history is required for each alter to develop neural networks capable of some independent, albeit limited, functioning. Further, it tends to happen where there is no recourse to other coping strategies. This is why we would expect the phenomenon to be the result of childhood traumas, rather than traumas encountered in adulthood. This is partly what distinguishes complex trauma and DID from 'simple' trauma and PTSD. The experiences are contained in a previous developmental stage which is not integrated with subsequent development. We would expect the different personalities to reflect in activation of separate neural networks as the sufferer moves from one personality to the next. Evidence for this has, in fact, been reported.

Carter (2010) notes that fMRI studies of the brains of DID sufferers showed patterns suggesting alters were not just acts. As one set of behaviours disappeared and another took its place, the neural patterns changed to match the altered demeanour. Brain scans showed a change in the memories available to each personality. When they were told anecdotes from their own trauma history, the neural networks activated by their reported recognition of the events matched that activated when they functioned in the corresponding alter. This appeared to confirm the relationship between their subjective dissociated state and the trauma origins. Carter reports another study that found brainwave coherence – a measure of which neural groups fire in synchrony – was completely different in each of the personalities of some DID patients, suggesting that they were thinking and feeling quite differently in each state.

Evelyn and her clinician were challenged with connecting what was disconnected, forging associations where none had existed for a long time. Yet how can the clinician re-integrate Evelyn's mind map so the alienated or fragmented alters are meaningfully connected to other aspects of her life? Somehow Evelyn needs to access the dissociated material she is strongly motivated to avoid. She has even formalized and authorized her alters by naming them. Recovery will involve repair to her mind map involving the restoration of all its parts, making sense of all her memories and experiences and roles, and forming an integrative whole so each can be accessed without undue suffering and without creating the tensions of incompatible roles and life experiences.

Complex trauma may also result in partial dissociation where there are no amnesic episodes nor hidden alters. Nevertheless, it appears something *is* in hiding – generally, emotions. Somehow bodily responses have become disconnected from emotions sourced in *I*. The person is aware of pain, but does not experience it as such – he or she feels numb, separate from the 'real me'. This sense of emotional disconnection where body and emotions no longer operate as effective expressions of *I* may prompt the person to acts of self-harm.[4] The resulting physical pain and the sight of bleeding provide feedback that *I* is 'alive', human, 'normal'.

Yet self-harm can escalate for the same effect to be achieved – it can become addictive. The skin becomes the canvas on which the evidence of life is etched, with every act of self-harm creating its own memory of success in enhancing self-awareness and capacity to 'feel'. But what causes it to become addictive? Do the endorphins released by pain also calm emotional distress that cannot otherwise be accessed; does self-harm serve a connective purpose; or is it simply a distraction from overwhelming life events? No doubt debate on these issues will continue. However we might understand these, self-harm occurs predominantly in adolescence, the tumultuous time of brain reorganization and of a changing mind map, where remembered traumas can contribute to anger, confusion, and anxiety, but also to dissociative processes. Once again, the challenge is to bring about the connections required for the effective expression of *I* through brain and body.

Part VI

Implications

Law, science, and the clinician

Chapter 20

The law, the brain, and *I*

The clinician's conundrum is also a judicial one. While much legal argument is about procedure and precedent, the *real* issues revolve around responsibility, guilt, accuracy of perception, and the faithful communication of those perceptions. To what extent does *I* have the capacity to properly manage brain and body, to make right choices, and to take responsibility for the body when drive and reasoned choice are not aligned? To what extent does *I* have access to accurate memories and to choose to present such remembered events with integrity, resisting drives to distort information for personal meaningfulness or self-protection?

These are the issues that confront both judge and clinician. The judicial system deals with external events and observed responses – a person's actions and their consequences – while *I* deals with perceptions mediated by its neural system and oriented by its mind map. Memories, judgements, decisions, and actions are determined by the extent to which a mind map faithfully replicates external realities. The judicial system normally holds me responsible for my actions, even though they may be determined as much by *I* as by a neural system capable of operating outside the intent of *I*.

The court holds me accountable for my words and actions, and for reporting things accurately. Is the truth being told? The brain suffers distortions and inaccuracies; but it is *I* that lies and deceives. Even if what the defendant is saying is largely true, chances are he or she colours the evidence they give in their favour, even if unconsciously. And so the clinician may be asked whether a defendant is malingering. Tests identifying personal biases might help make a call on the matter. But it also raises the question as to the reliability of evidence generally – how confident can we be that what the witness says is accurate? There are further issues. One might argue that I should only be accountable for that of which I am aware and for those behaviours I have the authority and power to control. That is, was it *I* that made and executed the decision, or was it a neural event independent of *I*, which *I* did not or could not control?

And so a clinician might be asked to prepare a report giving insights about a matter, or an apprehensive clinician might find himself in the hushed chamber of a law court, to give evidence in relation to a client. The dance between *I* and the brain creates dilemmas for the judicial process as much as it does for the clinician.

What the witness saw: Memory and the law

'I couldn't say, your honour – I don't remember.' How many a court proceeding has been frustrated by these few words? Could she *really* not remember? How do we know? And under pressure to provide the court with crucial evidence, how reliable is the evidence likely to be? The questions of reliability of memory and interpretation of witnessed events are not only an issue in relation to child witnesses. Many studies have been done on witness reliability in both children and adults, and the verdict has not been good.[1]

Memory is patchy, dependent on the focus of *I* at the time of the event, on the integrity of neural hardware, and on motivations, interpretations, perceptions, and subsequent reinterpretations and reconstructions of the event. Abstractions and approximations are better remembered than specific details, yet it is the detail the court wants: the more specific the desired information ('what did he *actually* say six months ago?'; 'what time was it when she rang a year ago?'), the more likely the witness might use creative imagination to reconstruct events to help the judge out. Timing and order of events is an early casualty, and the fragments that *are* remembered are readily juxtaposed so that distorted pictures emerge. Specific details that are so helpfully remembered for the court easily find their origin in associative processes, rather than the event in question.

And so I scan my neural networks in good faith, comfortable with my integrity, faithfully relaying what I find there ('I'm not lying, your honour, as God is my witness: that's what I remember'), but having no way of knowing that what I remember is not the same as the events that actually took place. Remembered material needs to fit into my mind map while the events that created the information have long passed. The better the 'memory' fits my mind map, the more I am convinced it is true, because it makes sense to me. It fits my reality, even though it only approximates external reality.

Moreover, I might be asked to remember material relating to traumatic events. Where these events were overwhelming, neural disconnections are likely to have occurred as part of a coping response – and with such disconnection, crucial information is lost. Here memories become more distorted, with disproportionate emphasis on small details:

> No, your honour, I can't remember what he looked like, what he wore, how tall he was, or when he entered. I *do* remember the little black gun in his hand partially covered by a green piece of cloth – or what *looked* like a gun under the cloth. I just can't get it out of my mind: I see it all the time.

What can the judge believe? How can the clinician help? When hypnosis does more to dissociate *I* from aspects of the mind map than it does to access accurate information, what tools are left for the clinician to throw light on the matter?

Free will, responsibility, and the law

There are essentially two ways in which I might be held responsible before the law. First, *I* might be held responsible for the management of brain and body, to effectively control the information and impulses the brain presents to *I*. Second, given the assumption of 'free will' – that is, the capacity and authority of *I* to attend to one thing or another and to make a decision accordingly – *I* might be held responsible for relational decisions, the position taken on various matters, the allegiances established, and the actions that proceed from them. Yet *I* is not always in control of its neural processes, and the making of a decision is more likely to be the making of a series of linked decisions, each limited by context and opportunity. The extent of control of *I* in that process may fluctuate. Some doubt whether we have free will at all. Although the judiciary, religious leaders, and the layman generally agree we have a free will, many philosophers and neuroscientists are less convinced, creating their own conundrum. While neural systems are clearly implicated in both attentional and decisional processes, I have proposed it is *I* that acts as the regulator. Yet we might ask: are these processes that *I* engages in free of constriction; do they reflect 'free will', unencumbered by neural demand? More troubling, are my attention and decisions determined by neural processes of which I have less control than I imagine?

The issue of free will interested Libet, who sought to discover whether it operated at neural level. To this end, he performed experiments in the 1980s and 1990s to find out how the timing of a conscious decision related to the brain processes that executed it. Controversially, he found that subjective reports of subjects indicated they experienced making their decision *after* (by some half a second) the *readiness potential* (the wave of brain activity that precedes an action) was detected in the brain. This was interpreted to mean that

> the unconscious brain kicks off a movement, and the conscious decision to make the movement comes in its wake, the implication [being] that the brain itself is the force that initiates the action. Rather than causing action, consciousness merely reflects what the brain is already doing . . . it follows that our behaviour is simply the end product of automatic brain processes – and our notion of a 'free will' is illusory.
>
> (Carter, 2010: 313)

Such a conclusion creates a potential problem in our legal system, but it is not the only way of interpreting the data.

Consider the possibility of *I* (*I* and consciousness not being the same) being source of decision making, as against neural processes. Yet my *awareness* of all things, including emotions, thoughts, sensations, intentions and decisions, requires the activation of neural networks, *whatever its source*. Awareness, therefore, comes *after the fact*. I am reliant on my brain to mediate the information and activities *I* partakes in – but that does not make my brain the *source*, nor does it mean my brain controls me (although it might sometimes – the clinician's conundrum). A decision made by *I* is neurally processed *after* it is made, such processing allowing awareness of that decision should *I* choose to focus on it (which it normally does not).[2] And this is what Libet found. But it does not follow that the brain made the decision rather than *I*, a deterministic process with *I* simply an accessory to the fact.

On the other hand, free will does not mean *I* decides independently of context, making a decision unpredictable. Whenever I make a decision, it has a basis: *I* scans its mind map for relevant parameters. What is the *right* decision? What is easiest and most comfortable? What takes me closer to my goal? Many decisions are hardly noticed – they logically flow from previous ones, or follow their pattern. It may be useful to make a distinction between decisions *I* makes consciously by weighing up several possibilities, and decisions that follow a predetermined logic or pattern – *if* the road is clear, *then* I'll cross it. Most decisions may be of the latter sort – these are simpler, taking less neural energy as the decisional process is narrower. *I* prefers to utilize these. But *I* has nevertheless programmed its neural software to create the logic algorithms used, which it can at any point over-ride.

In one sense, 'free' will is not 'free': all choice is limited and has a cost. Nevertheless, the idea of free will, however limited, is critical in that I can be held responsible for my actions. It is 'free' in the sense that I *have* a choice. If actions are predetermined rather than the result of choices *I* has made, then the very heart of morality and the legal system is in trouble. Choice normally involves judgement – a consideration of the alternatives and implications of a decision. It is not predetermined so much as it is (generally) the preferred or logical outcome in the prevailing circumstances. In this sense, the decision *I* makes is normally comprehensible, reasonable, and predictable to others who understand the prevailing circumstances. But the cost of choice is saying no to the alternatives, and herein lays a dilemma when the alternatives also invite embrace by *I*. With choice comes responsibility: that responsibility means I can be held accountable for the choices I make.

As important as 'free will' is, so is the converse: the ability to decide not to – 'free won't', the capacity to *inhibit* an impulse. To what degree did Charlie have the capacity to *not* act upon his perplexing thought that he should stab his girlfriend? Although he identified the thought not to be his, it nevertheless found expression in his neural system. What is the mechanism that leads to him choosing or not choosing to act upon it? It appears that his *I* still had the capacity to resist and inhibit the alien impulse, exhausting though it was at times.

The issue is not just one of free will versus determinism; it is also (perhaps more so) whether I have the *capacity to make judgement*. That is, am I able to interpret incoming information correctly? Am I in a position to access the information I need? This is true not only of access to external information, but also of the brain's capacity to 'weigh' internal information.

Making a decision is generally not a single *I* event – it is more likely a series of linked decisions limited by context and opportunity. The extent of control *I* has in the process may fluctuate, creating challenges in the ascription of moral and legal responsibility. Every decision I make affects the next one: the choices I make are limited by the choices I have already made. The small menu choice before me at a restaurant is the result of the earlier choice of restaurant, which in turn was the result of a choice as to whether to eat at home or eat out. Perhaps free will is better understood in the context of 'decision trees', each choice determining the parameters of the next. When I married, subsequent choices were (or should be) shaped by that decision. The choice I make narrows my focus; the narrowed focus determines my subsequent choice. And somehow, each choice, even decisions I made when very young, sets the context for later ones. By the time a client talks to the clinician about a life decision, the available choices have been greatly narrowed by choices already made. Yet the level of involvement of *I* in each choice may vary, which is why some find themselves before the judge unexpectedly.

For example, the decision to drive while intoxicated may have occurred well after *I* lost its capacity for judgement and control, a 'decision' based largely on remembered habits – can I be held responsible for this? This decision was preceded by one made while *I* had rather better capacity for judgement: to drink with no provision made should I become intoxicated – am I responsible for such a 'non-decision'? *This* decision, in turn, may have been preceded by one to join my mates at the hotel, a not irresponsible decision over which *I* had most control. Yet 'innocent' decisions eventually led to the illegal behaviour, now lost to memory, for which the judge holds me accountable. Decision making is complex, and the level of involvement of *I* can vary. A decision may represent a major turning point, or comprise multiple tiny decisions – almost imperceptible and of no apparent consequence, small shifts at the margin – adding up to a gradual, substantial shift in position. *I* is involved, but almost below awareness. Can I remain morally and legally culpable for decisions such as these, where the involvement of *I* is so tenuous?

One could argue that I should be culpable for all my actions, as I should retain full authority over my brain and body. My words and actions have consequences regardless of my intent, and so the imputation of guilt should be the rule rather than the exception – the assumption being that I *ought* to have control over my body, whose *very purpose* is to express the intent of *I*. Even though the external world creates demands, as does the body itself – for food, drink, rest, comfort, and so on – *I* can choose how to respond to these demands; *I* have authority to give expression to these impulses and demands, or refrain from doing so.

Alternatively, one could argue that, although I should be culpable for that over which I have authority and control, given the ongoing struggle between my brain and *I*, the extent of awareness and control will fluctuate, and so should my culpability. But how does one judge the extent of control *I* has at any point? This dilemma is reflected in setting the age for legal responsibility, when a person is considered capable of understanding what is required socially and legally to make right decisions, and when that person is considered capable to manage brain and body so to carry out those decisions. When is this? A young adolescent may be considered capable of deciding a life career choice, of entering into a sexual relationship, of resisting pressure to drink, do drugs, or commit crime, yet not be legally culpable – here is a conundrum. The problem is not only a developmental one.

Nevertheless, there is legal provision for 'decisions' in which *I* might have diminished control for which I may not be held accountable, leaving the judge to decide where to draw the line, given the potential for every *I* to be in conflict with its neural host. When am I not at the 'helm' of my brain? Am I responsible for what I do in my sleep or when under hypnosis or under the influence of drugs? Am I responsible for the decision to *not* act (especially if there was a clear likelihood of a bad outcome)? Responsibility requires that *I* has the capacity to make a decision. *I* needs to be able to make a judgement and precipitate a course of action. That is, *I* needs to have the capacity to accept or reject the information the brain supplies. The alternative, the idea that behaviour is determined by neural activity reflecting only biochemical processes and conditioning – the idea that there is no separate entity *I* to make independent judgement of the information at its disposal – would surely mean that there is no 'I' culpable for *any* behaviour, asleep or awake, drunk or sober, suffering schizophrenia or of a 'sound mind'.

For some, the ongoing struggle between *I* and the brain for supremacy can be difficult indeed: the learned and activated impulses of the brain can be like wild horses that *I* tries to subdue with varying success. Perhaps successfully for a time, then becoming exhausted;[3] or more likely, exhaustion befalls the neurons engaging in the conflict, perhaps leading to a lapse of attention or engagement by *I*, and the event – the criminal act – occurs. Who then is responsible before law? If *I* has authority over the body it lives in, does *I* remain responsible for the body's actions, even if these actions go against the intentions of *I*? Conversely, even if my body fails to carry out the wrongful intentions of *I*, does *I* still carry liability?

It was the voices, your honour

As it is, there is implicit distinction made in law between *I* and the brain: there is provision that people may do things for which they are not responsible. How can this be? To do something generally requires a decision based on choice, and such choice requires the making of a judgement. Is it possible to do something *without* making a decision to do it? And is it possible to make a choice *without* judgement? For the law to allow that a person can do something for which he or she is not responsible implies either that the person was not active in the decision itself, or that he or she was incapable of making the necessary judgement.

But if *I* was not active in the decision, then how was the action initiated? And if *I* was not involved in making a judgement, on what basis was the decision made? Can neural activation free from control of *I* (not just the conscious control of *I*) 'decide' something? *I* makes decisions, yet decisions also find origin in unprocessed and unhindered impulses and drives: crimes of passion and psychotic and dissociated states, where *I* is temporarily incapacitated, a state of affairs *recognized in law*. *I* is held responsible for my words and actions, not the brain; *I* makes judgements, not neural networks. Any attempt to reduce existence to complex biochemistry – the activity of neural networks evolved over time to protect and propagate the organism – founders upon the rock of ascribed responsibility. Without the capacity to make judgement and the ability to choose (even if neural networks are involved), the application of law becomes illogical. Then the only reasonable response is *corrective* – to fix the problem; not *moral* – you are guilty of doing a wrong thing. Social scientists that take a reductionist view can logically only arrive at the former conclusion – pragmatic responses replace moral or legal ones.

I make the assumption that it is *I* that chooses and the choice is then expressed physically, although it is possible for this expression to occur sometime after the decision is made. The expression may even be blocked altogether. A poor fit between a decision I make and its subsequent expression creates tension which is experienced as frustration by *I*: I might make a conscious decision to complete an assignment today, but procrastination finds it untouched by evening. The reverse may also happen: a man may make a decision to stop drinking, yet the drinking continues – his 'decision' fails to find expression. Decisions of *I* do not always convert to action. But equally, I may engage in actions that appear not to be the result of decisions by *I*. This might occur with various neural conditions or the ingestion of, or withdrawal from, medications. In each case, the question presents itself: to what extent can I be held accountable? Let us consider Caroline, Derek, and Martin.

Caroline had not been sleeping well, and so her doctor prescribed zolpidem. She took it that night and slept well. Before going to bed, she had a discussion with her husband about confidential work matters, which was unlike her. She also offered to drive to the corner shop as they had run out of milk. Her husband went instead, telling her to get the sleep she needed. The following day, when her husband referred to the conversation of the previous night, she had no memory of these events and was alarmed about the confidences she had compromised. Had she been asleep, even though she appeared to be awake? Or was she simply amnesic to these events? She certainly *appeared* awake and responsive to conversation. Her brain was responding appropriately – but was her *I* engaged? Certainly, there was no retrospective awareness of the event. Could she be held accountable for her actions? Her decision to take zolpidem was one her *I* controlled, but what of her subsequent behaviour?

Derek had been taking the antidepressant escitalopram for anxiety and depression. One day he decided to cease taking the medication because of its side effects. After initial euphoria, he became irritable, nauseous, and dizzy, and fought a migraine headache. Over subsequent days, this gave way to disorientation, agitation, paranoia, and irrational behaviours, culminating in an assault upon a friend, for which he was charged and came before the court. After his medication was restored, he was restored, and greatly distressed by what had happened. How does Derek now stand before the law? Was he able to make judgement about the outcome of his decision? Was his *I* in control when his brain reacted to the sudden withdrawal of his medication? Nevertheless, he was in control of his decision not to take his medication, even though he did not predict the consequences.

Martin had not been feeling well lately. He had become withdrawn, morose, and agitated, and increasingly spent time in his bedroom. There were enemies all around keeping close watch on him and his family, he said: it was very stressful. Fortunately, he had psychic abilities, and voices in his head kept warning him to take protective action against the surrounding gangs that were plotting the destruction of his family. So he started searching for listening devices and kept a baseball bat by his bed. One evening, he answered the door bell with baseball bat in hand and attacked the stranger at the door. The police were called, and he was taken into custody. He was subsequently prescribed the anti-psychotic risperidone, after which the watchful eyes of the nearby gangs became less intense, and the voices less compelling, and his unfortunate visitor kept his distance. How culpable was Martin for his actions?

For all three – Caroline, Derek, and Martin – the capacity of their *I* to make good judgements was compromised for different reasons. Yet their actions were the product of a neural system of which their *I* was expected to be at the helm, and at least for Caroline and Derek, distortions in neural functioning was the result of action based on earlier decisions (to take zolpidem; to *not* take escitalopram), at which time their *I was* at the helm, even though it had insufficient information to make good judgement. For Martin, I daresay his *I* retained some control – it was his judgement that was compromised. These issues have further application. Consider those who acquiesce to hypnosis, come under the spell of a brain-washing cult, or allow themselves to succumb to other trance states: can these be held accountable for their actions when their *I* has temporarily forfeited authority and control? For the decision to forfeit such control, I can surely be held accountable, but what about actions while 'under the influence'?

Chapter 21

Science, the brain, and *I*

Psychology as a discipline has had a vexed relationship with the world of scientific endeavour, the psychologist as practitioner even more so. Carl Rogers wrote in *Persons or Science? A Philosophical Question*:

> As I have acquired experience as a therapist . . . and as I have worked as a scientific investigator . . . I have become increasingly conscious of the gap between these two roles. The better therapist I have become, the more I have been vaguely aware of my complete subjectivity when I am at my best in this function. And as I have become a better investigator, more 'hard-headed' and more scientific, I have felt an increasing discomfort at the distance between the rigorous objectivity of myself as scientist, and the almost mystical subjectivity of myself as therapist.
>
> (Rogers, 1961: 200)

Things have not changed. The dialogue between clinician and researcher has generally been strained, with the researcher, quite rightly, viewing with some disdain hypotheses that enthusiastic clinicians propose on the basis of personal experience, often with minimal research 'evidence'; while the clinician, with equal justification, wonders about the clinical relevance and application of material published in scientific journals. Each is faced with the question of how to explain what they see; but the parameters, language, and logic of explanation are a constant point of tension.

Clinicians are encouraged to apply scientific knowledge and method to what they do. Their work needs to be 'evidence-based', and their techniques open to scientific investigation. They are asked about the efficacy of treatments, and they grapple with the associated issues of the focus of therapy, of outcome variables, of the valid and reliable measurement of those outcomes, and of the explanatory models used to guide the process – the model of how change occurs. But the chasm between laboratory and clinic is great, the difference between what is known and what clinicians are asked to respond to considerable.

The parameters of science

It is the scientist's privilege to define his parameters, isolate variables, control various conditions, and determine the scope of his research: 'I am studying the effects of release of dopamine on attachment behaviours'; or: 'I wish to discover the effect of age in children on auditory short-term memory capacity'; and so on. Indeed, his subject complexity compels him to limit his focus, but the cost is that his findings are not easily generalized to life situations where variables are never isolated and conditions never controlled. And it is the life situation that the clinician faces, with all its complexities, unseen variables, and unpredictable conditions. To adequately understand the current experiences and behaviour of his client, the clinician needs to deal with the total picture – the client's history, motivations, environment, neural integrity, the strength of *I*, and so on, both known and unknown. The scientist limits his measurements and explanations to the narrow focus of his research; the clinician is faced with the problem of how wide to cast his net to explain what is before him.

Both the measurement and categorization of the patterns of human experience and behaviour have proved elusive in the science of the mind. Despite decades of research and thousands of theses that seek to measure aspects of human functioning, it remains an inexact science. We really do not know *what* we are measuring or categorizing, or what we *should* be measuring or categorizing. The measurement of the many aspects of the neural bases of human experience remains beyond our grasp, fMRIs notwithstanding, although we have glimpses of its complexity. But even more difficult is the measurement of the activity of the intangible *I*, which plays a role in that experience. So inevitably we measure the reports of subjective experience or selected behavioural manifestations of such experience, whether we are considering depression, autistic spectrum disorder, psychosis, or anxiety. And despite the herculean efforts of teams of scientists and clinicians codifying 'aberrant' human experience for the *Diagnostic and Statistical Manual of Mental Disorders*, such categorization has done little towards understanding the dynamics that discriminate between these experiences.

Turning to mathematics to attain more objectivity does not really solve the problem: numbers need to retain meaningful relationship to events and the variables they are said to represent. Applying numbers to human experience and behaviour, both in measurement and in developing explanatory models and algorithms, has its own challenges. Whether we look to mathematical modelling or statistical evaluation, the meaningful interpretation of results and the drawing out of its implications for clinical practice can be problematic.

Acceptable 'evidence': The measurable and the repeatable

Psychologists have a great goal: to be 'evidence-based' – the 'scientist-practitioner' model of clinical intervention is commonly promoted. And to be sure, I *want* to be evidence-based. I *want* to be a scientist-practitioner. I *want* to use interventions that 'work'. But what does this mean? Generally, evidence acceptable to science is measurable and can be confirmed by subsequent and repeated investigation and observation. But evidence in relation to human experience generally does not lend itself to this. And what does it mean to be a 'scientist-practitioner'? Page observed that what we mean by the term 'science' varies according to the philosophy of science one embraces, so that 'the term scientist is so devoid of meaning that for an individual, a training program, or our professional society [the *Australian Psychological Society*] to profess allegiance to a scientist-practitioner model is gratuitous' (Page, 1996: 103). He further asserted that there 'is no single universally accepted philosophy of science that could provide a foundation for the scientist-practitioner model of psychology' (Page, 1996: 107).

To base psychological practice on science surely means mastering the subject matter – to understand the dynamics of the mind. Yet, perhaps because this has proved too difficult, much psychological research has turned to a pragmatic 'what works' in identifying and changing aspects of experience or behaviour in selected 'samples' of people, calling it 'evidence-based', without developing a working model of the mind. Surely an effective clinician needs to understand the dynamics of the mind, rather than simply applying pragmatic solutions that might 'work'. Even if we limit ourselves to the latter as an expression of science-oriented practice, the question of what is acceptable evidence remains. Evidence that a technique 'works' implies it accomplishes what we want it to. But what change in human experience are we seeking? Is it to help clients find meaningfulness in events, 'symptoms', and memories, or to remove unwanted 'symptoms' and uncomfortable memories? Is it to change the behaviour, thinking, and skills of the client to what *they* want, or to what *I* think ought to be? Or is it to bring about better alignment between the brain and *I* towards improved self-efficacy?

Accepting that the clinician has to deal with constructs that are difficult to measure, with variables that cannot be controlled, and with explanatory systems that need to allow for 'free will', what is the nature of 'acceptable evidence' in the model a clinician might use to explain what he hears and sees? Is evidence that is acceptable to the historian and the court acceptable to the scientist? When there is sufficient agreement in the accounts of a few witnesses, the evidence is sufficient for a judge to convict a man and send him to jail for many years. There is room to argue how to interpret the evidence, but the evidence *itself* becomes sufficient basis for 'knowledge' in a legal and historical sense. Now if a few people agree in their accounts of subjective experiences based on introspection, is this acceptable evidence for clinical purposes? Nevertheless, even if we agree on the legitimacy of such data, we might argue about its interpretation – of what is it evidence?

This, of course, is a question central to psychology: is reported subjective experience (a description or estimation, current or remembered) 'acceptable' evidence? For that matter, is experience *itself* (apart from whether it can be reported accurately) 'acceptable' evidence? Radical behaviourists devoted to making a science of psychology voted a resounding *no*,[1] while most clinical practitioners voted a resounding *yes*. Yet most psychological 'measurements' used in research, such as personality questionnaires, depression and anxiety measures, SUD scales, schema questionnaires, and so on, are based on self-report. All make use of reported subjective experience – and this includes introspection – as basic data.[2] These are used as both dependent and independent variables in countless 'scientific' studies.

Even should I leave behind the imprecise and subjective world of psychological measurements and focus on something less imprecise and subjective – the functions of the brain itself – will I have better success? Will it be better science? Yet even in researching the brain, especially its neural software, it is difficult to know whether I am measuring what I think I am measuring, or whether what I want to measure is a measurable entity. Take 'working memory'. Is this a measurable entity somewhere in the brain? If it *is* a function of some tangible neural entity, what might that entity be,[3] and how might it be reliably measured? The brain in interaction does not isolate its functions – how can I disentangle these in study? Furthermore, if the entity *I* presents a variable in brain functioning, how is *this* controlled for? *I* is neither a random factor nor determined by brain processing; yet the brain responds to *I*, just as *I* depends on the brain. And most disconcertingly, *I* has the capacity to make decisions – 'free will' – that creates unique non-repeated events.

We cannot *see* what is going on – even in brain imaging processes, all we see is evidence for neural activity. We do not see meanings being created. Because of this, our conclusions and speculations are inferential, no less so than it was for the psychological thinkers and investigators of a hundred years ago, who did not have our technology. But our technology does not allow us to see or understand actual brain dynamics – only some of its effects, from which we make inferential statements.

Consider the connection between an *I* event and a physical event activating certain neural networks. What, for example, is the connection between a smile, its neural correlate, and the corresponding *I* event? When *I* is happy, I might smile. Then again, there may be the perception of something 'funny', or an attempt to be friendly. And for some, a smile is a sign of nervousness. No doubt I can find correlations and publish graphs and statistical tables. But the interpretation of *this particular event* identified at neural level remains speculative regardless of the maths and graphs I have at hand. Alternatively, I can make 'sense' of the matter at the level of introspection and inferential logic, speculating about the intent of *I*, but how is this any different from psychoanalysis?

Science and the clinician: Rules of explanation

The problem of acceptable evidence and measurable events in the realm of human experience lead to other problems relating to explanatory models. Because 'scientific evidence' is generally open to inspection and objective measurement and relates to repeatable events, this kind of evidence is normally also pursued by researchers in psychology, resulting in a constant risk of forcing human experience into limited reductionist and deterministic models.

It is a problem not restricted to researchers in psychology. Both the neuroscientist and biochemist face the temptation to generate models of human behaviour and experience that reduce events to molecular level. It is like 'explaining' that my conversation is 'nothing more' than a series of sound-waves that leave my mouth and enter your ears. But science should not be about explaining things 'away', reducing life events to their most basic form. Rather, science is about generating models that help understand and predict the behavioural and experiential processes we are studying; models that best 'fit' what we observe and provide a way of conceptualizing and communicating about such processes. What is it we are trying to explain? For me as clinician, it is human experience and motivation, human decision making and perception, optimal functioning within the self and within relationships, and in particular, in relation to the client before me.

Nevertheless, although our interest is at macro level, the models we generate should not do violence to what happens at micro level. A model to explain what is happening, for example, when I have a conversation with someone, should work at the level of meanings and ideas exchanged, but should also allow that the conversation really *is* carried by a series of sound-waves from mouth to ear. To use another analogy, if I was to study the meanings of a novel, I might usefully narrow my focus to some key passages, and even, perhaps, to key words. But if I was to study the novel at the micro level of individual letters and their relationship to one another, I would never be able to make sense of what was going on in the novel, even though every letter is necessary and needs to be in *exactly* the right place.[4] The question of the entities I work with becomes a key issue in developing an explanatory model that makes meaning of the whole.

Although Freud has been criticized for the lack of 'science' in his psychoanalytic formulations, he was very much the scientist in training and orientation, albeit struggling with the vexed issue of applying 'science' to the mind. But Freud, too, sometimes succumbed to the problems of reductionism and determinism. In this regard, Frankl articulated the dilemma the clinician faces[5] – how is it that I can rise above my own biological and psychological conditions if I am defined by them? In much scientific research, not only has *I* become reduced to neural activity, 'nothing but' cells of the body, an expression of matter (even if seen as an 'emergent' function), but also the activation of the will and the expression of *I* in the decisions *I* makes have become reduced to the inevitable endpoints of predetermined forces in the body and the world in which the body moves, the chain of cause-and-effect governing the natural world.

Although the idea of 'self' or mind is often rejected by science purists, it remains in mainstream psychology because (in part) clinicians need it for their explanatory models. But the question of 'self', of *I* – largely defined by the subjective state of awareness – still presents the scientist-practitioner with the problem of the nature of 'acceptable explanation'. 'Science' needs clear objectively defined concepts and entities. It needs definitions with mathematical and conceptual precision, allowing us all to talk about *exactly* the same thing in experimental research. Yet no diagnosis, emotion, or subjective state qualifies. Instead, I use literary devices, such as analogy and metaphor, to communicate explanatory models.

My over-riding interest as clinician is to match my hypotheses with client experience and behaviour, rather than to other theories. Yet many scientists and clinicians use evolutionary theory to promote the utility or validity of their explanatory hypotheses; it then plays an important role in their conceptualizations. My starting point is not evolution, but the client's experience, and, given my role, this needs to be my focus.[6] I believe a goal of the 'true' scientist is to develop a model centred on the phenomena being explained, rather than conforming to an overarching theory.

There are many who might take issue with these sentiments, arguing that the proper brief of a clinician is the application of scientific research to the problems presented in the clinic. Any counsellor can develop idiosyncratic theories about human behaviour with associated ideas for intervention, but the clinician works with *evidence* – scientific evidence about the nature of the conditions being presented, so that he can give 'proper' diagnosis; and scientific evidence for what works in intervention, so he can oversee a successful and expedient recovery. Nevertheless, an explanatory model (that is, the application of a 'scientific' interpretation) must find meaning in the context of a client's subjective experience to be helpful. In any event, the diagnostic processes, scientific interpretations, and 'best practice' interventions are themselves under continual debate (as they should be), and are constantly changing as new formulations are developed for clinical issues.

I and scientific inquiry

In *The Man who Mistook his Wife for a Hat*, Sacks observed:

> Charcot and his pupils, who included Freud and Babinski as well as Tourette, were among the last of their profession with a combined vision of body and soul, 'It' and 'I', neurology and psychiatry. By the turn of the century, a split had occurred, into a soulless psychiatry and a bodiless psychology.
>
> (Sacks, 1985: 98)

Subsequent development of the discipline of psychology did little to restore the chasm: *I* remained suspect, and neurology appeared to have little to offer. Why did *I* remain suspect? Psychologists in academic circles have over the decades argued strongly that, because I cannot see, measure, locate, or test for the mind (here, think '*I*'), it is not a legitimate subject of inquiry for a scientist, and so has no place in the discourse of psychology as a scientific discipline. While this may be acceptable logic for the peer-reviewed researcher and publisher, it creates a problem for the clinician, who is daily confronted with issues involving *I*. Nevertheless, issues of mind also created problems for the science of psychology, forcing it to employ statistical paradigms where 'laws of behaviour' and 'laws of cognitive functioning' only provide approximate predictions for human behaviour.

The mind remains an invisible mediator, making internal (and often distorted) judgements in the completion of psychological measures. When testing is more 'objective', such as with IQ testing, we enter into debate as to what is *really* being measured. When 'cognition' slipped back into the scientific literature after the strictly 'scientific' behavioural approach proved frustratingly restrictive and incomplete in its conceptualization, other aspects of mind often accompanied it in subtle ways. Now, in an effort to recapture a scientific base, the growing popularity of building psychological understanding around neurosciecnce research (after all, neurons can be seen, measured, and subjected to experimental trials) will once again fall short of the conceptualizations clinicians need to effectively work with their clients' narratives.

Much of what we do 'scientifically' is what the brain is naturally wired to do: to make associations. And so a common enterprise in psychology is: what goes with what? Is *this* really related to *that*? Out of this, we hope to build our understandings. But this is inadequate to explain the complex dynamics that operate in any one person. Our scientific investigations have until now left us short-changed when we ask the question: what's really going on? Our correlations and t-tests and analyses of variance and more complex mathematical modelling only give us information about the statistical relationship between sets of variables. Yet the understanding of human experience, of the dance of *I* with the brain, requires an understanding of the unique and dynamic forces operating within and around the person. It is this uniqueness and dynamism that makes studies based on trends and averages so inconclusive. And it is this uniqueness and dynamism that creates the problem for the 'clinician as scientist'.

These problems are not restricted to psychology or even to neuroscience or biochemistry – but apply also to that queen of sciences, physics. Yet here some real progress appears to have been made in the conceptualization of dynamic forces. For the quantum physicist, light as a dynamic entity has the properties of a wave, but when frozen in time and space, it has the properties of a particle. The difficulty is in capturing a dynamic entity so that we might properly see and study it. A particle of light cannot be captured in time and space: it is only possible to talk of *probabilities* of its being in any one place at any particular time. And despite the endeavour to deal with the observable, the scientist cannot actually *see* light: only the *effects* of light can be seen.

Although physics remains deterministic in a way psychology cannot, the application to psychology is clear: the dynamic and interactive nature of *I* and the brain gives them properties that cannot be studied in a static context. Meaningfulness requires dynamic interchange – you cannot read anything by staring at the same few letters for a period, nor can you understand what I say by focusing on a sound-byte (which is dynamic, carried in wave form). Even though the words in this book are static, the reading process itself is dynamic – the meanings I apprehend are an outcome of the dynamic process. '*Aha*' is a 'coming together' by association in a moment of time. Although bits of information chunked together become unique static associations captured in neural association strings, these are established by the dynamic of the continuous stream of associations normally represented in daily living, and are themselves activated in dynamic processes. As with light and wind, I cannot see *I* – the *awareness* of *I* is only known through the *effects of I* in my body and neural system. I do not even have an awareness of how I manage neural software: I just *do* it, and this, too, is a dynamic process.

I have argued that human experience (perhaps like quantum physics) does not lend itself to the formulations of traditional science: however, I have *not* suggested that logic, reason, or evidence do not apply to explanatory models. Rather, I believe we need to revisit the rules of acceptable evidence and explanatory mechanisms if we are to do justice to human experience and to create appropriate conceptual frameworks the clinician can use.

Chapter 22

The clinician, the brain, and *I*

'I haven't done this before,' Susan tells me apologetically, as her eyes take in her surroundings at the beginning of her first session. 'I'm not sure what I should say, what you need to know. I don't know what to expect. Can you tell me how this works?'

What an excellent question, I think to myself. How *does* this work? What will I, her clinician, be trying to do once she has told her story? Change the landscape of her neural network connections that mediate her cognitive software so that she might think differently? Modify the pattern of release of neurotransmitters and neuropeptides so that she feels better? Encourage her to make new decisions so that her *I* takes a different position on matters? Work on creating hope and new plans for her future?

To begin with, I will simply listen. I will engage Susan's *I* as together we make sense of what she is experiencing. A clinician may, of course, do much more than this – but this is normally the beginning, and generally the greater part of a clinician's role – the verbal interchange between me and the other. Is the object of my focus another brain, to understand how it functions? No: it is to communicate with the other – Susan – who exists within the body sitting before me. Why would I do this? Perhaps, through the interaction we establish, we might decide on the meaning of things, I might help to alleviate the distress her *I* might be experiencing, or I might contribute to the solving of the life problems her *I* is struggling with. How can my talking with her accomplish this? Perhaps when I make an interpretation, I work in cooperation with Susan's existing drive to properly interpret those signals. An interpretation may elicit an 'aha' response in her, indicating that a connection has been made that is meaningful and remembered: it is verbal in nature, but connects emotional and sensory events to ideas.

Just as there is interaction between Susan's *I* and her brain, so there is interaction between me as clinician and the *I* in Susan. It is an interaction mediated by our brains and that has the potential to modify aspects of her mind map simply through my engagement with her *I* (but also an interaction that may suffer interference because of distortions created by our respective mind maps). Yet if the brain is about connection and disconnection, informing and protecting *I*; if it is about focus and discrimination and interpretation of events and meaningfulness, the dynamics of the interaction of *I* with the world; if it is about software systems supporting a mind map that informs *I*; then surely these processes are as much of interest to Susan's clinician as is the actual encounter with the other *I* that manages and responds to these systems.

The question of change in psychotherapy

How is all this possible? How can the interaction between clinician and Susan bring about neural changes, changes in her mind map, or changes in the position of Susan's *I* about various matters? What brings about change for Susan − if, indeed, this is the goal?

One of the first tasks the clinician undertakes is the establishment of rapport and empathy: 'Look out the other's windows. Try to see the world as your patient sees it . . . Patients profit enormously simply from the experience of being fully seen and fully understood' (Yalom, 2001: 18). Why? This sets the context for open exchange between the clinician's *I* and Susan's *I*. Why is this so important and helpful? And why is it sometimes not nearly enough? Why does the simple telling of the pain and distress Susan experiences resolve or, at least, help many things − yet not all things? What is the difference between that which gets resolved in the telling and that which does not? When I hear 'well' and interpret 'accurately', changes often occur: how is this possible? Is it simply in the naming of emotions, the accessing of troubling memories?

Susan says at the end of a session in which I have said little: 'Thank you. I feel like a load has come off my back − I feel much lighter.' What does she mean? She has not lost any kilos − how can she be 'lighter'? Mostly what I did was listen. Susan's *I* event became a 'we' event through the telling. Knowledge was shared and emotional intensity reduced. How did this happen? What if Susan was to tell her attentive dog what she told me − would the effect be the same? Is the effect in the telling, or does the nature of the interaction − the belief that I, her clinician, understand her − make a difference? And if so, why should it? Can communicating with me bring about a chemical change in her brain?

Apparently it can. Research has shown that 'naming an affect soothes limbic firing' (Siegel, 2009: 116). Articulating an emotion has the immediate effect of ameliorating its intensity as measured by neural activation, as though one form of expression has been replaced (to a degree) by another − amygdala and reticular formation activation replaced by frontal cortex activation. The work of the frontal cortex software to manage the material carried in the amygdala and reticular formation by way of the limbic system seems to be helped towards resolution by the articulation of the emotion. No doubt Carl Rogers would feel vindicated. The focus of neural activation and the meanings thus carried seems to be transferred from one part of the brain to another, or perhaps dissipated altogether by exiting the system through communication with another *I*. When I listened to Susan, there was a new endpoint in the communication process: it was no longer between Susan's *I* and her own brain. I become part of her resolution process. Perhaps the presence of a new endpoint (me) in our communication caused Susan's *I* and brain to align: perhaps her brain was forced into the role of mediator of *I* rather than source of the communication of emotion.

But psychotherapeutic change is not just about soothing limbic firing. Change is necessarily also about new learning, perhaps about unlearning, almost always about symptom relief, and ultimately about thriving in the world. What can a clinician hope to change? In Seligman's reflections upon what can and what cannot change in therapy, he introduces the idea of *depth* of a presenting problem. He suggests there are three aspects to this: the *biological underpinnings*; the *ease of confirming or disconfirming beliefs* underlying a problem; and the *power of the belief* underlying a problem (Seligman, 1994). He explains biological underpinnings as 'prepared' learning – that is, learning that is genetically predisposed or heritable, resulting from a single experience which is not rational or conscious, resistant to change, and selective only for objects of adaptive significance. 'Unprepared' learning – that is, a learned habit – is easier to change. With regard to ease of confirming or disconfirming beliefs, Seligman argues that the harder a belief underlying a problem is to disconfirm, the harder it will be to change. With regard to power of belief, Seligman suggests that the greater the range of experiences a particular belief explains, the greater its power, and the harder it is to change. 'Deep' problems centre on 'prepared' learning and beliefs that are 'powerful' and difficult to disconfirm. Seligman then outlines his views about the varying 'depth' in a range of psychological problems.

Translating these ideas into our terms, Seligman argues that problems rooted in predetermined hardware wiring ('prepared' learning), problems requiring a change of position of *I* contrary to my own rationale for my position (disconfirming a belief), and problems requiring profound changes in the structure of the mind map (a 'powerful' belief) are 'deep', and likely to be difficult or perhaps impossible to change. This certainly seems reasonable. Yet recent literature on neuroplasticity suggests there is potentially no limit to the changes that are neurally possible (Doidge, 2010). Nevertheless, neuralplasticity is not so much about learning in the sense of the normal establishment of neural pathways as it is the capacity of the brain to utilize alternative regions and pathways where the regions and pathways normally allocated to the task have ceased to function. Importantly, neuroplasticity is not about changing the decisions of *I*, or about changing the structure of the mind map, or about unlearning – the undoing of neural pathways.

Further to Seligman's thoughts on *depth* as a dimension of change, I would like to add the dimensions of *direction* and *domain* of change. In regard to *direction*, I propose that it is easier to learn than to unlearn a thing – the brain is primed to make connections governed by focus of *I*. In contrast, *disconnections* generally only take place under duress, and frequently without involvement of *I*. To be able to *unlearn* things would solve problems that addictions, anxieties, and obsessional thoughts create. Learned skills, such as language or motor skills, may 'get rusty' with neglect, but the neural connections remain. Under the right conditions, they will again be activated.[1] Possibly the only way to 'unlearn' something is through the creation of new meanings for existing material: while neural connections remain largely intact, *I* attributes new meanings, requiring adjustment of only a few connections.

The brain is primed to make increasingly efficient and complex connective systems to carry meanings for *I*. There appears to be little capacity to reverse the process, to dismantle the mind map and deconstruct meanings, except where there is corruption of the hardware systems, as happens in dementia or in extreme situations where functional dissociation is necessary for the survival of self. Being geared towards integrating new information, the brain is inherently resistant to changing established systems, whether those changes relate to the regulatory settings of automatic bodily functions, to changes in homeostatic balance, or to basic changes in a person's world view. A mind map that accommodates change in the sense of new 'superficial' learning is one thing; a mind map that itself needs to change (revising old 'foundational' learning) is altogether another.

A person's mind map needs to remain stable to function as a reliable orienting system with which *I* can interpret the ever-changing world. It provides a world view, values, life direction and goals, self-perception, and the principles around which expectations and judgements and interpretations are made. If the system works towards stability (resisting change), then it is necessary to sustain neural connections and association strings once established, which is why connections are so much easier to create than disconnections are to effect. To the extent therapy is about change, given the difficulties inherent in change, the art is to make maximum use of existing learning and to minimize the amount of change necessary to bring about the desired outcome, minimizing demand on the neural system.

With regard to *domain* of change, we have seen the complexity of various memory systems involved in learning: both implicit and explicit, covering different sensory modalities. Both the type and range of modalities covered will inform the extent, ease, and robustness of change. The most powerful learning incorporates multiple sensory modalities, requiring the activation of multiple neural networks (through the appropriate focus of *I*) involving the various senses. Change is easier when fewer modalities are involved.

Yet psychotherapy is not only about change: it is also about the management by *I* of the neural resources on which it depends and through which it expresses itself. The *I*–brain dynamic plays an important role both in the progress of many psychological problems and in making sense of life experiences. Each reacts to the other as partners do in marriage – *I* interpreting and reacting to neural signals, and neural networks in turn both mediating and reacting to *I*. Both clinician and client need to manage the internal struggle of *I* with the body's signals – while *I* directs thinking, planning, and forms intentions, the body communicates needs relating to homeostasis and self-preservation, processes largely determined genetically and developmentally. As both *I* events and neural events can occur outside consciousness, the clinician can have a challenge explicating the dynamic. It is the understanding of these subterranean forces emanating from both *I* and the brain – forces influencing behaviour below awareness – that became the holy grail of the psychoanalysts. However, although the brain creates meaning from incoming sensory and body events, it is generally unable to make meaningful interpretation of its own dysfunction. In this regard, accurate external feedback to help interpret these experiences can be important, assuming the client knows the relevant information to report.

The complexity of the clinician's task emerges. At what point does therapeutic intervention properly target brain functioning (or more accurately, neural dysfunction), as against *I* that the brain serves? If the brain normally works efficiently, should I understand many psychological problems as normal reactions to abnormal events, the brain's self-regulating responses protecting *I*? If neural disconnection, temporary neural shutdown, and other dynamics of neural homeostasis have a functional role, is it wise to intervene directly in the complex mediating neural processes when the problem may reflect a functional brain reacting to a disturbed *I*?

Nevertheless, brain hardware can fail, so that some form of direct neural intervention is sometimes justified. Sometimes the problem may relate to the brain reacting to *I*'s response to the world, as in trauma reaction, depression, and anxiety. At other times, the problem may relate to *I* reacting to a dysfunction in the brain, as with schizophrenia or one suffering stroke; and at still other times, the nature of the problem may be unclear, as with addictions and OCD. And then there are processes that once were adaptive, but are so no longer, such as childhood responses to trauma, or processes that once were a function of *I*, but no longer, such as we see in eating disorders. Where then should the therapeutic focus be?

And so we come to the question: what is the role of the clinician with respect to these different challenges? How can the clinician help make a difference – indeed, how does the clinician decide what he can reasonably do for Susan? When is the process about simply listening and acknowledging; when is it about facilitating change in thinking, experience, or behaviour; and when is it about making sense of and optimizing the *I*–brain relationship? Furthermore, who should properly 'drive' the process – Susan or her clinician?

The role of psychotropic medication in therapy

Before reflecting on the role of the clinician in therapy, I make some observations in relation to the role of psychotropic medication in psychotherapeutic change. Even the simplest of psychological conditions is surprisingly complex at neural level because of the interactive nature both of the neural networks themselves, but also of the neural networks with *I*. The separation of the primary neural event from its secondary effects is problematic, and this has implications for medical intervention: to what degree does psychotropic medication address the primary neural event, as against ameliorating the associated symptoms? The use of the same medications for different conditions, the use of different medications for the same conditions, and the variation of side effects seen in different people reflect the complexities and variation of neural systems between people, and the limited understanding we have of the nature of the conditions themselves. Further, even though medication may affect aspects of neural processing, it is indifferent to the issues of *I* in its interactive role with the brain.

I am sometimes asked by clients suffering depression whether or not they should take antidepressant medication. I am not in a position to offer an opinion, and I refer them on to their doctor or psychiatrist. But the question is an intriguing one and I see many clients who have been prescribed psychotropic (mostly antidepressant) medication (the range available is constantly growing) who talk of their experiences. And so I venture some observations in relation to antidepressants and antipsychotics.

By and large, the aim of antidepressants is to enhance the presence – either the production or the retention – of one or other of the neurotransmitters serotonin, noradrenaline, or dopamine.[2] Only a limited range of neurotransmitters assumed to relate to depression are currently targeted by medications. The most commonly used class of antidepressants appear to be SSRIs. These medications aim to discourage neurons from absorbing serotonin (a normal cellular action), so that more serotonin molecules remain in the relevant synapses. It is argued that, in a depressed person, serotonin levels are depleted, and some have hypothesized that this 'imbalance' is responsible for depression. It therefore seems logical that correcting this 'imbalance' should resolve the depression, and this is what the SSRI is designed to do.[3] But what actually happens? How might the brain react to such manipulation of a neurotransmitter system normally managed by the brain itself, influenced by *I* through its software?

A normal synaptic function of the neuron is its reuptake capacity, through which it regulates neurotransmitter activity. To selectively inhibit such uptake through antidepressant medication no doubt increases serotonin availability, but equally risks reducing neural sensitivity and regulatory responsiveness. Serotonin, like any neurotransmitter, needs to have the capacity to move from one neuron to the next as needed to do its job as gatekeeper: the reuptake process plays a role in this action. Further, the brain comprises many balanced systems: while neurotransmitters are released in one system, they are inhibited in another. Such selective activation underpins internal communication processes and occurs in rapid succession – the brain needs to be responsive to the changing demands made of it.

The need for such responsivity presents a problem for medications targeting neural systems, as medications make no discrimination between brain regions and their varying roles in overall information-processing tasks, nor are they time-sensitive. Any one type of neurotransmitter mediates information implicated in many interconnected neural networks. Compromising one type of neurotransmitter activity has implications for many networks, and the inhibition of one part of the brain activates another part, giving rise to side effects, which vary from person to person. And so any action by medication may have both beneficial and unwanted effects. While one aspect of neural functioning is slowed, another may be activated. The question is: which areas are thus affected? Further, in the brain's task to maintain homeostasis, it is likely to slow the production of a neurochemical it finds in sufficient quantity in the synaptic system: it is possible the brain may over time temporarily *reduce* its production of serotonin in the presence of SSRIs.

Nevertheless, antidepressants have some beneficial effect for many people suffering depression, although it is unclear how much this is due to contributing to the reinvigoration of depleted neurons. Perhaps a beneficial effect may relate to the reduction of neural sensitivity through the medication's moderating action. For a fatigued neural system (if this is what we are dealing with), this may be helpful in that medication may partially suppress the demands being made on the system. If the artificial interference in neurotransmitter activity has the effect of moderating the sensitivity of that neurotransmitter to the functions of *I* or to external signals, we might expect to find an experiential 'dulling' of experience and emotions, also affecting the relationship of *I* with the brain. To the extent that neurotransmitter activity is directly related to suffering in *I*, its partial attenuation might ameliorate suffering, but at the cost of the responsiveness of the neural system.

Subjective reports appear to support this notion. For example, Liam reported that after many months on the SSRI escitalopram:

> I feel clumsy-minded, unable to catch my thoughts. It feels messy in my head – there is no order or clear thinking. Sometimes I feel too relaxed – not calm – but as if I don't care anymore about my actions. I feel a loss of sense of responsibility or duty, unable to really carry things through.

Another client said of his experience with escitalopram: 'I feel detached, unemotional, objective. I know I have feelings down there, but they can't "climb out". I can't access them or express them anymore.' A client on moclobemide reported: 'I feel a bit spacey at times.'

Other clients on antidepressants have reported: 'Since taking the medication, I don't get down or angry as quick, but I have also largely lost my sexual desire: it has taken the passion away'; and: 'I am not really myself, but I'm coping better'; and: 'It cuts out the highs and the lows – there is more of a buffer between me and the world; but I feel a bit spaced out'; and: 'It takes the "edge" off my performance, my thinking and my emotion – I feel a bit foggy.' I am aware of no research that systematically explores clients' subjective experience of various psychotropic medications. However, I have observed that, although individual experiences of antidepressants vary, a common theme appears to be not so much a resolution of the various symptoms of depression or other conditions such as anxiety and OCD, but a numbing effect that renders the symptoms less concerning. This echoes Charlie's experience with sertraline.

These experiences suggest some alleviation of symptoms, but not the 'things are back to normal' experience we might anticipate if we had successfully corrected neurotransmitter 'imbalance'. Instead, the experience is frequently of the brain being affected by a substance interfering with normal neural responsiveness – in the areas of emotion, thinking, sexual desire, and general performance. Furthermore, there sometimes appears to be some interference with the control of *I* over the brain, as if a substance is blocking neural responsiveness to *I*. A decrease in emotional sensitivity can be helpful as it alleviates the suffering of *I* to some degree.

Further, the inhibition of some neural responsiveness may contribute to neural recovery. It may be that antidepressant medication can make a helpful contribution to recovery from depression, but not necessarily in the ways often conceptualized, nor in a consistent manner, as it also contributes to unintended inhibition and activation of other neural networks.

With bipolar disorder, even though it may be on a continuum with depression, reflecting dysregulation due to neuron depletion (using Birkmayer's model – although many will disagree with this conceptualization), the dysregulation process is different and generally more severe, and a different class of medication is typically used: lithium. This inert salt may reduce overall neural sensitivity, which in turn may aid in the regulation of the reticular formation. Torrey observes: 'like other antipsychotics, precisely *how* lithium works is as yet unknown; its effectiveness may be related to its ability to control the transport of substances across the cell membrane' (1988: 210). But, again, it is an intervention independent of the control of *I*, its potential for toxic side effects is significant, and it may also act to reduce the responsiveness of the system to normal neural demands.

Similar observations may be made with regard to other psychotropic medications. Nearly all major tranquilizers or antipsychotic medications block dopamine receptors (and also possibly the receptors for noradrenaline, acetylcholine, and other neurotransmitters). This seems to remove or at least reduce the experience of hallucinations, delusions, psychomotor agitation, thinking disorders, 'bizarre' behaviours, and symptoms relating to the 'over-acuteness' of the senses, but at cost of stiffness and tremor. It appears that dopamine plays a role in enabling problematic neural pathways that represent dysfunctional connections, although they mediate functional messages as well. And so there are side effects: blurring of vision, restlessness, diminished spontaneity (of physical movement, gestures, and speech), and slurring of speech. That is, a blunting and interfering in certain performance levels.

To reduce symptoms is one thing, but can these medications improve the functioning of people suffering psychosis – can they enhance the strength of sense of self, for example? Apparently not: Torrey notes they make little improvement on apathy, ambivalence, poverty of thought, or flattening of emotions (1988: 189). He points out that 'drugs do not *cure*, but rather *control*, the symptoms of schizophrenia', and: 'we do not know precisely how they work, but we suspect it is their ability to block dopamine (and other) receptors in the brain' (Torrey, 1988: 186).[4] Torrey cites the following experience of a patient administered antipsychotic medication:

> Whereas I lived in a fascinating ocean of imagination, I now exist in a mere puddle of it. I used to write poetry and prose because it released and satisfied something deep inside myself; now I find reading and writing an effort and my world inside is a desert.
>
> (Torrey, 1988: 197)

Again we find a *reduction* in neural capacities, rather than a 'cure' for the problem: the medications do not restore corrupted limbic pathways or disconnect unwanted ones.

Even medications designed to stimulate neural functioning appear to have a suppressing effect. The mother of a boy prescribed methylphenidate for ADD reported that her son had some improvement of concentration, but at the cost of difficulties getting to sleep, loss of appetite, a dulling of emotions, and loss of motivation. In other words, aspects of the regulatory function of his reticular activating system appeared to be compromised. It seemed to take away some of his 'spark': he was less happy, and with time he became depressed. Dextroamphetamine also appears to compromise neural functioning. Troy was in his thirties and had used dextroamphetamine for many years, but became concerned for his marriage:

> It helps me focus at work, although I become obsessive, and I no longer interact with my wife or with others. I don't care about things, I'm irritable, stressed, and don't listen. When I come off dextroamphetamine, at first I'm tired like a zombie, then after awhile, I get my personality back: I feel alive again.

Whatever the psychotropic medication, attempts to chemically change brain functioning may enhance, distort, or block neural communication processes. While chemical intervention can promote or disrupt neurotransmitter activity, and affect the relationship of *I* to its neural networks, *I* remains separate. Any issues centred in *I* need to be addressed differently, usually through encounter with another *I*. The use of psychotropic medications for psychological problems, while helpful in symptom management, generally does not *resolve* the problem, even where corruption or fatigue of neural hardware seems indicated.

The role of the clinician in therapy

Sometimes psychotherapy is about listening. Sometimes it is about change – difficult though this generally is. Sometimes psychotherapy is about establishing new meanings and integrating old ones. And sometimes it is about assisting another's *I* to manage neural processes, even where it is unable to bring about fundamental change.

We revisit depressed Helen. There are clinicians for whom assessment would mean the categorizing of Helen into one or other illness or disorder, so they can 'apply' the 'appropriate intervention' seen to be relevant to that category. Yet such categorization fails to provide the clinician with information of the mind map orienting Helen and informing her behaviour, nor does it reflect the complexity of processes between Helen's *I* and her brain wherein changing symptoms may shift her from one category to another. Furthermore, it can place the clinician in the stance of observer of Helen's *I* as an 'it' to be 'treated', rather than being in encounter with an *I* which happens to be struggling. Alternatively, the clinician may find himself in the role of teacher, encourager, or coach. Who has the power in the relationship: who makes the decisions in relation to the clinician's role or to the changes sought? Most would agree her clinician needs to respect the integrity of Helen's *I*: her perceptions, judgements, and decisions. Her clinician needs to support the changes *Helen* seeks, and help Helen's *I* to manage her neural software optimally.

The clinician's role is coloured by the way Helen's problem is conceptualized. An 'illness' needs healing; a 'problem' needs to be solved; a 'deficiency' in thinking or performance requires training or education; and a 'disorder' needs to be returned to order. Does Helen have a 'mental illness', disease, or sickness? If someone had a broken leg, suffered a head injury, spoke with a stutter, presented under the influence of heroin, or was afraid of heights, would we say they had an 'illness' or 'disease'? We need to distinguish between invading organisms (commonly regarded as sickness or disease); the effect of toxins (which might have a disease label, but not when administered by an anaesthetist or due to recreational drugs); physical injuries; the failure of neural systems to adequately perform their function; and the problems created by the decisions of *I*. The terms we use affect the questions we ask and the directions we turn to for answers.

There is a further conundrum. Because the clinician's efficient brain seeks to make sense of things, it is selective in the material it apprehends and it interprets the material on the basis of its pre-existing frameworks. The clinician encounters a troubling problem: if Helen reports experiences that do not fit well with the clinician's perceptual framework, is it valid for him to reinterpret Helen's perception in terms of his own framework, as if it were somehow superior or less distorted? That Helen's perceptions may be distorted or poorly interpreted may well be the case, but is the clinician free of this same problem? Does his knowledge of 'scientific' evidence necessarily make him a better judge? Already we have seen that 'scientific' evidence in psychology needs to be treated with care. Yet reinterpreting a client's experience is commonly done: a valid aspect of the clinician's role, to be sure, but one fraught with difficulty, especially when dealing with apparent perceptual distortions.[5]

We can choose not to be bothered by the veracity of Helen's interpretations and work with the material as remembered by her, making sense of the material within her conceptual framework. The art of 'making sense of things', whatever the original data may be, is central to the creation of a narrative. Such a narrative – the verbal representation of material comprising a client's mind map – allows for manipulation of remembered material, both by Helen's *I* and by her clinician, but always within a pre-existing framework. It employs a language both understand and can work with. It allows the retrospective creation of meanings of remembered events, a process of integration and reworking. It is not the same as the events themselves, nor the stored memories of the event, which are probably stored as images or abstract representations. Rather, it represents meaning subsequently imposed on the events.

Cozolino argues for the development of narrative as a key process in therapy:

> The co-construction of narratives between parent and child or therapist and client provides a broad matrix supporting the integration of multiple neural networks. Autobiographical memory creates stories of the self capable of

supporting affect regulation in the present and the maintenance of homeostatic functions into the future. Memory, in this form, may maximize neural network integration as it organizes vast amounts of information across multiple processing tracks. Stories serve to bridge and integrate neural networks both in the present moment and through time.

(Cozolino, 2002: 63)

My role as clinician may be ancillary – Helen is largely responsible for the creation of her own narrative.

The access to psychological problems by way of language provides clinician and client with a powerful tool. Both neural networks and language serve the same function – to carry a message. Yet both can fail to deliver. Neural networks mediate the message within; language generally mediates the message without. Still, it is not the language but the *message* that *I* apprehends and responds to, although without language to carry it, the message is not delivered. It is the incoming message that is abstracted from language; it is the encoded message that is sent. Central to the identity and function of *I* is one who receives and sends messages – messages to bless or to curse; messages of love, value, and encouragement, or messages of destruction and dismissal; messages that embrace and connect, or messages that withdraw and disconnect.

The clinician ultimately works with words to carry messages, although there are other mediums, such as art, music, massage, or movement. The clinician needs to take great care in the messages he sends, and how accurately he interprets incoming messages. He needs to craft outgoing messages so they are accurately received. The use of story and metaphor can play an important role in such communication.[6] The process is an enormous challenge – not only because of the limitations of language, but also because of differences or distortions in the respective mind maps that can confuse and misrepresent messages.

To what can I liken the role of clinician? Perhaps we might conceive of Helen's *I* negotiating its neural territory and mind map, partly known and understood, partly not – like a soldier negotiating foreign territory, partly known, partly not, in order to subdue it. The soldier depends on external intelligence to know what is before him and how to negotiate the territory, while the external intelligence needs to know the position and capacities of the soldier. The clinician is the 'external intelligence', with some knowledge of the territory Helen's *I* faces, but needing to know Helen's 'position' and capacities (that is, to understand the mind map orienting her *I*) in order to provide useful feedback. Whatever assistance might be given through medication (to push the soldier analogy – the provision of aerial support) or external information, Helen's *I* still needs to take authority over her neural region, just as the soldier needs to establish a physical presence in the territory he is occupying.

The clinician's role encompasses different processes reflecting the complexities of the client's experience. At times the clinician simply listens and acknowledges; at times he interprets and helps create new meanings, improving the orientation of the client. At times the clinician helps plan change strategies in relation to unwanted behaviour or thinking; at times he encourages and motivates towards such change. At times the clinician teaches and trains, accurately distinguishing between his client's *I* and neural processes. The clinician needs to judge when to do what, to time things well, and to understand the readiness, capacities, and orientation of the client. Manualized 'evidence-based' treatments applied upon the basis of the categorization of a client into one disorder or another risks being untimely and counterproductive, although such procedure applied appropriately can help create structure for therapy. But there is no substitute for good clinical judgement.

Epilogue

With the rapid developments in technology translating into developments in the neurosciences, a fundamental question for the clinician is: what do I learn from these developments that help me address the problems with which my clients present me? As researchers enthusiastically map out the neural correlates to subjective experiences with fMRI technology, what are they finding that helps me in my clinical work tomorrow, apart from being able to explain to clients which parts of their neural landscape are being activated when they engage in particular thoughts and feelings? Do these advances help me in my interaction with the other *I* that uses a marvellous and complex system through which to express itself?

When I went to school, my mathematics teacher made various statements – generally not towards me – that belied his awareness of this deep mystery. He would say: 'Use your brain'; and: 'Did you leave your brains behind today?' Clearly, he understood there was a distinction between *I* and my brain. Even though I relied on my brain to receive messages from my environment (my maths teacher and my textbooks in this case), to process these messages, and then to remember them so that I could pass my maths tests, it was *I* that pursued the knowledge and understanding my maths teacher wanted me to have. Although *I* was intimately connected with the work of my brain (provided I chose to use my brain in this way), *I* was not the same as the message carriers, encoders, decoders, processors, storage systems, and all the other tasks my brain performed.

This is my proposal. Many neuroscientists and reductionist-scientists, however, might protest this is not *science* – this is speculation. Nevertheless, the idea has been around for a long time, and for good reason. I am loath to jettison ideas that fit clinical experience well, simply because 'science' has not yet been able to establish 'scientific evidence' or a sound mathematical model to support the notion. After all, many basic propositions in physics began as speculation before becoming orthodoxy.

Although I have described a paradigm that may be unsatisfactory to many cognitive and neural scientists, it represents a working model, or at least an alternative perspective, for clinicians: one that accounts for many clinical phenomena with which clinicians are confronted, and who need to make 'sense' of what is heard and seen. It is, I believe, the clinician's task to engage the *I* in his client, in one way or another, to ameliorate the suffering in that client through finding new meanings or moving to new 'positions' in relation to a matter, and developing ways to better manage neural demands. But perhaps the most challenging question remains: where the client's *I* is weakened, where *I* has lost a degree of authority over the neural system through which *I* expresses itself and through which it establishes a degree of power and control over the environment, then how might that authority begin to be restored; how might *I* be strengthened to better manage brain and body?

Notes

1 *I*: The elusive subjective self

1 Some grammatical issues in the use of *I* emerge. Normally, I will refer to *I* as *I*; but occasionally I will refer to *I* more generally as *it*. This immediately creates a problem when I link to Martin Buber's (1958) thesis, in which he uses the term *it* in distinction to *thou*. On the other hand, I do not want to commit to the notion of *I* as he or she – it may be that sexuality is a function of the body rather than of *I*. So I have a semantic problem. Also, normally the preposition *am* would be used with 'I' but clearly this will not work with *it*, so I am forced to use the preposition *is*. I am keenly aware that *it* refers to inanimate objects, which is clearly not what I have in mind. But for now I will adopt this approach. You will also notice that I refer to the hypothetical clinician as 'he', even though the majority of clinical psychologists happen to be 'she'. My only excuse for doing so is that I am indirectly referring to myself, who happens to be a 'he'.
2 The fragments of case studies in this book, unless taken from published material, were encountered in my practice. The accounts are short to ensure anonymity. Names have been changed and, where necessary, composite case studies have been created.
3 The notion of metacognition – thoughts about thoughts – follows a similar approach.
4 See also Feinberg's (2001) account of 'split-brain' subjects who maintained an experience of a unified 'I'.
5 At times I use the terms 'body' and 'brain' interchangeably, and sometimes the term body/brain to mean the physical self in distinction from the subjective entity *I*.
6 See also neurophysiologist Charles Sherrington's (1941) discourse in relation to the unity of *I*.
7 Many volumes provide good historical and theoretical perspectives. See, for example, Entralgo's *Mind and Body* (1955) for a history from a medical perspective. For a summary of the issues from a philosophical perspective, see Shaffer's *Philosophy of Mind* (1968). For more recent debate in the area, see, for example, the works of David Chalmers, John Searle, and Daniel Dennett. Todd Feinberg also provides an excellent summary, including his own important notion of 'nested hierarchies' in *Altered Egos* (2001).

2 *I* expressed through the body

1 It may be contended that *I* is equivalent to Descartes' 'centre of consciousness', formulated as an observer watching what is happening in the brain: the *homunculus* problem in philosophy. The inevitable next question is: where *is* this internal observer, and how does it, in turn, perceive things? However, I will argue that the brain does all the processing and integrating of the incoming information – no *homunculus* does this. The brain is

necessary for the *mechanics* of thinking and decision making. *I* represents the endpoint of the brain's work and the source of its initiatives, comprising a dimension different from the physical processes of the brain. Scientists are likely to charge that this represents a 'ghost in a machine' that is not open to 'scientific' investigation. They may well have a point, but just because it does not appear to be amenable to scientific investigation does not make it an illegitimate notion – it may just be an awkward notion to work with. Nevertheless, it remains a necessary aspect of our explanatory model, given the nature of the dynamics we are seeking to address. I note that, while many are dismissive of Descartes' dualism, the relationship of the objective with the subjective self remains far from being solved.

2 There is the question as to whether the body can have life without the presence of *I*. It seems to me that if it *is* possible for the body to have life without the presence of *I*, it would surely be short-lived, as the body would cease to exercise its purpose as the vehicle of expression of *I*.

3 Siegel offers the following formulation of mind:

> The human mind is a relational [flowing between and among people] and embodied [in the brain and throughout the body] process that regulates the flow [shaping the characteristics, patterns, and direction] of energy [the neural energy used when we think, talk, listen, and read] and information[anything that symbolizes anything other than itself, something that carries meaning].
>
> (Siegel, 2009: 52)

This formulation resists the notion of the mind being explainable by molecular activity, as Francis Crick suggests on behalf of many neuroscientists: 'most neurologists now believe that all aspects of the mind, including its most puzzling attribute, consciousness or awareness, are likely to be explainable in a more materialistic way as the behaviour of large sets of interacting neurons' (Crick, in Carter, 2010: 332). While Siegel's definition is useful, consider what happens when I substitute *I* for 'mind': '*I* am (is) a relational and embodied process that regulates the flow of energy and information.' *I* becomes a *process* and the focus of this process becomes the 'regulation of the flow of energy and information'. The sense of *I* as an animated, sentient presence that interacts with other *I*s and responds meaningfully to the external world is lost.

4 This to varying degrees, perhaps like the peak body–self alignment or 'flow' Goldman talks of in *Emotional Intelligence* (Goldman, 1995).

5 I use the terms 'communication' and 'information' in the widest sense possible, not limiting them to the formal receptive and expressive language that encapsulates ideas.

6 The notion that *I* apprehends ideas that have an existence separate from the neural software that mediates them is reminiscent of Plato's *Theory of Ideas*.

7 To talk of any aspect of the brain being 'designed' or having a 'purpose' is to imply intent in its makeup; and intent necessarily has a source. For example, a chair is designed by someone with the intent it is sat on. I can also sit on a rock – but that is not the *purpose* of the rock. It has no design with such intent, although one may *position* a rock with such intent. Some things necessarily require the notion of 'purpose' to properly explain. The notion of a 'chair' is most reasonably described by its purpose, given its varied physical manifestations: inevitably, its existence is the result of someone's design intent. Not allowing such explanatory reasoning in models of science makes an assumption about the origin of those things we are trying to explain: that is, there *is* no design origin. However, this is an assumption, not a logical fact, and one by which I do not wish to be constrained in developing an explanatory model. See also note 13 in Chapter 5 on the use of the term 'purpose'.

3 *I* separate from the body

1 Specifically, the temporoparietal junction is identified. This appears to play a role in mul-tisensory integration and is implicated in the experience of body ownership (Moseley, 2011): stimulating this region can result in an out-of-body experience. Yet how are we to interpret this? That such stimulation creates an out-of-body perceptual illusion? Or that changes in the neural body map resulting from temporoparietal junction activation interferes with the capacity of *I* to interact with the body? Not only is the out-of-body event a *perceptual* one, it also results in *loss of volitional control* by *I* of the body, and *the suspension of sensory signals* to *I* from the body. There appears to be multiple disengagement of *I* from the body. In contrast, an illusion typically results from misleading or insufficient information in only one or other sensory domain.

2 See, for example, the first systematic study on the subject by Green (1968), and Fein-berg's more recent accounts (Feinberg, 2001). Feinberg observes:

> Besides epilepsy and migraine, autoscopia has been associated with typhoid fever, influenza, various forms of brain infections, alcoholism, drug intoxications, brain tumours, and brain haemorrhages . . . [and] in people with a variety of psychiat-ric conditions, including hysteria, obsessive-compulsive disorders, schizophrenia or depression.
>
> (Feinberg, 2001: 82)

However, the term *autoscopia* refers to visual hallucination of the self projected into the outside world – it makes assumptions about the nature of the experience.

3 A process called *apoptosis*: see Cozolino (2006). Such rapid change of brain chemicals after the ceasing of internal communication systems – that is, death – creates a problem for post-mortem neurological examination.

4 Parenthetically, is it reasonable to suggest that just as the repair of damaged supporting biochemical structures might restore healthy neural communication processes affected by the damage, likewise promoting effective neural communication processes might act to restore damaged supporting biochemical structures?

5 Sacks tells the extraordinary case of amnesic Jimmie G. in *The Lost Mariner* (Sacks, 1985), who lost time – thirty years, in fact – although he (his *I*) presented as 'charming and intel-ligent'. He was diagnosed with Korsakov's syndrome, caused by alcoholic destruction of the mammillary bodies (part of the hypothalamus). He was convinced he was nineteen when he was, in fact, forty-nine. Without his neural timekeeper (which is bound, it seems, with the neural software involved in creating new memories), his *I* had no way of recognizing time.

4 The brain: Computers and neural processing

1 These ideas have been further developed by cognitive psychologists in attempts to con-struct *artificial neural networks* – with some limited success: see Friedenberg and Silverman (2012).

2 The inevitable objection will be raised: if we wish to argue for design, there must be a designer – but who designed the designer? But this problem remains whether or not we invoke the presence of a 'designer' – ultimately, we are faced with the problem that somewhere, somehow, the creation of something was precipitated from nothing. I only raise this here because issues of brain design and origin are regularly speculated upon in scientific literature, and the position authors take in this matter plays a role in shaping their theories (consider, for example, Paul MacLean's notion of the *triune brain* [MacLean, 1990]).

3 The three 'contributors' to brain design suggested are not independent forces. Even the expression of the genes comprising DNA is affected by other activity in the cell's environment (the study of this relationship is called *epigenetics*). Any genetic contribution to psychiatric problems is moderated by external factors.

4 The idea that the nature of the ultimate source should be beyond my comprehension is unsurprising: if the entity *I*, which I know so well and whose existence I comfortably acknowledge, is so difficult to comprehend, why should I be disturbed that the source of *I* is at least equally difficult to comprehend?

5 The brain: Mind maps and meaning

1 I propose that that which is communicated between *I* and the other, between the communication's source and its destination, may be measured in 'units of meaningfulness'. Being a function of neither time nor space, 'units of meaningfulness' are of another dimension and not reducible to neural cell parameters. While connections between cells are space/time events, the meanings thus made possible are not.

2 See Frankl's *Man's Search for Meaning* (1992) and *The Doctor and the Soul* (1980).

3 See, for example, Neisser (1967) and the subsequent information-processing literature.

4 The role of associations and connections, especially those of a temporal nature, is a key principle in the behavioural tradition.

5 An association string might also be understood as a fundamental memory unit – memory is 'an association between a group of neurons so that when one fires, they all fire, creating a specific pattern' (Carter, 2010: 261).

6 New association strings are continually being formed, and old ones reinforced. Each neuron co-opts other cells to create association strings, yet the key defining a string (or unit of meaning) is probably found in a single neuron. I suggest that a copy of the association string key may be found in some or all neurons comprising the particular network, a redundancy creating robustness. In this case, the number of cells carrying keys may reflect the resilience of the network to decay. Thus each cell becomes both a component and a key to at least one neural template or association string. I suspect each neuron is capable of multiple functions: it carries the key to a particular network; it participates with other associated networks; it regulates neurotransmitter and neuropeptide activity to stimulate other physical events; it houses DNA; and it regulates its own life processes. Association strings are stored throughout the brain, so that if any one part of the brain is damaged, only a small part of the template library is lost. Many such templates are not language based; also, their lifespan will vary, depending on use.

7 The notion of meanings being imposed in the brain's perceptual processing is a foundational principle in gestalt psychology. Although I only make passing reference to this tradition, I believe its principles provide an important perspective in understanding brain processing.

8 Arden and Linford (2009a) refer to networks or 'communities of cells' involved in more specialized functions as *neural modules*.

9 That is, the essence contained in the idea being communicated.

10 See, for example, Searle (1992). There are different formulations for how the neural elements might be 'drawn' or 'held' together to form a whole which is 'more than', or has properties 'different from' that of the component parts. Searle argues for consciousness as a property of the brain as a whole, but not of its parts, just as, for example, the properties of water at a macro level are different from those at a micro level. These are attempts to conceptualize how we might abstract an integrated meaningful whole as represented by our perception or subjective experience from the many elements drawn from the flood of incoming signals.

11 Feinberg's *nested hierarchies* model forms a bridge between neural hardware systems and

the meanings *I* subsequently apprehends, and is a conceptually more solid model than one centred on an 'apex of neural functioning' (see Feinberg, 2001). However, he proposes that 'in the hierarchy of our conscious awareness, it is meaning that provides the constraint that "pulls" the mind together to form the "inner I" of the self' (Feinberg, 2001: 131). In contrast, I propose that meaning provides the constraint that "pulls" the *mind map* together, which the "inner I" subsequently apprehends. It is the *mind map* that comprises the integrated complex of meanings the neural system supports. These meanings are not the same as *I*: even though *I* apprehends the meanings, and the meanings form the basis of the expression of *I*, the meanings remain external to *I*. Meaningfulness is carried by the message; *I* is the destination of that message.

12 One approach to explicating clients' unique networks of associations comprising their system of 'constructs' (another way of conceptualizing aspects of the mind map) is in the use of the *Repertory Grid*, formulated for Kelly's *Personal Construct Theory* (Kelly, 1955). Some may also recognize similarities between the *mind map* and Bowlby's *internal working models* (see, for example, Pietromonaco and Feldman Barrett, 2000). Bowlby's conceptualization of internal working models tends to revolve around the development of interpersonal relationships, focusing on the development of expectations of the self, significant others, and the relationship between the two. My conceptualization is broader than this, but from a dynamic perspective, internal working models and the mind map have many features in common, including the interconnection of many aspects of cognitive and affective functioning; the interpretation of current events in the context of remembered material; and the need for inherent stability, yet with capacity for these internal representations to change over time. Furthermore, many aspects of the self-awareness are necessarily mediated by the mind map, as dimensions of self-identity involve the memory systems bound in the mind map. (See, for example, the extensive work of Klein *et al.*, 2002.) The focus of traditional psychodynamic therapists is also largely about the explication of aspects of the client's mind map, with a view that the resulting insights contribute to subsequent integration and emotional resolution.

13 The notion of 'purpose' used in relation to various aspects of the *I*–brain dynamic is philosophically contentious. The attribution of purpose is called *teleological thinking*, and is generally dismissed when used in scientific explanatory models as inherently illogical. A more acceptable approach in science is to talk of *teleonomic processes* – see Feinberg (2001). It is beyond the scope of this book to explore this issue at length. However, as noted earlier regarding the use of the term 'design', the issue is that 'purpose' and 'design' implies intent; and intent implies the existence of one who has brought about the process in question and whose actions are governed by such intent. I use the term deliberately, aware of the debate it invites about what we can assume about the nature of things. Whatever standpoint is taken, an assumption needs to be made as to whether the notion of purpose is valid: proof either way is difficult to come by.

14 The question of what is an illusion is a perplexing one. In one sense, it could be argued that *all* experience is an illusion in that it is a construction of the neural system rather than the reality itself. But normally, we refer to an illusion as a distorted perception or faulty meaning resulting from inadequate or misleading information. Generally, inaccurate interpretation is a function of limited cues or information to which the brain has access in making judgements. When there are sufficient cues based on disparate incoming sensory signals, distortion in perception is avoided. In relation to the perception of *I* as an entity distinct from my brain, what cues or information do I need to ensure my perception is 'accurate' rather than an illusion?

15 In this regard, it could be argued that the sense of *I* being one with my body is as much an illusion created by my mind map as is the experience of *I* being external to my body. Yet each 'illusion' constitutes the reality of my experience, of which I seek to make sense from the available data.

16 Gregory writes:

> there are various kinds of receptors, almost all signalling only changes in illumination and very few giving a continuous signal to a steady light. Some signal when a light is switched on, others when it is switched off. These various kinds are named 'on', 'off', and 'on-off' receptors. It seems that these receptors, sensitive only to change of illumination, are responsible for signalling movement, and that *all eyes are primarily detectors of movement* [my emphasis].
>
> (Gregory, 1972: 92)

17 Investigators have identified 'fast' and 'slow' neural systems in relation to emotional responses, with slow systems involving more conscious control (Cozolino, 2002). Speed of processing is, then, a relevant factor.
18 Support for this notion was first reported in 1908 and is referred to as the *Yerkes-Dodson Law*.
19 Walsh argues that tactile stimuli may play a key role in creating a sense of the ownership of the body as represented in the mind map:

> We know that our body parts 'belong' to us without having to move, contract or otherwise test the body part in question. Presumably, the brain develops the map of what belongs to it by using sensory information . . . touch seems ideal for identification of ownership as any tactile stimuli that are perceived must, by definition, be occurring against the brain's own body – we do not usually perceive tactile stimuli on anything that is not part of our body.
>
> (Walsh *et al.*, 2011: 3010)

20 Feinberg (2001) describes an unusual condition, *asomatognosia*, wherein a stroke patient no longer recognizes a part of his body (such as his right foot) as 'belonging' to him. Here it seems the internal foot ambassador has been disconnected from the rest of his still-functioning neural networks. However, the sense of *I* to whom the foot once was recognized as belonging remains intact.

6 The brain: Neural hardware and software

1 The background material on neurons and synaptic activity is largely based on Guyton (1981), Cozolino (2002), Carter (2010), Arden and Linford (2009a), and Siegel (2009).
2 The material on various neurotransmitter correlates is largely based on research reported by Cozolino (2002, 2006), Reeve (2005), Carter (2010), and Doidge (2010).
3 In this environment, the startle response becomes more resistant to habituation to subsequent milder and novel stresses – the startle response also contributes to my perception of the world as a dangerous place.
4 What actually *is* this 'pressure' or 'compelling urge' that *I* seeks to resist? What is the origin of such 'pressure'? It seems the brain wants to *react*, while *I* seeks to *respond* by interposing judgement and thought in the stimulus–response cycle. As we shall see, different neural regions appear to be involved in this process.

7 Neural cartography and *I*

1 As I write, Dr John Mazziotta of the Department of Neurology of University of California in Los Angeles, director of UCLA's Brain Mapping Centre and principal investigator of the International Consortium for Brain Mapping (ICBM), is leading a team of researchers from six countries to create the world's first comprehensive 'atlas' of the

structure and function of the human brain, which no doubt will also need to incorporate interpersonal neural variability.

2 You may notice books normally refer to the *amygdala* and the *hippocampus* in the singular form: there are in fact two regions for each, one to the right and one to the left, whose functions differ a little. So technically we should be speaking of *amygdalae* and *hippocampi*. However, to retain consistency with the literature, I will generally use the terms amygdala and hippocampus.

3 It is unclear whether damage is the problem or whether hippocampal functioning is inhibited, fatigued, or 'stressed' by the glucocorticoids due to ongoing vigilance.

4 The resonance circuits also comprise the mirror neurons associated with capacity for empathy.

5 The *binding problem*: see Feinberg (2001) and Singer (1996).

8 Early development: *I* weaves a mind map

1 I note here my earlier proposal that conscious awareness begins as *I* makes successful interaction with my neural system. If consciousness is in part a function of *I* and necessary for attention, there is a strong basis for arguing that *I* is present at least from birth, even if I have no memory of those early months.

2 This process is partly mediated by mirror cells, where the encounters and imitative dance between Rachel and Sarah activate identical neural patterns in their respective brains. See also Winnicott's early work in regard to the mirroring process between mother and child (in particular, Winnicott, 1967; for further references, see Arden and Linford, 2009a).

3 Tallal (see Schwartz and Begley, 2002) believes dyslexia results from a child's difficulty with fine discrimination. Her research found that a child's brain can be trained to make fine discriminations through practice and slowing input slightly to allow *I* opportunity to notice differences not noticed before, that then become recorded in neural networks. She found that establishing better ability to discriminate sounds allowed better discrimination to read letters on a page. Things had been slowed enough to *notice* and shape the neural landscape accordingly. When attention shifts too rapidly, little neural shaping occurs because there is insufficient focused repetitive activity.

4 That is, the remembered presence of others, creating expectations of ongoing availability – Erikson's sense of *basic trust*.

5 Bowlby observed:

> Principal determinants of the pathway along which an individual's attachment behaviour develops, and of the pattern in which it becomes organized, are the experiences he has with his attachment figures during his years of immaturity – infancy, childhood and adolescence . . . On the way in which an individual's behaviour becomes organized within his personality turns the pattern of affectional bonds he makes during his life.
>
> (Bowlby, 1985: 41)

The attachment patterns thus created comprise the *internal working models* Bowlby described (see Pietromonaco and Feldman Barrett, 2000).

6 See, for example, Bowlby (1971), Ainsworth *et al.* (1978), Arden and Linford (2009a), and Siegel (2009).

7 Sustained higher levels of metabolism continue to pump sodium into neurons, eventually overwhelming the ability of cells to transport it out again, resulting in destruction of the cell membrane and cell death. This process has been found to be particularly damaging to cells within the hippocampi, leading to a variety of memory deficits (Cozolino, 2002).

8 That is, Piaget's 'concrete-operational' stage, following the earlier 'preoperational' stage (Peterson, 2004).

9 Entering adulthood: Mind map transformations

1 Piaget's *formal-operational* cognitive stage.
2 Erikson notes:

> Identity is a psychological process reflecting social processes . . . it meets its crisis in adolescence, but has grown throughout childhood and continues to re-emerge in the crises of later years. The over-riding meaning of it all, then, is the creation of a sense of sameness, a unity of personality now felt by the individual, and recognised by others as having a consistency over time.
>
> (Erikson, 1968, quoted in Peterson, 2004: 376)

3 In this discussion, by 'body' I mean 'brain and body'.
4 The picture I have of the recognition process is that there exists in the person who knows me a neuron dedicated to recognition of me. The cell will never be isolated because in isolation it immediately dies. Besides, it would lose its capacity to function even if it *did* stay alive, because its task of recognizing me is made possible only by its connections with other cells that carry the components for recognition. There are cells carrying some abstraction of visual memories; cells dealing with voice recognition; cells carrying aspects of our common stories or narrative. But should this connecting cell atrophy, the different aspects required to allow recognition would be disconnected – although the memory of the parts remains, the 'whole' made possible by the connecting 'recognition' cell is lost, and the other would no longer recognize me.

10 *I* considers self

1 By *I* event, I mean an event whose origin is *I*, not consciousness per se.
2 This raises the question of the 'proper' basis for self-evaluation. Some would argue that *all* self-evaluation is unhelpful, whether or not *I* has control over the circumstance: general self-acceptance is advocated.
3 Long before positive psychology established its mandate, Victor Frankl was writing on the will to meaning, which was also about resilience. Watching how fellow prisoners survived in the concentration camps of Kaufering and Theresienstadt, Frankl found 'the prisoner who lost faith in the future – his future – was doomed. With his loss of belief in the future, he also lost his spiritual hold; he let himself decline and became subject to mental and physical decay' (Frankl, 2006: 74). Yet what actually is the key to resilience: a strong *I*, or a resourceful mind map that allows *I* to access various coping strategies? The first may be a quality inherent in *I*; the latter a set of skills that may be learned. Nevertheless, a recent extensive research programme seeking to establish whether resilience against adolescent depression can be taught through training coping skills (Spence, 2010) returned disappointing results. If there is a resilience factor, it may reside in strength of *I*, rather than in a set of abilities or an outlook that is taught.

11 *I* encounters thou

1 The decision to love another involves judgement about the other *I*, establishing a position of one *I* towards the other. This easily becomes confused once a sexual encounter is involved, as this creates its own agenda – an attachment agenda, which has a

neurochemical basis. If *I* has not made a clear decision *before* the sexual relationship establishes attachment, confusion easily results when a subsequent adverse decision is at odds
with the developing attachment: that is, after all, *I* does not love the other even though
intimacy has been entered into.

12 *I* preserves experiences: Focus and memory

1 Lindsay and Norman note:

> It is clear that thought processes must operate on some internal coding – a coding
> that reflects the meaning of the material being thought about, not its physical real-
> ization. In order to make the most efficient contact with the storage of information
> in the long term memory, it would be useful for all information to be transformed
> into some common form.

(Lindsay and Norman, 1972: 340)

2 The involvement of *I* in working memory is also suggested by Miller's (1956) discovery
   that working memory appears restricted to around seven (plus or minus two) units of
   information at a time. These units appear to be units of meaningfulness, implicating *I*,
   rather than data points. If the brain was simply processing data points like a computer,
   there would appear to be no logical reason for such restriction.
3 Stress releases glucocorticoids that over time can damage the hippocampi so that long-
   term memory is affected, although I suspect such glucocorticoid action might also cause
   temporary inhibition of hippocampal function as protection from long-term memories
   of an emerging history of negative events. The temporary inhibition of hippocampal
   function may also free processing space for the immediate demands of scanning for danger and general readiness for action.
4 This 'video-clip' is frequently a visual memory attached to the strong emotion that is
   relived. The right amygdala has strong connections with the visual association cortex,
   separate from frontal cortex involvement – herein no doubt is a neural basis for the flashback phenomena in PTSD (Simmons *et al.*, 2004).
5 Music appears to play a unique connective role in emotion and memory. It mediates
   both the *stimulation* and the *expression* of emotion. It seems that music and accompanying
   motor movement releases dopamine, leading to 'feeling good'. Music can trigger many
   emotions – confidence, aggression, grief, happiness; dopamine is not the only neurotransmitter pathway it activates. The chordate is also activated, planning and organizing body
   movements in response to rhythms. The corpus callosum tends to be very busy with
   rapid interchange of information from one side of the brain to another, generally melody
   on the right, words on the left. It seems the brain is hard-wired for melody and musical
   structure – there is a neural disposition to relate to melody patterns and sequences, along
   with a strong memory capacity for these patterns from a very early age. Music seems to
   improve memory generally, a connection teachers have long used in the classroom to
   enhance new verbal learning, beginning with memorizing the alphabet. The capacity of
   music to enhance memory may be both because a melody line establishes simple association strings that can be utilized to anchor other associations, and because it can activate
   emotions, which increases neural arousal to aid memory processing activity. Not only
   does music readily engage an emotional response, it also engages the brain intellectually,
   it enhances memory, and it frequently elicits visualizations: learning a musical instrument
   seems to improve brain development generally.
6 This may also happen naturally when someone is in a state of shock – that is, emotionally numb – *while* an event occurs: 'I felt I was watching a movie.' That is, the person
   becomes disconnected from the current reality when disconnected emotionally.

7 William James noted that attention:

> is the taking possession by the mind, in clear and vivid form, of one out of what seems several simultaneously possible objects or trains of thought. Focalization, concentration, of consciousness are of its essence. It implies withdrawal from some things in order to deal effectively with others.
>
> (James, in Norman, 1969: 7)

8 Generally, theories developed to explain both mechanisms of attention and mechanisms of memory deal with hardware and software processing aspects (see, for example, Lindsay and Norman, 1972) or are constructed around mathematical models – the interactive function of *I* (or mind or psyche) receives little attention.

9 See, however, LaBar (2007) and Kensinger (2009) in relation to research linking emotion and memory.

10 See, for example, Anderson and Levy (2009) and Bergström *et al.* (2009).

13 *I* disengages: Unconscious states

1 In respect to the latter, Reeve notes that unconscious 'non-Freudian' neural activity is 'simple, automated, and capable of performing only routine information processing. It carries out habitual or automatic processing, such as that which occurs when driving a car, or playing the piano (that is, unconscious procedural knowledge)' (Reeve, 2005: 389). This habitual processing also operates in sleep activities I might engage in.

2 The saturation or habituation effect that causes the brain to cease its 'work' of establishing meaning, allowing it to 'down tools', can also be experienced by staring at a written word that ordinarily conveys meaning and associations, but ceases to do so after awhile as habituation takes effect. In addition to these signals, my body is also sensitive to the relationship of ambient temperature to body temperature – too great a discrepancy interferes with the shut-down process.

3 The *locus coeruleus* is linked to sleep regulation, control of arousal and stress responses, and dysregulation of affect (Leahy and Gradisar, 2012). Dahl (1996) argues high arousal is incompatible with sleep.

4 Guyton (1981) proposes the following mechanism for the sleep–wake cycle. When the RAS is completely rested and sleep centres no longer activated, the wakefulness centres begin spontaneous activity. This excites the cerebral cortex and peripheral nervous system. Positive feedback from these areas to the RAS activates the RAS further, so that a natural state of wakefulness is sustained. After the brain has been activated for many hours, the neurons within the activating system fatigue. The positive feedback cycle between the cerebral cortex and the peripheral nervous system and the RAS begins to fade, until a few of the neurons in the RAS become inactive, so eliminating part of the feedback stimulus to the other neurons. As these, too, become fatigued and inactive, the process spreads through neuronal networks, leading to transition from wakefulness to sleep. During sleep, the excitatory neurons of the RAS gradually become more excitable because of the prolonged rest, while the inhibitory neurons of the sleep centres become less excitable, leading to a new cycle of wakefulness. No doubt this relates to the activity of adenosine mentioned earlier.

5 Besides recovering from fatigue, the brain is involved in some constructive tasks during sleep, including the consolidation of new memories mediated by hippocampal activity. Memories of the previous twenty-four hours are revisited, allowing more simultaneous firing of the new neural templates, contributing towards their establishment. Neuroimaging studies show activation patterns during sleep that mirror those recorded during learning of tasks from the previous day (Carter, 2010). Lack of sleep interferes with this consolidation process and can leave me feeling 'scattered'.

6 Delta waves are commonly observed in infancy and when performing certain 'continuous attention tasks'.
7 See Green and McCreery (1994).
8 This disengagement process leaves me vulnerable and unguarded, so that sudden and unexpected stimuli can create a strong startle response when I sleep. Similarly, I can get so engrossed in a daydream or other activity where I enter a trance-like state that I can similarly experience a startle response. In a daydream, *I* is 'at play': *I* plays with the memories and ideas and desires found in the neural networks; *I* is not in an alert and guarded state.
9 Morphine affects pathway activity by inhibiting the release of several different neurotransmitters, including noradrenaline, acetylcholine, and the neuropeptide substance P, the latter associated with pain experience.
10 See, for example, Carter (2010).
11 Such interpretation normally involves the judgement that the reported supernatural experience is out of keeping with a person's normal religious beliefs, or are linked to bizarre beliefs or an overall 'delusional system'. Often the difference is clear to see, but there are times when the difference between 'normal' and 'abnormal' religious beliefs is not so clear.

14 *I* feels: Complex emotions

1 For example, see Dalgleish and Power (1999) and Scherer *et al.* (2001).
2 Guilt itself, of course, has more to do with a moral or legal judgement than emotion: I may or may not *feel* guilty; the fact of *being* guilty is something else.
3 This assumes 'love' is an identifiable emotion. However, even more than anger, 'love' covers many meanings and has many nuances.
4 See my earlier notes regarding the notion 'purpose' (Chapter 2, note 7, and Chapter 5, note 13). In this context, the conundrum is whether *I* is the source of the intent relating to emotional expression, or some other, or indeed whether some emotions are altogether without intent, and therefore without purpose.
5 All, that is, except my heart. Others see my eyes, tears, and smile; but who sees my heart? My heart is a lesser-known form of emotional expression. Many think of the heart as an organic pump, but, like my face, my heart is capable of many emotional expressions through its changing physical shape and pumping rhythm. Take the discovery of how a heart responds to intense sadness or trauma – the ballooning of the left ventricle like a Japanese octopus pot. Language also reflects the emotion expression of the heart: I may have a 'hard heart' or 'broken heart'; or experience a 'heart-stopping' event; or watch a 'heart-rending' movie; and so on. These heart expressions are directly controlled by the cardiac centre in the brainstem through neurotransmitters such as adrenaline and noradrenalin, which in turn receives messages from various 'higher centres' of the brain. But it operates in reverse too. When I focus attention on my heart, both a physiological reaction and an awareness of intense emotions can be triggered (Siegel, 2009) – my heart is sending the emotion message to my 'higher brain centres' to interpret.
6 See, for example, Cozolino (2006) and Siegel (2009).
7 Yet the task of grief is for *I* to 'let go' of the object of attachment, and for the brain, which remembers the many old life patterns and meanings connected with the object of attachment, to bring these memories and meanings to the attention of *I*, so that these also might be 'let go', allowing the perceptual framework within which *I* operates to be reworked.
8 I have not included the *venting* of Rachel's anger as a form of resolution: venting might allow temporary release of emotional tension, but actually resolves nothing. The tension release may in fact reinforce her venting behaviour. A clinician might also consider

physiological issues (such as fatigue or depression), dispositional issues (perhaps a tendency to perfectionism, or fear of inadequacy), general distress (due to loss or pain), or coping issues (perhaps an expression of empowerment or moral assertion). Such complexity creates many challenges. Assessment might usefully differentiate between the role of *I* and neural activity in anger. Rachel might need to address neural processes creating vulnerability to, or maintaining, her anger, as well as perceptions and meanings her *I* apprehended that generated the anger response.

9   Rachel is an adult: she can make a judgement about my judgement. What, though, if the clinician works with a minor? Should the parents then seek a clinician who agrees with their moral judgements, even though their children may not share their view? To complicate things, the parents themselves may differ in their judgements on the matter. Emotional or adjustment issues can be entwined in moral ones.

10 Nevertheless, CBT is an effective tool at combating the brain's natural tendency to processing for efficiency rather than accuracy – taking thinking short-cuts that lead to illogical, inaccurate, and distressing thoughts. The process of disputing illogical thinking is not the problem: the issue is the sometimes inappropriate application when dealing with emotion where there is no misperception: emotions are not necessarily the result of distorted and illogical thinking.

15 *I* suffers: Anxiety and pain

1   It is this illogic that CBT seeks to address. However, it needs to enlist the involvement of *I*, the very *I* that is losing control of its bodily responses; the *I* that does not need to be convinced of the illogic – it knows it already. When bodily responses run out of control, it is time for *I* to disengage from the anxiety cycle, perhaps through mindfulness strategies.

2   In this sense, the brain acts as its own regulator. If it does not function in the way it deems necessary and judges that it doesnot have the required resources, alarm signals or anxiety result. It is not only *external* events that are responsible for these signals; the brain's assessment of *internal* capacities can do so as well. This notion of automatic brain processes operating independently of the fiat of *I* is referred to in cognitive therapy as *automatic thoughts*.

3   To find logic in the illogicality of anxiety by reference to evolutionary processes (that is, the anxiety was functional in prehistoric times, but is no longer so) makes for interesting speculation, but I suspect that chronic anxiety would have been as dysfunctional for the caveman and tent-man as it is for us now, leading eventually to debilitating depression. It comes as no real surprise to find evidence from the beginning of recorded history of the search to trust in a higher being to compensate for the perceived inadequacy of one's own coping capacities and for the vulnerabilities the unknown creates.

4   Bray and Moseley write:

> There is mounting evidence that the body schema is disrupted in people with back pain . . . although the current work does not demonstrate a causative link between back pain and disrupted working body schema, it raises the possibility that one exists, which in turn raises the possibility that therapeutic strategies that normalise working body schema may be helpful in rehabilitation.
>
> (Bray and Moseley, 2011: 171)

5   I note here that the anterior cingulate, which would have been chronically activated by Una's emotional distress, is the same region implicated in the pain experience. Incidentally, this process probably also occurs in the somatization experienced in depression: that is, chronic emotional distress can give rise to pain signals. Neural correlates between

social stress and physical pain are reported elsewhere, pointing to *I* as the initiator of the process. Cozolino notes that the anterior cingulate is activated 'when we, or those we love, experience physical pain or social stress', and 'the common neurobiology of physical pain and social rejection may provide a clue as to why healthy, intimate relationships consistently correlate with better cardio-vascular health, immunological functioning, and resistance to stress' (Cozolino, 2006: 106).

16 Depression: *I* and neural fatigue

1 See, for example, White (1982) and Parker (2008).
2 *Glutamate* is an essential power source for the neuron, providing energy for both neurotransmitter production and neural firing. *Glial* cells in turn make the metabolic process possible. Both are needed to power the neuron. There are also *trophic factors* that energize the neuron. Phelps (2006) mentions three such factors: *brain-derived neurotrophic factor*; *Bcl-2*; and the recently discovered *BAG-1*. I mention these only because they become relevant to the story of depression.
3 We see an aspect of specific momentary neural fatigue when we focus on a word or sound long enough: that word or sound eventually loses meaning, suggesting the neural connections establishing meaning are attenuated through fatigue, although we could conceive of the apprehension of meaning as a dynamic event so that when the contrasting signals enabled by dynamic activity are compromised, effective processing is interrupted. Either way, the neural fatigue phenomenon is exploited in the clinical setting in desensitization procedures, where neural adaptation (also known as *habituation*) is utilized to reduce the power or meaning of a message or link, such as those relating to disturbing emotions.
4 See, for example, Hammen *et al.* (1985) and Kessler (1997).
5 This also has cardiovascular implications.
6 Researchers (e.g. Lesch *et al.*, 1996, and Caspi *et al.*, 2003) have found differences in the alleles of the 5-HT gene that appear to affect a person's ability to manage stress and their subsequent likelihood of suffering depression.
7 Schore observes: 'Early stress leads to a vulnerability for depression later in life. This, in part, is mediated by deficient organization of frontal circuitry and the establishment of lower levels of excitatory neurotransmitters and growth hormones during critical periods' (Schore, 1994, in Cozolino, 2002: 312).
8 Cruwys and O'Kearney observe:

> in instances of chronic, intense arousal, the excessive levels of glutamate and corticosteroids impact severely on the hippocampus, causing oxidative stress, excitotoxity and subsequent neurodegeneration associated with diminished functioning capacity of the hippocampus . . . [N]eurodegeneration of the hippocampus caused by severe and/or chronic stress may lead to disruption of this feedback system, promoting dysregulation of cortisol and resulting in chronic hypoarousal or hyperarousal (or intermittent periods of each).
>
> (Cruwys and O'Kearney, 2008: 71)

9 Interestingly, however, there is some evidence for *increase* in the volume of the amygdala region. It is as though the chronic disquiet and distress of *I* finds expression in amygdalic activity, which over time increases in volume, reflecting the high use and the strength of pathways subsequently established in the region. However, this is at the cost of neural regions that moderate, integrate, and make sense of things. These latter regions are more likely to become fatigued and atrophy, resulting in volume decrease. However, hippocampal atrophy may also be attributed directly to chronic excess stress-induced cortisol.

10 In this regard, Cozolino suggests that increasing serotonin levels would increase hippo-campal volume, moderating the amygdalae and its fear circuits. He argues that the person is overwhelmed by negativity which is not held in the light of logic and reality testing. If the hippocampal function is thus fatigued, CBT as an intervention becomes difficult to implement, given the very system that it utilizes is depleted of energy. As with the amygdala region, the functions of the hippocampal region are suppressed in depression.

11 Arden and Linford explain that BDNF is a key element in neuroplasticity and neuro-genesis. It is a 'sort of naturally occurring neurofertility drug that stimulates the growth of new dendritic branches and releases the reproductive capacity of existing neurons, resulting in the creation of new neurons' (Arden and Linford, 2009a: 213).

12 A protective shut-down may result from different circumstances. Most commonly it is a response to neural stress corresponding to various external and internal events – includ-ing substances the body might ingest – where the demands made of neurons outstrip biochemical resources. But it may result from feedback from fatigued or stressed organs (like the heart), seeking to protect those organs from possible damage caused by excessive demands; or from a learned history of inhibition of 'positive' emotions due to miserable life experiences, or from a decision made early in life to not express emotion because it was not safe to do so, therefore preventing resolution.

13 See also Weissenburger and Rush (1996). Although there are many different neural correlates to the depression experience, some will be primary (the depletion process) and some will be secondary (the dysregulation of systems) as the brain reacts to its own deficiencies.

14 With regard to the challenge of *I* to exert control over regulatory functions, there is a strong neural tendency to establish consistency between current mood state, perception (the world is a positive or negative place), and activity (driven by arousal levels), rather than consistency of perception and activity over time in defiance of mood fluctuations. The tendency to align perception and activity with mood to maintain internal consis-tency and minimize dissonance may lead to reduced awareness by *I* of the mood fluctua-tions, as lack of dissonance creates no clear signal that things are changing. This makes the regulatory process more difficult.

15 The symptoms that he attributed to the exhaustion syndrome (not all of which are neces-sarily seen at any one time) included:

> lack of activity, indecision, tiredness, inhibition, depression, haziness, sopor, stupor, somnolence, bradycardia, hypotension, low muscle tonus, poor tendon reflexes, vasomotor vertigo, slow thinking, incapability of perceiving relationships, lack of self-confidence, impaired concentration, apathy, lethargy, tired facial expression, limp posture, weak tuneless voice, disinclination to work, and cheerlessness.
>
> (Birkmayer and Pilleri, 1966: 91)

He was here describing depression, linking it to neural exhaustion.

16 That the heart may be at risk in this process is not surprising. If neural activity suffers fatigue in depression, it is not so much the heart itself at risk, but its regulatory mecha-nisms in the fatigued RAS that become compromised. Following Birkmayer, we would predict cellular depletion to lead to dysregulation of *all* systems governed through the brainstem, including sleep cycle, breathing, heart, and mood regulation. (For research on the disruption of deep sleep and dysregulated REM patterns in depression, see Berger and Riemann, 1993).

17 To say there is an 'imbalance in brain chemistry' is misleading. One gets a picture of a gardener testing soil pH: 'There's an imbalance here – more lime needed to reduce acidity levels!' While there is every reason to believe the neural system is not releasing enough serotonin or dopamine or other neurotransmitter, this is better understood as

a problem in *neuron responsiveness* rather than *chemical imbalance*. The point is that neurotransmitters are normally released and absorbed according to momentary requirements mediating timely neural messages. It is a dynamic action of the neuron, not a static state of the brain.

18 This spiral is seen in young children suffering emotional and social disconnection. Seriously neglected children from Romanian orphanages found after the Ceausescu era at first were distressed, with many engaging in self-stimulatory behaviours characteristic of autism, but they eventually became passive and withdrawn, and in time experienced developmental delays and general neural atrophy, at times leading to a fatal shutting down (Arden and Linford, 2009b).

19 Just as Helen's depression process results in disconnection and loss of meaning, the reverse is also true: disconnection and loss of meaning contributes to her depression process.

20 Frankl notes:

> In the case of melancholia, psychophysical insufficiency is experienced in uniquely human fashion as tension between what the person is and what he ought to be . . . In melancholia the insufficiency feeling magnifies the gap between what is and what ought to be.
>
> (Frankl, 1980: 202)

21 Hope, an attribute of *I*, is a critical factor in human survival which has received minimal attention in clinical literature, except perhaps in the related concept of optimism, which is more cognitive and expectational without the connotation of perseverance (Peterson, in Sander and Scherer, 2009). Why is it that hope – the looking forward to something meaningful and fulfilling, the imagination and dreams a person has – should make a difference to physical wellbeing? Is it that *I* embraces its stay in the body because something positive keeps it there: otherwise, suicide becomes an option? Less dramatically, depression can lead to a 'lost interest in life', a passivity or disinterest that can lead to death in a gradually weakening body.

22 CBT is best used in relation to cognitive distortions that generally result from the brain's drive to efficiency. Similarly, it may be useful in addressing brain processing problems as reflected in dysfunctional 'automatic thoughts' and in unhelpful mental images. Dealing with unresolved emotions, with ideas embraced by *I* and long embedded in a person's dysfunctional mind map, or with a fatigued neural system, however, create other challenges. Not all thoughts are the result of brain efficiencies or processing problems: many thoughts find their origin in *I* based on decisions and values embraced by *I*. This requires a different approach.

23 Having said this, I note Arden and Linford's observation that it appears 'some antidepressants stimulate the production of BDNF and enrich our neuroplastic capacities as well as inhibit the reuptake of neurotransmitters' (Arden and Linford, 2009a: 212).

24 Birkmayer lists among the observed symptoms of the 'excitation syndrome' pole:

> hyper-awareness; hyper-agility; overzealousness; mental agitation; enhanced powers of association; flight of ideas; increased drive; restlessness; irritable mood; excitation; uninhibitedness; uncritical attitude; anxiety; insomnia; tachycardia; sweating fits; high basal metabolic rate; hypertension; exaggerated reflexes; increased muscle tonus; excessively erect posture; tense facial expression; and increased need of contact and communication.
>
> (Birkmayer and Pilleri, 1966: 91)

All of which we recognize as bipolar symptoms.

25 Some suggest ADD/ADHD may be related to bipolar disorder (e.g. Phelps, 2006, Arden and Linford, 2009b) in that they share many symptoms, and ADD/ADHD often leads

to a later bipolar diagnosis. Perhaps ADD/ADHD also find origin in neural fatigue (and accompanying dysregulation – see Cozolino's thought about vagal dysregulation in ADD/ADHD; Cozolino, 2006), perhaps due to neural stress or chronic ANS arousal in infants, making it conceptually the externalizing pole of childhood depression (Achenbach, 1991). Additional problems include compromised neural connectivity with implications for brain development and subsequent specific learning difficulties, including dyslexia. The significant relationship between maternal depression and childhood ADHD becomes suggestive (consider the possible role of mirror neurons), as does the use of *atomaxetine* (a norepinephrine reuptake inhibitor targeting concentration and motivation) in the management of ADHD. However, the usefulness of stimulant medication for some ADHD sufferers suggests the need to activate overall neural readiness potential (especially in the frontal cortex) for improved focus. Depression is frequently identified (or comorbid) with ADHD. Poor regulation of emotion signals (which influence attention) and weakness of *I* (as agent of focus) must surely play a central role in ADHD. Neurally, reduced volumes in the frontal lobe have been found as well as cingulate and basal ganglia deficits (Arden and Linford, 2009b) – perhaps as a *result* of chronic fatigue and dysregulation in the developing brain.

17 Battle for the mind: Psychosis and *I*

1 We see this principle in sensory deprivation experiments which stimulate internal hallucinatory experiences that 'fill the gaps' of missing external data.
2 Cozolino suggests that the schizophrenic's problem relates to excess dopamine overloading the sensory processing capabilities (Cozolino, 2002).
3 Torrey's more recent research also implicates a possible viral factor present in early childhood that leaves a weakened neural system and later vulnerability to psychosis (Fox, 2011).
4 Frankl writes:

> the schizophrenic experiences himself as if he, the subject, were transformed into an object. He experiences psychic acts as if they were being rendered in the passive mood. While the normal person experiences himself thinking, watching, observing, influencing, listening, eavesdropping, seeking, and persecuting, taking still or moving pictures, etc., the schizophrenic experiences all these acts and intentions, these psychic functions, as if they were rendered in the passive; he 'is being' observed, 'is being' thought about, etc. In other words, in schizophrenia there takes place an experiential passivizing of the psychic functions. We consider this to be a universal law of the psychology of schizophrenia.
>
> (Frankl, 1980: 209)

5 This effect has long been known: see, for example, Heron *et al.* (1956). Kingdon and Turkington (2005) also refer to these phenomena in their discussion of hallucinations in schizophrenia.

18 When *I* loses control: Addictions and OCD

1 The idea that there may be a neural predisposition – a genetic wiring – to addiction in general (that is, an 'addictive personality') or alcoholism in particular seems to lack supporting evidence, as found in Vaillant's longitudinal research (Seligman, 1994: 208).
2 The terms 'reward' and 'reinforcement' are used in the behavioural literature as explanatory mechanisms for the learning process. However, this involves a conceptual problem: what makes a 'reward' rewarding? (This, of course, becomes a problem with those

suffering depression, where the 'reward' value of rewards is lost.) Similarly, 'reinforce-ment' is defined as that which causes the behaviour to increase – but then the behaviour is said to increase because of the reinforcing value of the contingency (Sulzer-Azaroff and Mayer, 1977), presenting a circular argument. The idea of 'reward' or 'reinforcement' relating to an inherent drive to neural homeostasis provides a more satisfying explanatory argument, although how *I* apprehends the positive sensations relating to the rewarding event continues to present explanatory challenges.

3 Schwartz, a psychiatrist specializing in OCD who integrates Buddhist mindfulness phi-losophy with neuroscience, writes:

> When someone with the disease experiences a typical OCD thought . . . some part of his mind is standing outside and apart from the OCD symptoms, observing and reflecting on their sheer bizarreness . . . The insistent thoughts and images of OCD, after all, are experienced passively, the patient's volition plays no role in their appearance . . . [Yet] although the passive stream of the content of consciousness may well be determined by brain mechanism, the mental and emotional response to that stream may not be.
>
> (Schwartz and Begley, 2002: 13)

4 See, for example, Meyer *et al.* (1974), Foa and Wilson (2001), and Rees (2009).
5 The homeostatic principle operates as counterpoint to the adaptation principle, which finds expression in neuroplasticity.

19 Dissociation and exile of *I*

1 Dissociative experience in trauma comes in many forms: it may involve focusing on non-threatening irrelevant detail at the time of the trauma; viewing the event from a distance – being an onlooker, as it were, rather than a player; blacking out altogether; or having an out-of-body experience. And so, for example, Una Glennon writes: 'I feel strangely disconnected with everything that is unfolding around me, as if I am on the sideline looking in' (Glennon, 2010: 21).
2 Flashbacks are not a function of *I*: they are intrusive events that find their origin in a poorly integrated neural memory – they recreate bodily and emotional responses, and reactivate distress in *I*. Typically, *I* is passive in the process. Direct pathways between the right amygdala and the visual cortex enable this connection, free of frontal-cortex involvement.
3 See, for example, Seligman (1994) and Foa and Riggs (1992).
4 I note that general self-alienation – hatred of, or anger with, self – may also be the basis of self-harm, where *I* gets some relief through self-punishment.

20 The law, the brain, and *I*

1 See, for example, Zaragoza *et al.* (1995).
2 Every sportsman can attest that the rapidity of both the decisions and the enacting of decisions they make during a game outpaces any possible awareness they might have of the same. I also note that the 'readiness potential' Libet measured is not the same as a decision, but that such potential necessarily precedes awareness – whether of a decision, or of anything else.
3 Research suggests that the very *process* of decision making demands considerable neural energy. An exhausted brain greatly compromises decision-making processes: see, for example, the work of psychologist Roy Baumeister (in particular, Baumeister and Tier-ney, 2011).

21 Science, the brain, and *I*

1 For the interested reader with a philosophical bent, Taylor's (1964) detailed critique of the problems inherent in the deterministic and mechanistic formulations undergirding the explanation of human behaviour by the behaviourists is worth reviewing.

2 The dependence on introspection to argue that subjective experiences (partly defining *I*) are not the same as physical brain states is criticized by Friedenberg and Silverman on the basis that 'introspection is a weak form of evidence and can be wrong . . . What is required is objective proof that such experiential states are not physical' (Friedenberg and Silverman, 2012: 32). Yet the scientist is burdened with the equally daunting task of proving that experiential states *are nothing more* than physical brain events.

3 If we are to argue that working memory is a function of an entity called 'the brain', we come into some logical problems if we understand the brain as a complex system comprising both hardware and software that interacts with *I*. Is 'working memory' a function of the hardware, the software, or the interaction of *I* with the brain?

4 Here we can see how the application of traditional methods of 'science' is not appropriate for some endeavours. What if I was to apply 'science' to studying and understanding a novel? How would I *measure* a novel? By measuring the number of words, or the number of times a particular word is used? By 'measuring' theme or genre? I could gather statistics – a beautiful bell curve emerges when measuring the word length of novels. I could try to list symptoms of 'dysfunctional' novels, and categorize novels according to 'symptoms' (features) I have observed and decided to be significant. Then what mathematics would I apply to 'understand' the novel and its dysfunctions? Is this 'science'? Analysis, certainly. Measured and categorized, yes. Application of mathematical models, perhaps. But does this really *explain* the novel? Has my knowledge and understanding been advanced? No – I have lost the novel along the way: the content and message have gone missing.

5 Frankl observed:

> there is danger inherent in the teaching of man's 'nothingbutness' [reductionism], the theory that man is nothing but the result of biological, psychological and sociological conditions, or the product of heredity and environment. Such a view of man makes a neurotic believe what he is prone to believe anyway, namely, that he is the pawn and victim of outer influences or inner circumstances. This neurotic fatalism is fostered and strengthened by a psychotherapy which denies man is free . . . Man is not fully conditioned and determined but rather determines himself whether he gives in to conditions or stands up to them. In other words, man is ultimately self-determining . . . Therefore, we can predict his future only within the large framework of statistical survey referring to a whole group; the individual personality [with which the clinician works], however, remains essentially unpredictable. The basis for any predictions would be represented by biological, psychological or sociological conditions. Yet one of the main features of human existence is to rise above such conditions, to grow beyond them . . .
>
> (Frankl, 2006: 130–131)

6 Where evolutionary theory is one's starting point, it is logical that the idea of *I* – the subjective self – be explained as an emergent function of a complex neural system, whether it be apex of a hierarchical system or emerging in a nested hierarchy, as argued by Feinberg (2001). It is logical because evolutionary theory is built on the notion of emergent processes, beginning with primitive forms and developing into very complex ones with different properties from the simpler forms. Yet logical as the notion is *in the context of evolutionary theory*, it fails to answer the perplexing question of how or why a subjective self or *I* might emerge from non-subjective events. Freedom from the parameters of evolutionary theory allows for different explanatory mechanisms.

22 The clinician, the brain, and *I*

1 I say this, the notion of extinction in behaviour therapy notwithstanding. Extinction refers to 'reduction of rate of behavioural response', generally as a result of the absence of 'reinforcing contingencies' (Sulzer-Azaroff and Mayer, 1977). But the extinction process does not result in 'unlearning' – that is, in disconnection of the relevant neural association strings – it simply reflects an inhibition of performance. Because I no longer ride my bike, use a pencil, or speak the language of my early childhood does not mean I have lost these skills.

2 There are antidepressants that inhibit the reuptake of serotonin (SSRIs, such as escitalopram and sertraline), noradrenaline, or both serotonin and noradrenaline (NRIs, such as venlafaxine), or both noradrenaline and dopamine (NDRIs – these are not available in Australia). Then there are selective serotonin reuptake enhancers and noradrenaline–dopamine disinhibitors (NaSSAs, such as mirtazapine). Tricyclic antidepressants (TCAs) block the reuptake of noradrenaline and serotonin, and monoamine oxidase inhibitors (MOAIs, such as moclobemide) help to prolong the life of dopamine, serotonin, and noradrenaline. Of course, research continues, and a new generation of antidepressants targeting the neurotransmitter melatonin has become available (e.g. agomelatine, which targets certain serotonin receptors and melatonin receptors).

3 The mechanism of the actions of SSRIs remains subject to debate. One theory is that SSRIs increase serotonergic transmission in the 'mood pathways', reducing activation of the frontal cortex, which some argue is involved in the pathogenesis of depression.

4 Since Torrey, questions continue to be raised, not only in relation to the extent of the clinical efficacy of antipsychotic medication, but also in relation to how the associated research may reasonably be interpreted. See, for example, Lepping *et al.* (2011).

5 There are many subjective experiences that raise genuine questions: the things that some 'see' and 'hear', which others do not – are they neural aberrations, hallucinations, or dream-like manifestations because of neural pathway loops or shut-downs, or misattributions; or are they forms of communication apprehended by *I* from unknown sources, a world lesser known? Having said 'lesser known', there is no shortage of accounts of these inexplicable experiences that for some become familiar indeed. How can I as clinician develop confidence about the accuracy and meaning of my perceptions and experiences? One form of 'grounding' or validating of my perceptions must be in socially shared perceptions, a vital link to 'reality'. Yet even here, 'shared perceptions' vary – how experiences are interpreted and what is validated as a 'real' event will shift from one social context to another.

6 See, for example, Burns (2001).

Bibliography

Achenbach, T.M. (1991) *Manual for the Child Behaviour Checklist/4–18 and 1991 Profile*, Burlington, VT: University of Vermont Department of Psychiatry.

Ainsworth, M.D., Blehar, M.C., Waters, E., and Wall, S. (1978) *Patterns of Attachment: A Psychological Study of the Strange Situation*, Hilldale, NJ: Lawrence Erlbaum Associates.

American Psychiatric Association (2000) *Diagnostic and Statistical Manual of Mental Disorders* (4th ed.), Washington, DC: American Psychiatric Publishing.

Anderson, M.C. and Levy, B.J. (2009) 'Suppressing Unwanted Memories', *Current Directions in Psychological Science*, 18: 189–194.

Anscombe, E. and Geach, P.T. (1970) *Descartes – Philosophical Writings*, London: The Open University.

Arden, J.B. and Linford, L. (2009a) *Brain-Based Therapy with Adults*, Hoboken, NJ: John Wiley and Sons.

Arden, J.B. and Linford, L. (2009b) *Brain-Based Therapy with Children and Adolescents*, Hoboken, NJ: John Wiley and Sons.

Baumeister, R.F. and Tierney, J. (2011) *Willpower: Rediscovering the Greatest Human Strength*, New York: Penguin Press.

Beck, A.T. (1976) *Cognitive Therapy and the Emotional Disorders*, New York: International University Press.

Beck, A.T. (1996) 'Beyond Belief: A Theory of Modes, Personality, and Psychopathology', in: Paul M. Salkovskis (ed.), *Frontiers of Cognitive Therapy*, New York: The Guilford Press.

Beck, J.S. (1995) *Cognitive Therapy: Basics and Beyond*, New York: The Guilford Press.

Berger, M. and Riemann, D. (1993) 'REM Sleep in Depression – an Overview', *Journal of Sleep Research*, 2: 211–223.

Bergström, Z.M., de Fockert, J., and Richardson-Klavehn, A. (2009) 'ERP and Behavioural Evidence for Direct Suppression of Unwanted Memories', *Neuroimage*, 48: 726–737.

Birkmayer, W. and Pilleri, G. (1966) *The Brainstem Reticular Formation and its Significance for Autonomic and Affective Behaviour*, Basle: F. Hoffmann-La Roche & Co.

Bowlby, J. (1971) *Attachment*, Harmondsworth: Penguin Books.

Bowlby, J. (1985) *Loss: Sadness and Depression*, London: Penguin Books.

Brand, P. and Yancy, P. (1993) *Pain: The Gift Nobody Wants*, New York: Harper Collins.

Bray, H. and Moseley, L. (2011) 'Disrupted Working Body Schema of the Trunk in People with Back Pain', *British Journal of Sports Medicine*, 45:168–173.

Bromiley, G.W. (1985) *Theological Dictionary of the New Testament*, Exeter: The Paternoster Press.

Buber, M. (1958) *I and Thou*, Edinburgh: T. & T. Clark.

Burns, D.D. (1980) *Feeling Good: The New Mood Therapy*, Maryborough: Information Australia Group.

Burns, G.W. (2001) *101 Healing Stories: Using Metaphors in Therapy*, New York: John Wiley and Sons.

Carter, R. (2010) *Mapping the Mind*, London: Orion Publishing Group.

Caspi, A., Sugden, K., Moffitt, T.E., Taylor, A., Craig, I.W., Harrington, H., McClay, J., Mill, J., Martin, J., Braithwaite, A., and Poulton, R. (2003) 'Influence of Life Stress on Depression by a Polymorphism in the 5-HTT Gene', *Science*, 301: 386–389.

Clark, D.A. and Steer, R.A. (1996) 'Empirical Status of the Cognitive Model of Anxiety and Depression', in: P.M. Salkovskis (ed.), *Frontiers of Cognitive Therapy*, New York: The Guilford Press.

Cozolino, L. (2002) *The Neuroscience of Psychotherapy*, New York: W.W. Norton and Company.

Cozolino, L. (2006) *The Neuroscience of Human Relationships*, New York: W.W. Norton and Company.

Cruwys, T. and O'Kearney, R. (2008) 'Implications of Neuroscience Evidence for the Cognitive Models of Post-traumatic Stress Disorder', *Clinical Psychologist*, 12: 67–76.

Dahl, R. (1996) 'The Regulation of Sleep and Arousal: Development and Psychopathology', *Development and Psychopathology*, 8: 3–27.

Dalgleish, T. and Power, M. (eds) (1999) *Handbook of Cognition and Emotion*, Chichester: Wiley.

Doidge, N. (2010) *The Brain that Changes Itself* (revised ed.), Melbourne: Scribe Publications.

Dominus, S. (2011) 'A Mind of Their Own', *The New York Times Magazine*, 25 May.

Eccles, J.C. (1986) 'Do Mental Events Cause Neural Events Analogously to the Probability Fields of Quantum Mechanics?', *Proceedings of the Royal Society of London. Series B: Biological Sciences*, 227: 411–428.

Ellis, A. (1988) *How to Stubbornly Refuse to Make Yourself Miserable About Anything, Yes, Anything!* Sydney: Pan Macmillan Publishers.

Entralgo, P.L. (1955) *Mind and Body (Psychosomatic Pathology: A Short History of the Evolution of Medical Thought)*, London: Harvill Press.

Erikson, E.H. (1968) *Identity: Youth and Crisis*, New York: W.W. Norton.

Feinberg, T.E. (2001) *Altered Egos: How the Brain Creates the Self*, New York: Oxford University Press.

Foa, E.B. and Riggs, D. (1992) 'Post-Traumatic Stress Disorder in Rape Victims', *American Psychiatric Press Review of Psychiatry*, 12: 273–303.

Foa, E.B. and Wilson, R. (2001) *Stop Obsessing! How to Overcome your Obsessions and Compulsions*, New York: Bantam Doubleday Dell.

Fox, D. (2011) 'The Insanity Virus', *Discover Magazine*, Fall ed.

Frankl, V. (1980) *The Doctor and the Soul*, New York: Vintage Books.

Frankl, V. (2006) *Man's Search for Meaning*, Boston, MA: Beacon Press.

Freed, P.J., Yanagihara, T.K., Hirsch, J., and Mann, J.J. (2009) 'Neural Mechanisms of Grief Regulation', *Biological Psychiatry*, 66: 33–40.

Friedenberg, J. and Silverman, G. (2012) *Cognitive Science: An Introduction to the Study of the Mind* (2nd ed.), Los Angeles: Sage.

Glennon, U. (2010) *Ciara's Gift*, Crawley: UWA Publishing.

Goldberg, E. (2001) *The Executive Brain: Frontal Lobes and the Civilized Mind*, New York: Oxford University Press.

Goldman, D. (1995) *Emotional Intelligence*, New York: Bantam Books.

Goleman, D. (1995) 'The Brain Manages Happiness and Sadness in Different Centres', *The New York Times*, 28 March.

Green, C. and McCreery, C. (1994) *Lucid Dreaming: The Paradox of Consciousness during Sleep*, London: Routledge.

Green, C.E. (1968) *Out of the Body Experiences*, London: Hamish Hamilton.

Gregory, R.L. (1970) *The Intelligent Eye*, London: Weidenfeld and Nicholson.

Gregory, R.L. (1972) *Eye and Brain: The Psychology of Seeing*, London: World University Library.

Griffiths, K. (1997) *A Guide to Understanding Head Injury*, Melbourne: Shannon Books.

Guyton, A.C. (1981) *Textbook of Medical Physiology* (6th ed.), Philadelphia, PA: W.B. Saunders Company.

Hammen, C., Marks, T., Mayol, A., and Demayo, R. (1985) 'Depressive Self-Schemas, Life Stress, and Vulnerability to Depression', *Journal of Abnormal Psychology*, 94: 308–319.

Heron, W., Doane, B.K., and Scott, T.H. (1956) 'Visual Disturbances after Prolonged Perceptual Isolation', *Canadian Journal of Psychology*, 10: 13–16.

Joyce, J. (1968) *Ulysses*, London: Penguin Books.

Kelly, G.A. (1955) *The Psychology of Personal Constructs*, New York: Norton.

Kensinger, E.A. (2009) 'Remembering the Details: Effects of Emotion', *Emotion Review*, 1: 99–113.

Kessler, R.C. (1997) 'The Effects of Stressful Life Events on Depression', *Annual Review of Psychology*, 48: 191–214.

Kingdon, D.G. and Turkington, D. (2005) *Cognitive Therapy of Schizophrenia*, New York: The Guilford Press.

Klein, S.B., Rozendal, K., and Cosmides, L. (2002) 'A Social-Cognitive Neuroscience Analysis of the Self', *Social Cognition*, 20: 105–135.

Kuijpers, H.J., van der Heijden, F.M., Tuinier, S., and Verhoeven, W.M. (2007) 'Meditation-Induced Psychosis', *Psychopathology*, 40: 461–464.

LaBar, K.S. (2007) 'Beyond Fear: Emotional Memory Mechanisms in the Human Brain', *Current Directions in Psychological Science*, 16: 173–177.

Lambert, K.G. and Kinsley, C.H. (2011) *Clinical Neuroscience: Psychopathology and the Brain*, New York: Oxford University Press.

Leahy, E. and Gradisar, M. (2012) 'Dismantling the Bidirectional Relationship between Paediatric Sleep and Anxiety', *Clinical Psychologist*, 16: 44–56.

Lepping, P., Rajvinder, S., Whittington, R., Lane, S., and Poole, R. (2011) 'Clinical Relevance of Findings in Trials of Antipsychotics: Systematic Review', *The British Journal of Psychiatry*, 198: 341–345.

Lesch, K.P., Bengal, D., Heils, A., Sabol, S.Z., Greenberg, B.D., Petri, S., Benjamin, J., Müller, C.R., Hamer, D.H., and Murphy, D.L. (1996) 'Association of Anxiety-Related Traits with a Polymorphism in the Serotonin Transporter Gene Regulatory Region', *Science*, 274: 1527–1531.

Lindsay, P.H. and Norman, D.A. (1972) *Human Information Processing*, New York: Academic Press.

MacLean, P.D. (1990) *The Triune Brain in Evolution: Role of Paleocerebral Functions*, New York: Plenum.

Marlatt, G.A. and Witkiewitz, K. (2009) 'Addictions', in: D. Sander and K. Scherer (eds), *The Oxford Companion to Emotion and the Affective Sciences*, Oxford: Oxford University Press.

Meyer, V., Levy, R., and Schnurer, A. (1974) 'The Behavioural Treatment of Obsessive-Compulsive Disorders', in: H.R. Beech (ed.), *Obsessional States*, London: Methuen.

Miller, G.A. (1956) 'The Magical Number Seven, Plus or Minus Two: Some Limits on our Capacity for Processing Information', *Psychological Review*, 63: 81–97.

Moseley, G.L. (2011) 'Cognitive Neuroscience: Swapping Bodies in the Brain', *Current Biology*, 21: 584.

Neisser, U. (1967) *Cognitive Psychology*, New York: Appleton-Century-Crofts.

Norman, D.A. (1969) *Memory and Attention*, New York: Wiley and Sons Inc.

Page, A.C. (1996) 'The Scientist-Practitioner Model: More Faces than Eve', *Australian Psychologist*, 31: 103–108.

Parker, G. (2008) 'How Should Mood Disorders be Modelled?', *Australian and New Zealand Journal of Psychiatry*, 42: 841–850.

Persinger, M.A. (2001) 'The Neuropsychiatry of Paranormal Experiences', *The Journal of Neuropsychiatry and Clinical Neurosciences*, 13: 515–524.

Peterson, C. (2004) *Looking Forward Through the Lifespan*, Frenchs Forest: Pearson Education Australia.

Phelps, J. (2006) *Why Am I Still Depressed?* New York: McGraw-Hill.

Pietromonaco, P.R. and Feldman Barrett, L. (2000) 'The Internal Working Models: What Do We Really Know About the Self in Relation to Others?', *Review of General Psychology*, 4: 155–175.

Rees, C.S. (2009) *Obsessive-Compulsive Disorder: A Practical Guide to Treatment*, Melbourne: IP Communications.

Reeve, J. (2005) *Understanding Motivation and Emotion*, Hoboken, NJ: John Wiley and Sons.

Rogers, C.R. (1961) *Becoming a Person*, Boston, MA: Houghton Mifflin Company.

Sacks, O. (1985) *The Man who Mistook his Wife for a Hat*, London: Macmillan Publishers.

Sacks, O. (2008) *Musicophilia: Tales of Music and the Brain*, London: Picador.

Sacks, O. (2010) *The Mind's Eye*, New York: Random House.

Sander, D. and Scherer, K. (eds) (2009) *The Oxford Companion to Emotion and the Affective Sciences*, Oxford: Oxford University Press.

Scherer, K.R., Schorr, A., and Johnstone, T. (eds) (2001) *Appraisal Processes in Emotion: Theory, Methods, Research*, New York: Oxford University Press.

Schwartz, J.M. and Begley, S. (2002) *The Mind and the Brain*, New York: HarperCollins.

Searle, J. (1992) *The Rediscovery of the Mind*, Cambridge, MA: MIT Press.

Seligman, M.P. (1994) *What You Can Change, and What You Can't: The Complete Guide to Successful Self-Improvement*, Milson's Point: Random House.

Seligman, M.P. (1995) *The Optimistic Child*, Sydney: Random House.

Shaffer, J.A. (1968) *Philosophy of Mind*, Englewood Cliffs, NJ: Prentice-Hall.

Shapiro F. (2001) *EMDR: Eye Movement Desensitization and Reprocessing: Basic Principles, Protocols and Procedures* (2nd ed.), New York: Guilford Press.

Sherrington, C. (1941) *Man and his Nature*, New York: Macmillan.

Siegel, D.J. (2009) *Mindsight*, Carlton North: Scribe Publications Pty Ltd.

Simmons, A., Matthews, S., Stein, M., and Paulus, M. (2004) 'Anticipation of Emotionally Aversive Visual Stimuli Activates Right Insula', *NeuroReport*, 15: 2261–2265.

Singer, W. (1996) 'Neuronal Synchronization: A Solution to the Binding Problem?', in: R. Llinas and P.S. Churchland (eds), *The Mind-Brain Continuum: Sensory Processes*, Cambridge, MA: MIT Press.

Spence, S. (2010) 'Are We Close to Being Able to Prevent Depression and Anxiety in

Young People?', Presentation at the *27th International Congress of Applied Psychology*, Melbourne.

Sperry, R.W. (1964) 'The Great Cerebral Commissure', *Scientific American*, 210: 42–52.

Sulzer-Azaroff, B. and Mayer, G.R. (1977) *Applying Behaviour-Analysis Procedures with Children and Youth*, New York: Holt, Rinehart and Winston.

Takahashi, H., Yahata, N., Koeda, M., Matsuda, T., Asai, K., and Okubo, Y. (2004) 'Brain Activation Associated with Evaluative Processes of Guilt and Embarrassment: an fMRI Study', *Neuroimage*, 23: 967–974.

Taylor, C. (1964) *The Explanation of Behaviour*, London: Routledge & Kegan Paul.

Taylor, J.B. (2009) *My Stroke of Insight*, New York: Plume Books.

Tononi, G. (2010) 'The Big Sleep', *Discover*, Fall ed.

Torrey, E.F. (1988) *Surviving Schizophrenia*, New York: Harper and Row.

Turk, D.C., Meichenbaum, D., and Genest, M. (1983) *Pain and Behavioural Medicine: A Cognitive-Behavioural Perspective*, New York: The Guilford Press.

van Lommel, P., van Wees, R., Meyers, V., and Elfferich, I. (2001) 'Near-Death Experience in Survivors of Cardiac Arrest: a Prospective Study in the Netherlands', *Lancet*, 358 (9298): 2039–2045.

Walsh, Lee D., Moseley, G.L., Taylor, J.L., and Gandevia, S.C. (2011) 'Proprioceptive Signals Contribute to the Sense of Body Ownership', *The Journal of Physiology*, 589: 3009–3021.

Weissenburger, J.E. and Rush, A.J. (1996) 'Biology and Cognitions in Depression: Does the Mind Know What the Brain is Doing?', in: P.M. Salkovskis (ed.), *Frontiers of Cognitive Therapy*, New York: The Guilford Press.

White, J. (1982) *The Masks of Melancholy*, Leicester: Inter-Varsity Press.

Winnicott, D.W. (1967) 'Mirror-role of the Mother and Family in Child Development', in: P. Lomas, *The Predicament of the Family: A Psychoanalytical Symposium*, London: Hogarth.

Yalom, I.D. (2001) *The Gift of Therapy: Reflections on Being a Therapist*, London: Piatkus Books.

Young, J.E. and Klosko, J.S. (1993) *Reinventing your Life*, New York: Penguin Group.

Yung, A.R. and McGorry, P.D. (1996) 'The Prodromal Phase of First-episode Psychosis: Past and Current Conceptualizations', *Schizophrenia Bulletin*, 22: 2.

Zaragoza, M.S., Graham, J.R., Hall, G.C.N., Hirschman, R., and Ben-Porath, Y.S. (eds) (1995) *Memory and Testimony in the Child Witness*, Thousand Oaks, CA: Sage Publications.

Index

For Product Safety Concerns and Information please contact our EU
representative GPSR@taylorandfrancis.com
Taylor & Francis Verlag GmbH, Kaufingerstraße 24, 80331 München, Germany